Crystal clear

WordPerfect

Covers Version 6 for DOS

Gordon Nelder-Adams

Contributing author:
Susan Plumley

Crystal Clear WordPerfect 6

Copyright ©1993 by Que® Corporation

All rights reserved. Printed in the United States of America. No part of this book may be used or reproduced in any form or by any means, or stored in a database or retrieval system, without prior written permission of the publisher except in the case of brief quotations embodied in critical articles and reviews. Making copies of any part of this book for any purpose other than your own personal use is a violation of United States copyright laws. For information, address Que Corporation, 201 West 103rd Street, Indianapolis, IN 46290.

Library of Congress Catalog No.: 93-85040

ISBN: 1-56529-359-2

This book is sold *as is*, without warranty of any kind, either express or implied, respecting the contents of this book, including but not limited to implied warranties for the book's quality, performance, merchantability, or fitness for any particular purpose. Neither Que Corporation nor its dealers or distributors shall be liable to the purchaser or any other person or entity with respect to any liability, loss, or damage caused or alleged to have been caused directly or indirectly by this book.

95   94   93   6   5   4   3   2   1

Interpretation of the printing code: the rightmost double-digit number is the year of the book's printing; the rightmost single-digit number, the number of the book's printing. For example, a printing code of 93-1 shows that the first printing of the book occurred in 1993.

Screen reproductions in this book were created with Collage Plus from Inner Media, Inc., Hollis, NH.

Publisher: David P. Ewing

Associate Publisher: Rick Ranucci

Director of Publishing: Michael Miller

Managing Editor: Corinne Walls

Marketing Manager: Ray Robinson

Composed in Stone Serif and MCPdigital by Que Corporation

Credits

Series Director
Shelley O'Hara

Creative Consultant
Karen Bluestein

Acquisitions Editor
Sarah Browning

Product Director
Robin Drake

Production Editor
Anne Owen

Editor
Chuck Hutchinson

Technical Reviewer
N. Christine Pichereau

Book Designer
Amy Peppler-Adams

Graphic Image Specialists
Teresa Forrester
Dennis Sheehan
Susan VandeWalle

Indexers
Michael Hughes
Joy Dean Lee

Production Team
Angela Bannan
Claudia Bell
Diane Bigham
Charlotte Clapp
Anne Dickerson
Joelynn Gifford
Heather Kaufman
Bob LaRoche
Tonya Simpson
Mary Beth Wakefield
Michelle Worthington

About the Author

Gordon Nelder-Adams is the WordPerfect expert for the Sacramento PC Users Group and a Computing Assistant at the University of California, Davis. He is the leader of the WordPerfect Special Interest Group for both organizations. He has used WordPerfect extensively since Version 4.0 and has been a beta tester for many WordPerfect products. He was a contributing author for Que's *Using WordPerfect for Windows*, Special Edition, and *Using WordPerfect 6 for DOS*, Special Edition.

Trademarks

All terms mentioned in this book that are known to be trademarks or service marks have been appropriately capitalized. Que Corporation cannot attest to the accuracy of this information. Use of a term in this book should not be regarded as affecting the validity of any trademark or service mark.

WordPerfect is a registered trademark of WordPerfect Corporation.

Contents

more ▶

PART III

PART IV

PART V

APPENDIX A

INDEX

Change the font size, "Changing the Font Size," p. 62

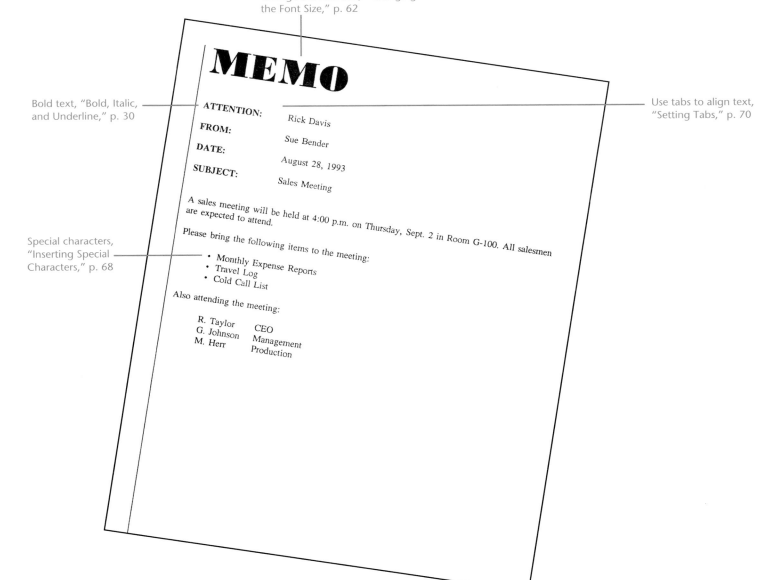

MEMO

ATTENTION:

Rick Davis

FROM:

Sue Bender

DATE:

August 28, 1993

SUBJECT:

Sales Meeting

A sales meeting will be held at 4:00 p.m. on Thursday, Sept. 2 in Room G-100. All salesmen are expected to attend.

Please bring the following items to the meeting:

- Monthly Expense Reports
- Travel Log
- Cold Call List

Also attending the meeting:

R. Taylor   CEO
G. Johnson   Management
M. Herr   Production

Bold text, "Bold, Italic, and Underline," p. 30

Use tabs to align text, "Setting Tabs," p. 70

Special characters, "Inserting Special Characters," p. 68

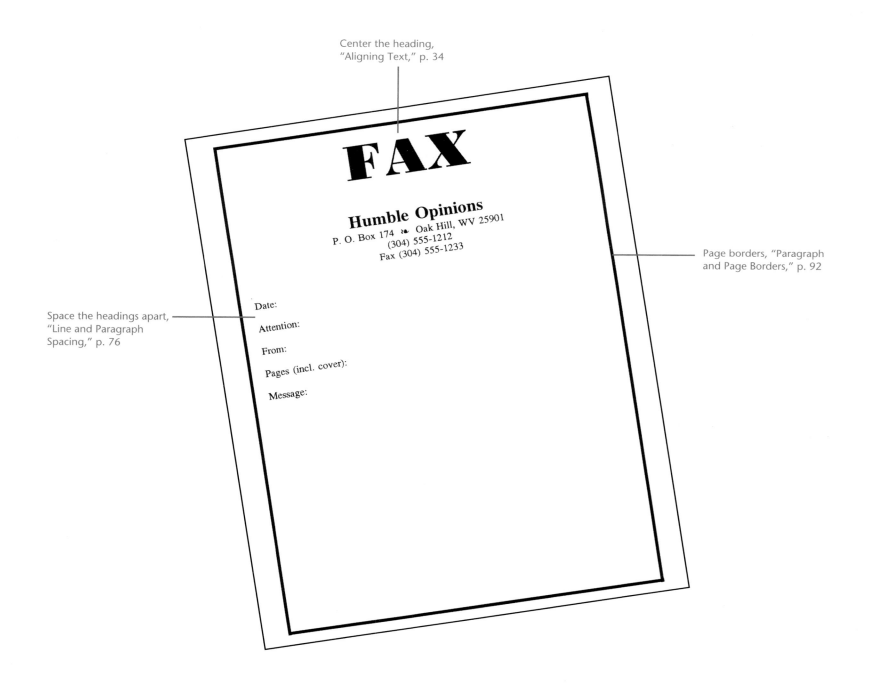

Center the heading, "Aligning Text," p. 34

FAX

Humble Opinions

P. O. Box 174 ✒ Oak Hill, WV 25901
(304) 555-1212
Fax (304) 555-1233

Page borders, "Paragraph and Page Borders," p. 92

Space the headings apart, "Line and Paragraph Spacing," p. 76

Date:

Attention:

From:

Pages (incl. cover):

Message:

BRENDA PAINTER
2113 Summerlee Road
Fayetteville, West Virginia 25901
(304) 555-9194

EMPLOYMENT OBJECTIVE
To utilize my extensive management, problem-solving, computer, and interpersonal skills for production management of medium to large print shop.

JOB EXPERIENCE

➤ Initiated, organized, and managed pre-press department consisting of twelve typesetters and six artists.

➤ Developed and managed a computer scheduling system for tracking jobs from the typesetting department to the bindery.

➤ Effectively implemented personnel policies that lead to a 23% increased efficiency rating over a three-year period.

➤ Coordinated work-flow of pre-press, camera, press, and bindery departments.

➤ Implemented successful on-the-job training program for employees wanting to learn cross-over skills.

EMPLOYMENT HISTORY
Seabold Printing Company, Beckley, West Virginia
Production Manager (1988-1993)

Seabold Printing Company, Beckley, West Virginia
Manager of the Pre-Press and Camera Departments (1984-1988)

Bender Printing Company, Charleston, West Virginia
Purchaser and Customer Relations (1982-1984)

Bender Printing Company, Charleston, West Virginia
Typesetter and Commercial Artist (1978-1982)

EDUCATION
BA -- Art and English, Marshall University, Huntington, West Virginia (1976)
Post-graduate work in Printing and Management, West Virginia Institute of Technology, Montgomery, West Virginia (1984-1988)

SPECIAL SKILLS
Computer literate including IBM Compatibles and Macintosh.
Experienced with high-resolution image typesetters and rastor image processors.
Experienced in operating small presses and binder equipment.

Arrow characters, "Insert Special Charac ters," p. 68

Horizontal lines separate parts of the document, "Creating Lines," p. 194

Indenting text, "Indenting Paragraphs," p. 76

Desktop Publishing Convention

New Haven Resort
September 16-17, 1993

Different fonts draws the eye, "Changing the Font," p. 58

PROGRAM

Thursday, September 16, 1993 .... John Rose

9:00 a.m.	Welcoming Address .... Jane Berry Rm. 312
9:30 a.m.	Buying a Personal Computer .... Sara Franks Rm. 312
10:00 a.m.	Personal Computers in Business .... Business Software Rm. 323
11:00 a.m.	Round-Table Discussion Speakers: David Wilson, Jane Berry, Wayne Smith, Dan Patten, Deb Rose Rm. 312
12:00 noon	Lunch .... Satar, Inc.
1:00 p.m.	Software Demonstrations .... Software Training Rm. 322
2:00 p.m.	Round-Table Discussion Speakers: Cheryl Franklin, Donnie Wyatt, Jim Sanders, Debra Dickerson Rm. 312
3:00 p.m.	Demonstrations .... PCs and Software Packages Rm. 323

Aligning numbers, "Aligning Text," p. 34

Right alignment, "Changing Justification," p. 72

Dot leaders, "Setting Tabs," p. 70

Changing case, "Converting Case," p. 46

Two-column format, "Newspaper vs. Parallel," p. 170

Paragraph spacing, "Line and Paragraph Spacing," p. 76

Underlining, "Bold, Italic, and Underline," p. 30

Graphic elements, "Retrieving an Image, " p. 198

BIRD WATCHERS

West Virginia Chapter

MIGRATIONS

Ever noticed in recent years you don't see as many yellow-throated vireos or hooded warblers as you used to? Here's something else to blame on the destruction of the tropical rain forests.

These birds, and many others, were migrants that wintered in tropical America. With the destruction of the rain forests, these migrant birds have no place to winter. Populations of these birds have been greatly reduced as a result.

BIRD CALLS

Some bird calls warn against preditors, defend territories, or attract mates. A bird's call can be most useful in identifying it-- especially when you can't see the bird. It may help you identify a bird's call if you put words to it.

For example, the song of the Black-capped Chickadee sounds like its name--chick-a-dee-dee-dee. Whereas the Steller's Jay call is a harsh waah, waah, shaak. One we find particularly interesting is the Towhee's drink-you-tea.

We're very interested in gathering more bird calls in this form. If you have a list of bird calls you can identify by putting them into words, please send them to us. Perhaps yours will be in the next issue of BIRD WATCHERS.

BIRD WATCH

HUMMINGBIRD FAMILY
(Trochilidae)

In this issue of BIRD WATCHERS, we focus on the Ruby-throated Hummingbird, often seen not only in West Virginia but in most of the Eastern United States. The Ruby-throated Hummingbird is the only hummingbird that lives in the eastern half of the continent.

The Ruby-throated hummingbird, or Archilochus colubris, averages 3 1/2 inches. His wings, as most hummingbird's wings, beat up to 80 times per second.

The plumage is shimmering green above with spots of blue. With a whitish belly, the bird's neck is usually pure white. The male Ruby-throated Hummingbird has a brilliant red throat patch and a black chin.

The hummingbird's call is a soft chew, chew and is usually heard when they are chasing each other.

Hummingbirds take nectar from a variety of flowers and also feed on sap oozing from holes drilled by Sapsuckers. There are over 100 flower species in North America that the hummingbird is attracted to, including bee balm, columbine, fuschia, petunia, and larkspur. Note that most of the flowers have very bright coloration; and the most popular color is red.

You can attract hummingbirds using a sugar-water dispenser. Hang several dispensers around your yard to attract the hummingbirds; they are often territorial. Be sure you wash the dispenser every three or four days; there's always the danger of sugar water becoming infected with a mold that is fatal to hummingbirds. And by the way, you don't need to use red food coloring in the water; if the feeder doesn't already contain red, paint it red to help attract the birds.

Humble Opinions
P. O. Box 174
Oak Hill, WV 25901
(304) 555-1212

August 23, 1993

J. L. Bender
212 Washington Blvd.
Huntington, WV 25701

Dear John:

Thank you for requesting information on the training specials for September. We are pleased to announce an additional 20% discount for customers who have taken training from us in the past six months--that means your total discount comes to 35% on all training you take in September!

Following is a list of the classes we offer in September:

CLASS	DAYS OFFERED	HOURS	COST
Desktop Publishing	Mondays	9-4	$260
Word Processing	Tuesdays	9-4	$245
Spreadsheet	Thursdays	9-4	$245
Accounting	Fridays	9-4	$320

I'm enclosing brochures containing information about each class. Don't hesitate to call if you need more information.

Sincerely,

B. N. Crowder

Justified text, "Changing Justification," p. 72

Tables are easy to create, "Creating Tables," p. 176

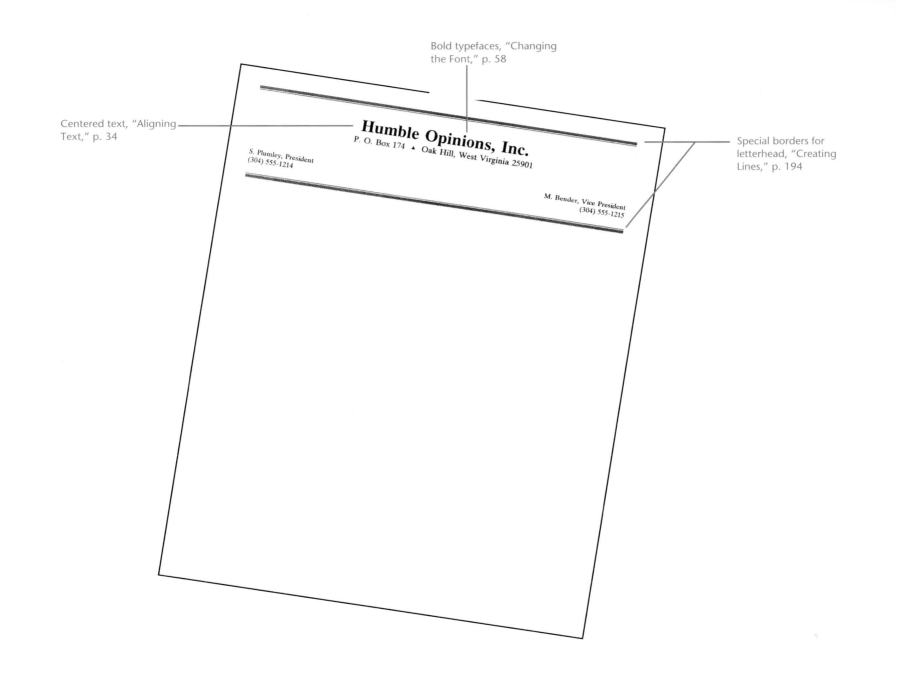

Bold typefaces, "Changing the Font," p. 58

Centered text, "Aligning Text," p. 34

Special borders for letterhead, "Creating Lines," p. 194

Humble Opinions, Inc.

P. O. Box 174 ▲ Oak Hill, West Virginia 25901

S. Plumley, President
(304) 555-1214

M. Bender, Vice President
(304) 555-1215

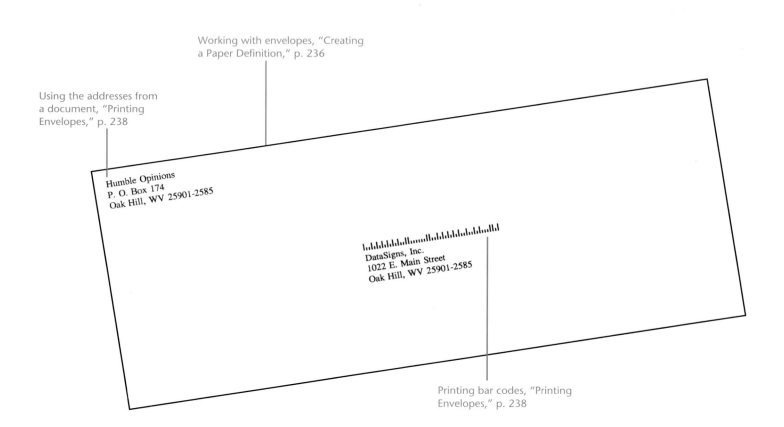

Working with envelopes, "Creating
a Paper Definition," p. 236

Using the addresses from
a document, "Printing
Envelopes," p. 238

Humble Opinions
P. O. Box 174
Oak Hill, WV 25901-2585

DataSigns, Inc.
1022 E. Main Street
Oak Hill, WV 25901-2585

Printing bar codes, "Printing
Envelopes," p. 238

Chapter 11

Go Eat Worms

Working with multiple documents, "Switching between Documents," p. 114

Our upbringing was full of superstitions misremembered and often spoke. I knew them by heart. I knew that if two people made a bed one was sure to get pregnant, that if I put my shoes on the bed I'd have bad luck and that if I put my nightgown on backwards I should leave it that way. When two people walked around obstacle on opposite sides, you better say "Bread and Butter" or an argument would soon follow. Sharp objects as gifts, like knives for instance, could cut off a relationship so you had to be sure to get a penny from the recipient, as if they were actually paying for it. And I knew that deaths happen in threes.

Using styles, "Paragraph Styles," p. 156

All kinds of odd rules and rhymes whistled through my head; there was one for every occasion. "Find a penny pick it up, you will always have good luck." "Sing before breakfast, cry before supper." "Rain before 7, sun after 11." "A bird in the house means a death in the family." (It was this that I was worried about.) If your palm itched, money was coming. If it was your nose that itched, it was company. I'm not sure what the itchings of other body parts portended.

On New Year's Day, we were all obligated to eat at least a bite of cabbage, carrot, black-eyed peas, and corned beef. Somewhere along the lines the turnip was added, probably because my dad likes turnips.

Page numbers, "Adding Page Numbers," p. 82

1

Shading boxes, "Changing the Box Borders," p. 212

SALES REPORT

Executive Summary

Italic text, "Bold, Italic, and Underline," p. 30

- Sales increased 15% this year.
- Five new products were introduced.
- Operating costs continued to rise, with a 8% increase this year.

Divisional Sales

The following table shows a breakdown of sales by division. As you can see, the East and North divisions continued to dominate sales. The fourth quarter increase can be attributed to the introduction of three new products that quarter.

	1st Quarter	2nd Quarter	3rd Quarter	4th Quarter
East	120,000	150,000	135,000	225,000
West	80,000	90,000	85,000	160,000
North	100,000	125,000	135,000	200,000
South	70,000	60,000	60,000	120,000

New Products

The following new products were released this year:

Dinosaur Robots
Dressie-Bessie Dolls
Dressie-Bessie Wardrobes
Battling Tree Trolls
Tree Troll Treehouse

Footers, "Using Headers and Footers," p. 86

Introduction

WordPerfect 6 is one of the most powerful word processing programs ever written. It performs hundreds of functions, most of which have many options. Although each of these options may be simple, choosing the best option for a particular task can be difficult.

Crystal Clear WordPerfect 6 provides a window of clarity into this powerful and complex program. Here's how:

◆ This book is broken down into articles so that the information is easy to find. Rather than wade through a 40-page chapter in a manual or book to find something, you can quickly and easily turn to the topic of interest in this book.

◆ The articles in this book explore the majority of WordPerfect 6's features and functions but don't attempt to give exhaustive coverage of every option. Each article provides the most useful and important information about that function.

◆ The steps to use a feature or to get a certain result are easy to find and follow. If you're interested in only performing a certain task, look for these steps and skip the rest.

◆ The other information in an article provides more background information, suggests related features or articles you may want to look at, provides tips on how to best use the feature, and explains how to undo a task. If you want more information, read the entire article.

◆ Numerous illustrations provide examples of the menus and dialog boxes you see when you perform an action. The illustrations also show you the results of the action. This visual orientation helps you follow along with the steps and see what the results are beforehand.

When you complete this book, you'll be able to use the program more productively than many people who have used Word-Perfect for years.

Part One

Section 1—Getting Started

WordPerfect is a word processing program designed to help you create and edit almost any type of document, whether you're writing a one-page letter or a thousand-page manuscript. The best thing about a word processing program is the ease with which you can make changes. This section covers the basic editing and formatting tasks. Most of what you do with WordPerfect will be covered in this section. You will find that you use these techniques with almost every document you create.

Section 2—Editing

WordPerfect is an editor's dream. It includes features that make it easy to make changes and spot errors. For instance, you can use the Speller to check spelling, look up words with the Thesaurus, and check your grammar. Use the tools here to fine-tune your writing.

Section 3—Formatting

To change a document's appearance, you change its format. You can create many types of documents by using WordPerfect—letters, memos, reports, magazines, contracts—the list is endless. Although you use the same WordPerfect tools to create all types of documents, the appearance of one type of document varies from another type because you use different formats. For example, you don't want a newsletter to look like a legal document or vice versa. This section shows you many ways to change your document's format.

Before you can start typing your "Great American Novel" or an important report, you need to start WordPerfect.

Before you can start writing, you need to turn on your computer and start WordPerfect.

Turn On the Computer

If you haven't done so already, turn on your computer and monitor. After the computer is on, you see a prompt (c:\> or something like that) on-screen. This prompt is called the *DOS prompt*. From this prompt, you type the command to start WordPerfect.

> **TIP**
>
> Instead of running programs from the DOS prompt, you can use the WordPerfect Shell, a program menu automatically installed with WordPerfect. If you see a menu of options after turning on your computer, look for the one titled WordPerfect. Then press the letter or number associated with that option.

Nothing Happens?

If nothing happens when you turn on the computer, check the following:

◆ Are both the computer and monitor on? You probably have power buttons for both.

◆ Are the monitor's brightness and contrast controls set right? Try adjusting them to see whether the monitor is on, but the contrast is too high or low.

◆ Do you use a power strip? If so, is it on?

◆ Are any connections (cables connecting the monitor to the computer, for example) loose?

◆ Do you have power? (Hey, it's happened. A famous technical support call involved someone that couldn't get the computer to come on. When the tech support rep asked her to check the connections, she said she couldn't. When he asked why, she said "Because it's dark in here. The power's out." Oops!)

The Document Editing Screen

After you start the program, WordPerfect's startup logo appears briefly and then the program displays its document editing screen. The screen may appear in Text mode, with gray letters against a blue background, or in Graphics mode, with black letters against a white background.

The document editing screen always shows the status line, insertion point, and document window. The menu bar is optional but so useful that you will probably always want it on-screen.

You can display the editing screen in different ways, called display *modes*. In Text mode, you can't see graphics images or formatting changes (such as italic text) on-screen, but the program is fast. In Graphics mode, you can see images and fonts, but the program is slower. To change modes, see the article "Changing the View."

Start WordPerfect from the DOS Prompt

1. From the DOS prompt, type **wp**.

2. Press Enter.

Troubleshooting

◆ When you turn on your computer, if you see Windows (a colorful screen with little pictures and Program Manager at the top), you need to exit Windows to get to the DOS prompt. Press Alt+F4, then press Enter.

◆ The first time you start WordPerfect, the program appears in Text mode. You can press Ctrl+F3 and then **G** to choose Graphics mode.

◆ The status line displays information about the current document: current font or document name, document number (Doc), page number (Pg), line number (Ln), and position of the cursor (Pos).

◆ The cursor shows you where text will appear when you start typing.

◆ The menu bar appears along the top of the screen.

◆ The mouse pointer appears when you move your mouse, and disappears as soon as you begin typing.

◆ You can also display additional editing tools on-screen. See the article "WordPerfect's Screen Tools."

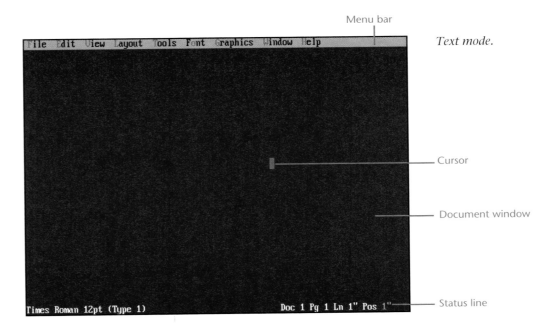

Text mode.

Menu bar

Cursor

Document window

Status line

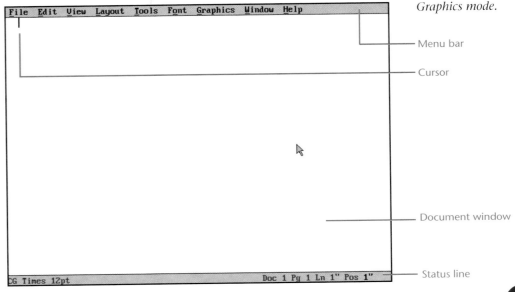

Graphics mode.

Menu bar

Cursor

Document window

Status line

When you want to do something in WordPerfect—change the font, get help, and so on—you can use the menus. Selecting a menu command is as easy as pointing to what you want and saying OK.

With WordPerfect, you can issue commands in several ways: by using the pull-down menus with the keyboard, by using the pull-down menus with the mouse, and by using function keys.

None of these methods is "right" or "wrong." You should experiment to find the methods you're most comfortable with. For the sake of clarity and simplicity, this book uses pull-down menu commands unless otherwise noted.

Pull-Down Menus

You will probably find the pull-down menus easiest to use. The menus are arranged logically, with related functions and commands grouped together. If you can't remember where to find something, you can usually make a good guess; you can also browse through the menu structure until you find what you're looking for.

Function Keys

If you have used a previous version of WordPerfect, you may be more comfortable using function keys to access commands. The command arrangement is somewhat random and difficult to remember, but you may be used to that. To help you keep track of the function keys, WordPerfect provides color-coded decals for the Shift, Alt, and Ctrl keys, and a template for the function keys.

How Menus Work

The menus follow several conventions:

◆ Every menu item contains a *mnemonic letter*. Mnemonic letters are often, but not always, the first letter in the menu item's description. In Text mode, WordPerfect displays mnemonic letters in bold; in Graphics mode and Page mode, the program underlines mnemonics. You can select the menu command or option by typing this mnemonic letter.

◆ A check mark next to a menu item means that that item is already activated. In most cases, selecting a checked item turns off that item, such as the Button Bar.

◆ Some menu items also list shortcut keys in addition to the item's description. Many, but not all, shortcut keys are function key combinations. For example, the shortcut key for Bold is F6, but the shortcut for Italic is Ctrl+I.

◆ Some menu items also contain one of two symbols: a triangle (►) or an ellipsis (...). Selecting a menu item with a triangle displays a submenu. Selecting a menu item with an ellipsis displays a dialog box. See the article "Using Dialog Boxes" for help.

◆ If a menu item appears with gray letters instead of black letters, that means you can't choose that item at the moment. For example, you can't choose **P**aste before you cut or copy something to be pasted.

Select a Menu Command with the Mouse

1. Click the menu name you want to open.

   Note: This book uses the term "choose" when referring to making a menu selection. Keep in mind that you can use the mouse or the keyboard.

2. Click the command name you want.

Select a Menu Command with the Keyboard

1. Hold down the Alt key and press the mnemonic letter key in the menu name.

   The mnemonic letter is underlined.

2. Press the mnemonic letter key in the command name.

Troubleshooting

If you choose the wrong menu, you can press Esc to leave the menu without making a selection.

Menu name

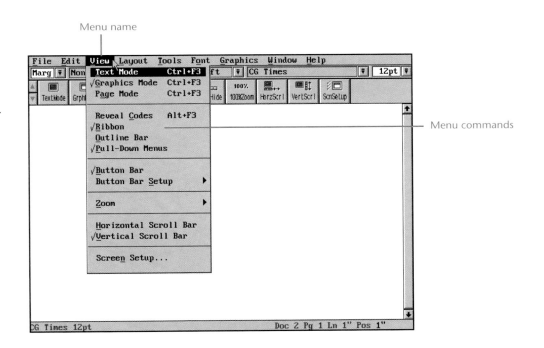

Menu commands

When there's a whole slew of options available relating to the same command, you see a dialog box. This box enables you to pick which options you want.

If all of WordPerfect's features were listed in the pull-down menus, the menu structure would be impossibly complex and difficult to use. Imagine all of the font, font size, and font appearances listed on one menu. It would take you a long time to find what you wanted. Instead, the menus contain only the most important items. For other commands, a dialog box appears that prompts for additional information.

Dialog Box Options

In most dialog boxes, you can make several different selections at the same time. Dialog boxes can contain many different kinds of items, such as these:

◆ *Buttons*. You can select any button by clicking it with your mouse or by pressing a mnemonic letter or shortcut key. If the button doesn't have a mnemonic or shortcut, press Tab until the button is highlighted with the marquee—a dotted line that surrounds the currently-selected dialog box item. Then press Enter.

◆ *OK, Cancel, and Close*. Most dialog boxes have an OK button and a Cancel button, and some also have a Close button. After you have made one or more selections in the dialog box, choose OK to implement your selections and close the dialog box. Choose Cancel or press Esc to close the dialog box without implementing any selections you may have made.

Choose Close to save any settings you change in the dialog box but not carry out any actions, like selecting a different printer but not actually printing a document.

◆ *Check boxes*. When an item contains several options, *check boxes* indicate that you can select several options at once.

◆ *Radio buttons*. When an item contains several options, *radio buttons* indicate that you can select only one option at a time.

◆ *Combination buttons*. A *combination button* is a push button that contains a short list of options. WordPerfect identifies combination buttons with a pair of opposing triangles.

◆ *Text boxes*. A *text box* is an empty box in which you can type an entry, whether it's a word, a phrase, or a number. Some text boxes designed to hold numbers have *increment buttons*, you can click with your mouse to increase or decrease the number displayed.

◆ *List boxes*. When an item contains more entries than can fit in the dialog box, WordPerfect displays the entries in a *list box*.

◆ *Drop-down lists*. A *drop-down* list also contains a list of entries, but usually displays only the currently selected entry. When you want to change the selection, the list "drops down" in front of other dialog box items.

Select Dialog Box Options with the Mouse

1. To select a check box, click in the check box with your mouse.

2. To select a radio button, click the button with your mouse.

3. To select a combination box option, point at the button with your mouse and hold down the left mouse button to display the list of options. Then drag up or down to select an option.

4. To select a drop-down list entry, click the drop-down button with your mouse to display the list, then double-click an entry to select it.

5. Choose OK for WordPerfect to act on your choice(s).

Troubleshooting

Until you choose OK, you can always "back out" of a dialog box by choosing Cancel. If you choose OK by mistake, immediately choose **E**dit, **U**ndo, or press Ctrl+Z.

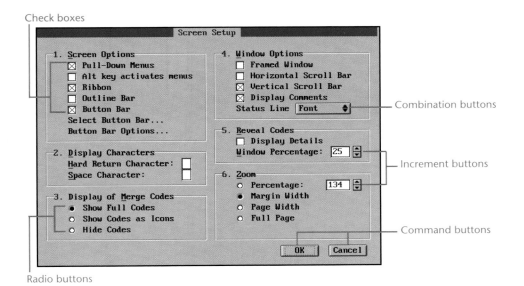

Check boxes

Radio buttons

Combination buttons

Increment buttons

Command buttons

Use the Keyboard

The mouse is the easiest way to select items in a dialog box. If you don't have a mouse, use these keyboard methods:

◆ To select a check box, press the mnemonic letter for the group of check box items, then the letter for that item.

◆ To select a radio button, press the mnemonic letter for the group of radio button items, then the letter for that item.

◆ To select a combination box option, press the mnemonic letter to display the list of options, then press the desired option's mnemonic letter. Or use the up or down arrow to highlight the option and press Enter.

◆ To select a drop-down list entry, press the mnemonic letter to display the list, then use the up or down arrow to highlight the entry and press Enter.

Just as you can keep different things on your desk (calendar, stapler, whatever), you can choose to display different tools on the WordPerfect screen.

If you use a mouse, WordPerfect's screen tools provide you quick access to frequently used commands. If you don't have a mouse, you can't use these screen tools, so turn them off.

The screen tools WordPerfect 6 provides include the Ribbon, the Button Bar, and the Horizontal and Vertical scroll bars.

> **TIP**
>
> All of WordPerfect's screen tools perform valuable functions; however, when you're not using a tool, it wastes space on-screen which otherwise can be used to display text. Turn off any screen tool you're not using; when you need the tool again, you can turn it on with the same few keystrokes or mouse clicks.

The Ribbon

The *Ribbon* appears immediately below the menu bar, and contains six drop-down list boxes for some of the most frequently changed settings: zoom, paragraph style, columns, justification, font, and font size.

To change any setting, click its drop-down button, then double-click the desired entry. After you display a drop-down list by using your mouse, you can use the keyboard to type a font name, size, or style name.

The Button Bar

The *Button Bar* normally appears below the Ribbon, but you can select one of several other locations if you prefer. Button Bar buttons are the mouse equivalent of shortcut keys; a Button Bar button exists for every pull-down menu item and for a number of other features.

See the section "Button Bars" for more information on Button Bars.

The Scroll Bars

The *Horizontal scroll bar* and *Vertical scroll bar* appear across the bottom and along the right side of your screen, respectively. The size and position of the scroll box in the middle of each scroll bar is in proportion to the document's size and the cursor position.

Clicking the Vertical scroll bar's up or down arrows is equivalent to pressing the up- or down-cursor keys. Clicking above or below the scroll box is equivalent to pressing the screen-up or screen-down keys (see the article "Moving the Cursor"). You can also move to the top or bottom of your document by dragging the scroll box to the top or bottom of the Vertical scroll bar.

> **TIP**
>
> Another way to customize the way the screen looks is to use a different view. The next article covers how to select the view you want.

Turn On a Screen Tool

1. Choose **V**iew.

2. Do one of the following:

Choose **R**ibbon.

Choose **B**utton Bar.

Choose **H**orizontal Scroll Bar.

Choose **V**ertical Scroll Bar.

Troubleshooting

The same command that turns on a screen tool also turns it off again. If you make a mistake, simply repeat the steps.

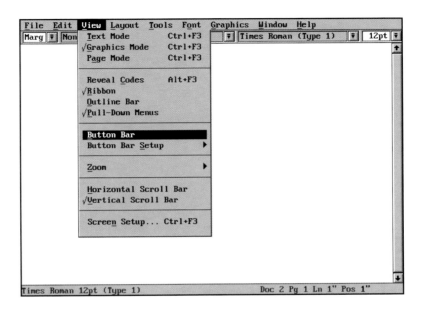

The View menu.

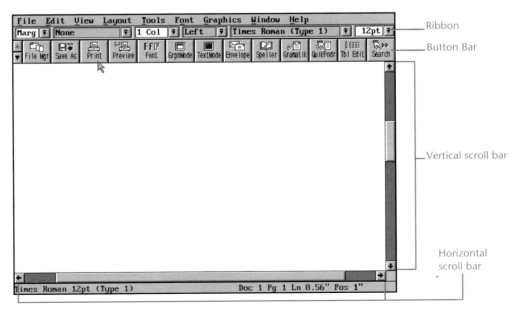

Ribbon

Button Bar

Vertical scroll bar

Horizontal scroll bar

WordPerfect's Screen Tools   13

Depending on what kind of work you're doing in the document, you might want to view it a little differently. Graphics mode works well when you're doing formatting. Text mode is good for straight typing—when you want a lot of speed.

WordPerfect lets you look at your document in different views (called *modes*): Text mode, Graphics mode, and Page mode.

Text Mode

Here's what you see in Text mode:

◆ WordPerfect uses fixed-width characters to display your text. Each character and space appears the same width on-screen.

◆ WordPerfect uses different screen colors to indicate different text attributes such as bold, italic, and underline.

◆ WordPerfect doesn't display graphics lines at all and displays graphic images as empty boxes.

> **TIP**
> Text mode is the fastest View mode to work in. Displaying graphical information on-screen uses a significant part of your computer's processing power; in Text mode, WordPerfect doesn't even try to use graphics, so your computer can devote the majority of its power to other tasks.

Graphics Mode

The benefits of working in Graphics mode are overwhelming. Because you can see your fonts and graphics on-screen while you work, you can spot many formatting mistakes when you make them. You can also see more information on-screen than in Text mode.

Here's what you see in Graphics mode:

◆ WordPerfect displays your fonts and graphics on-screen roughly as they will appear when printed.

◆ Dialog boxes, push buttons, and scroll bars appear sculpted, and the Button Bar can display icons and text.

◆ You can also see graphics lines and images in your documents.

> **TIP**
> On computers with an 80286 processor or only one megabyte of memory, for example, Graphics mode may be too slow for any productive work.

Page Mode

Page mode displays text, graphics, and other WordPerfect features in the same manner as Graphics mode, but it also displays your document's headers, footers, page numbers, and footnotes. To help you judge the position of these elements on the page, WordPerfect also displays the proper amount of space for your top and bottom margins.

Page mode is slightly slower to use than Graphics mode because WordPerfect displays more information on-screen. When you need to confirm the placement and appearance of page numbering and other page elements, Page mode becomes, in effect, an editable Print Preview.

Change the View

1. Choose **V**iew.

2. Do one of the following:

Choose **T**ext Mode.

Choose **G**raphics Mode.

Choose P**a**ge Mode.

Troubleshooting

If you choose the wrong View mode, repeat the steps and choose a different mode.

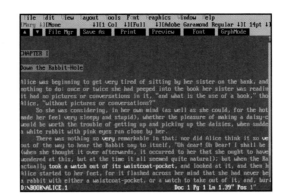

Text mode.

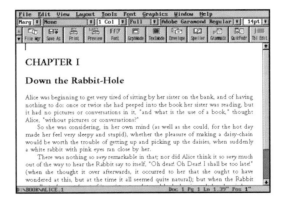

Graphics mode.

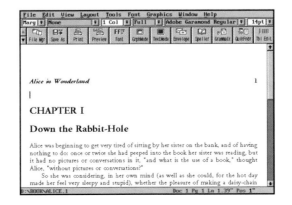

Page mode.

GETTING STARTED

It's hard to remember how to use each and every feature. When you want a quick on-screen reminder of how to do something, use WordPerfect's Help system.

As you learn and use WordPerfect, you may not always need the same kind of Help. At the beginning, you need to learn basic concepts of word processing. Later, you may need to understand a particular procedure or an unfamiliar term. If you don't use a feature frequently, you may need to be reminded about where to find it in the menus. WordPerfect's Help system provides these kinds of Help and much more.

Using the Help Index

The core of WordPerfect's Help system is the *Index*, an extensive alphabetical list of WordPerfect's features. You can navigate through the index in several ways:

◆ To find an entry, you can scroll through the list, or you can jump to an entry by choosing **N**ame Search and typing the first few letters of a feature you need help in. Each entry has a short description of the feature's purpose and a concise description of the steps required to use the feature.

◆ Double-click any underlined terms with your mouse to see a definition of the term.

◆ Related topics are shown in bold; you can double-click any bold topic to jump to the Help entry for that topic.

◆ Choose the Previous button to return to a previous topic.

Other Help Tools

You'll also find several other Help sections useful, particularly while you're learning the program. You can choose the following features from the Help menu:

◆ The *Tutorial* provides on-screen lessons of WordPerfect's basic features; it describes the features and gives you step-by-step instructions. If you make a mistake, the Tutorial waits until you make the proper selection. The Tutorial doesn't cover advanced features, but it does provide good hands-on training in the basics.

◆ *How Do I* contains descriptions similar to the Index, but it's organized by task, in a manner similar to this book. If you want to perform a task but don't know the name of the related feature, this Help section can be useful.

◆ The *Glossary* contains definitions of terms.

◆ The *Template* is a map of the function-key layout.

◆ *Keystrokes* lists WordPerfect's cursor-movement and text-editing keys.

◆ *Shortcut Keys* lists WordPerfect's built-in Ctrl+key shortcuts.

◆ *Coaches* contains minitutorials that provide instruction for performing more advanced tasks.

◆ *Macros* is a separate Help file for recording, editing, and writing macros.

Get Help

1. Choose **H**elp, **I**ndex.

2. Choose **N**ame Search.

3. Type the first few letters of the item you're searching for (for example, type **ind** for *Indent*), then scroll to find the exact entry.

4. Press Enter to display the entry and read the item.

5. To view a definition or related topic, double-click with your mouse a phrase that is underlined or boldface; or highlight the phrase and press Enter.

6. When you're done, choose Cancel.

Troubleshooting

To exit Help, choose Cancel.

Shortcut Key	
Help	F1

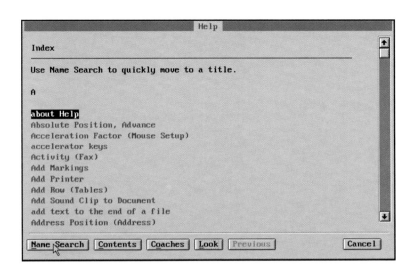

The Help Index.

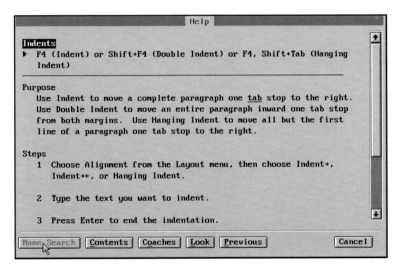

Help on Indents.

Whether you can type 100 words per minute or you use the "hunt and peck" method, typing text in WordPerfect is almost like typing on a typewriter—only better. If you make mistakes, just delete the typos and type them again.

When you type with WordPerfect, you see the letters on-screen as you type. Unlike a typewriter, however, the letters aren't committed to paper, so you can correct mistakes.

Text Wrap

The main difference between WordPerfect and a typewriter is the way each handles line breaks. When you use a typewriter, you must decide where to end each line. A typewriter rings a bell to warn you when you're near the right margin, but you must press the carriage return to start a new line.

When you type in WordPerfect, you never have to worry about line endings. The program calculates the amount of information on each line, and when you reach the end of a line, WordPerfect automatically moves the following word to the beginning of the next line. Adjusting your text in this manner is called *text wrap*.

No matter what changes you make to a document in WordPerfect, the program automatically adjusts each line ending to include as much text as possible. If you add words to a line, WordPerfect wraps down to the following line any words that no longer fit (and then adjusts the following line if necessary). If you delete words, WordPerfect wraps text up from the following line.

Remember: Don't press Enter at the end of each line. Let WordPerfect break the lines for you.

The cursor represents your position in a document. In Graphics mode, the cursor is a blinking vertical bar. In Text mode, the cursor is a blinking underline.

As you type, the characters appear on-screen, and the cursor moves along with the text. When you type a character, it appears to the left of the cursor.

Deleting Text

There are many reasons for deleting text. You may have used the wrong word in a document, or more importantly, your editor or boss may think so. You may need to shorten an article to fit a certain length. You may have typed gibberish because your fingers were on the wrong keys. Or you simply may have made a typo. This article includes the key combinations for deleting text. For information on deleting a block of text, see the article "Move, Copy, and Delete Blocks."

Type Text

1. Type on the keyboard as you would on a regular typewriter keyboard. Don't press Enter at the end of each line.

2. When you want to end a paragraph, press Enter.

Troubleshooting

◆ You can make simple corrections as you type in WordPerfect by pressing Backspace, which erases the character to the left of the cursor. To delete characters to the right of the cursor, press Del.

◆ If you delete some text by accident—whether a word, a block, or a page—you can undelete the text. See the article "Using Undelete and Undo."

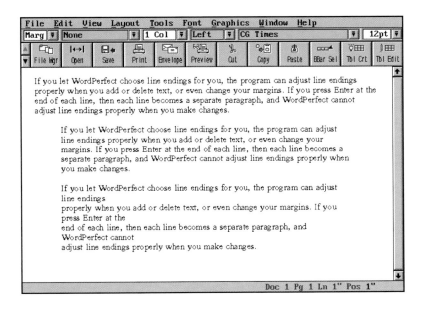

Word wrap.

Keystroke	Action
Del (Delete)	Delete a character to the right of the cursor (in Text mode, the character above the cursor)
Backspace	Delete a character to the left of the cursor
Ctrl+Backspace or Ctrl+Del	Delete the current word
Home, Del	Delete the part of a word after the cursor
Home, Backspace	Delete the part of a word before the cursor
Ctrl+End	Delete to the end of the line
Ctrl+Page Down	Delete to the end of the page (WordPerfect asks for confirmation. Type **Y** to confirm.)

If you want to make a change somewhere in a document, you have to move the cursor to that position first.

You can move the cursor by using the keyboard or mouse.

Using the Keyboard

The table on the next page lists keyboard methods for moving the cursor. If two keys are listed with a plus sign in between, press and hold down the first key. Then press the second key. If the keys are separated by commas, press and release the first key. Then press and release the next keys.

Using the Mouse

You can also use your mouse to move the cursor in a document. If you want to move to another position on-screen, simply move the mouse pointer to the new location and click the left mouse button. The cursor appears in the new location.

Moving Quickly To a Certain Page

Scrolling through a document that is several pages long isn't the quickest or easiest method to move to the page you want. In this case, use the GoTo command to move to the page. When the Go To dialog box appears, type the page number you want. WordPerfect will take you right to that page.

Using the Scroll Bars

If you want to move the cursor to a position off-screen, you must use the scroll bars.

◆ Click the Vertical scroll bar's up arrow to move up one line.

◆ Click the Vertical scroll bar's down arrow to move down one line.

◆ Drag the scroll box within the scroll bar to move the cursor to an approximate location in the document. The top and bottom of the scroll bar are equivalent to the top and bottom of the document; the middle of the scroll bar is the middle of the document.

Move to a Specific Page

1. Choose **E**dit, **G**o To.

2. Type a page number.

3. Press Enter.

Troubleshooting

If you use a cursor movement command by mistake, choose **G**o To twice (Ctrl+Home, Ctrl+Home). WordPerfect returns the cursor to its previous position.

Shortcut Key	
Go To	Ctrl+Home

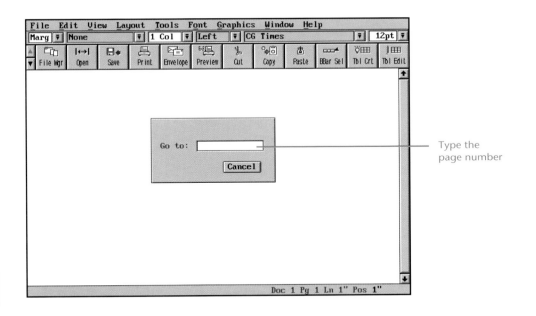

Type the page number

Keystroke	Movement	Keystroke	Movement
→	Move right one character	Home, ↓	Move to the bottom of the screen
←	Move left one character	Home, Home, ←	Move to the beginning of the line
↑	Move up one line	Home, Home, → or End	Move to the end of the line
↓	Move down one line	Home, Home, ↑	Move to the beginning of the document
Ctrl+←	Move left one word	Home, Home, ↓	Move to the end of the document
Ctrl+→	Move right one word	Home, Home, Home, ↑	Move to the very top of the document (before any formatting codes)
Ctrl+↑	Move up one paragraph		
Ctrl+↓	Move down one paragraph	Home, Home, Home, ↓	Move to the very end of the document (after any formatting codes)
Home, ←	Move to the left edge of the screen		
Home, →	Move to the right edge of the screen	Page Up	Move to the previous page
Home, ↑	Move to the top of the screen	Page Down	Move to the next page

One of the basic things you do over and over in WordPerfect is select a section of text—a phrase, sentence, paragraph, or the entire document. And then you do something to that text. You may want to copy the text, change the font, or do any number of things.

WordPerfect calls a section of text a *block*. You use the Block feature to highlight the text you want. You may want to move the block, copy it, or delete it. You may want to change the block's appearance—to make it bold or change its font. Whatever the reason, you must be able to select exactly the block of text on which you want to act.

When you choose the Block command, WordPerfect displays Block On on the status line and highlights any text you select in reverse video (with white letters on a black background).

> **TIP**
> When Block is on, if you type a character, WordPerfect extends the block to the first occurrence of that character. You can type a period (.) to block an entire sentence, or you can press Enter to extend the block to the hard return at the end of the paragraph.

> **TIP**
> If you perform an action, such as making text bold, and then need to reselect the same block to perform another action, choose Block and then choose Go To twice (Alt+F4, Ctrl+Home, Ctrl+Home).

Ways To Block Text

WordPerfect offers several ways to select a block: you can use the mouse or the keyboard. Pick whichever you prefer.

If you want to select a sentence, paragraph, or page, you can use a menu command:

◆ Choose **E**dit, **S**elect, **S**entence to block the current sentence.

◆ Choose **E**dit, **S**elect, **P**aragraph to block the current paragraph.

◆ Choose **E**dit, **S**elect, P**a**ge to block the current page.

Select a Block with the Keyboard

1. Move the cursor to the beginning of the text you want to block.

2. Choose **E**dit, **B**lock.

3. Use any of the cursor movement commands to extend the block in any direction.

Select a Block with the Mouse

1. Move the cursor to the beginning of the text you want to block.

2. Hold down the mouse button and drag across the text you want to select.

3. Release the mouse button.

Troubleshooting

If you want to cancel a block before you perform an action, simply press Esc or click the left mouse button.

Shortcut Key

Block	Alt+F4 or F12

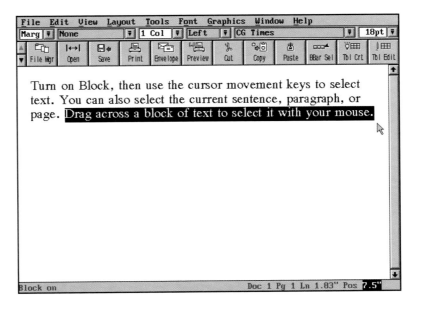

Selected text.

Turn on Block, then use the cursor movement keys to select text. You can also select the current sentence, paragraph, or page. Drag across a block of text to select it with your mouse.

GETTING STARTED

One of the best things about a word processing program such as WordPerfect is the ease with which you can rearrange text. Don't like where a paragraph is? Move it. Like another paragraph a lot? Copy it and use it again. Hate a paragraph? Delete it.

You can certainly delete text at one location in a document and retype it in another, but deleting and retyping wastes time and effort. Once you type something in WordPerfect, you never need to type it again. You can rearrange your text in any way you like, as many times as you like.

What Happens during Move and Copy?

Here's what happens during a move and copy:

- When you cut a block of text, you don't leave a hole behind. WordPerfect adjusts your text to fill in the gap. When you insert the block in its new location, the program adjusts the text again to make room for the block.

- When you cut or copy text, WordPerfect places the text in a temporary holding spot called the *clipboard*. Once the information is in the clipboard, you can choose Paste to insert a copy of the information in a new location.

- Once your text is in the clipboard, you can make more than one copy (like making several prints from a photographic negative). You can choose Paste as many times as you like to insert multiple copies of a block of text into your document.

- Each time you choose Cut or Copy, WordPerfect deletes anything in the clipboard to make room for the information you just selected. If you're moving a block of text, therefore, make sure that you paste it in its new location before you cut or copy another block.

- In WordPerfect, you can Cut and Paste or Copy and Paste by using a single combined command. After you select a block, you can choose one of these combined commands, move the cursor to a new location, and then press Enter to have the program paste your block automatically.

- You can copy or move information between two documents as easily as you can between locations in a single document. The "Files" section describes how to open and switch between more than one document.

What Happens When You Delete Text?

WordPerfect stores the last three deletions you make. So if you make a mistake and delete something accidentally, you can usually undelete it. See the article "Undelete and Undo."

Move Block of Text

1. Select a block of text.

2. Choose **E**dit, Cu**t** to cut the block.

3. Move the cursor to a new location.

4. Choose **E**dit, **P**aste.

Drag and Drop Moving

1. Select a block of text.

2. Press and hold the left mouse button.

3. Drag the cursor to a new location.

   When you release the mouse button, WordPerfect moves the selected text to the new location.

Troubleshooting

If you cut text by mistake, choose Edit Undo to undo the deletion.

Shortcut Keys

Cut	Ctrl+X
Paste	Ctrl+V
Cut and Paste	Ctrl+Del
Move	Ctrl+F4

more ▶

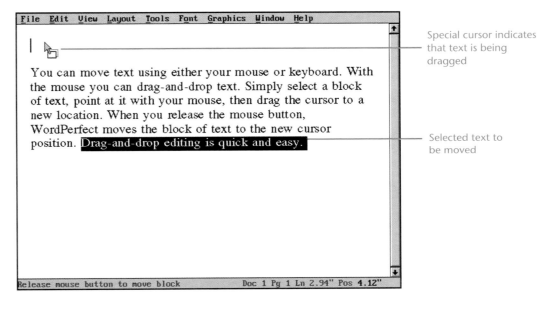

Special cursor indicates that text is being dragged

Selected text to be moved

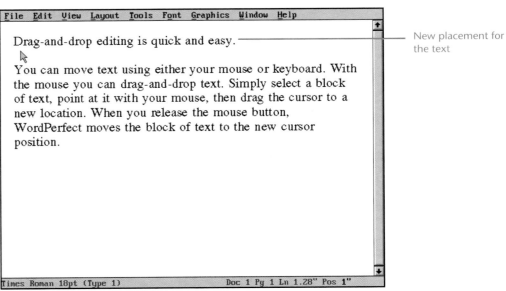

New placement for the text

GETTING STARTED

Copy a Block of Text

1. Select a block of text.

2. Choose **E**dit, **C**opy to copy the block.

3. Move the cursor to a new location.

4. Choose **E**dit, **P**aste.

Drag a Copy

1. Select a block of text.

2. Press and hold the left mouse button; also press and hold down the Ctrl key.

3. Drag the text to a new location.

Troubleshooting

If you copy text by mistake, choose Edit Undo or just delete the copied text.

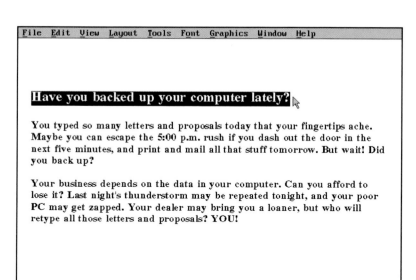

This headline will be repeated in the body of the document.

File Edit View Layout Tools Font Graphics Window Help

Have you backed up your computer lately?

You typed so many letters and proposals today that your fingertips ache. Maybe you can escape the 5:00 p.m. rush if you dash out the door in the next five minutes, and print and mail all that stuff tomorrow. But wait! Did you back up?

Your business depends on the data in your computer. Can you afford to lose it? Last night's thunderstorm may be repeated tonight, and your poor PC may get zapped. Your dealer may bring you a loaner, but who will retype all those letters and proposals? YOU!

Block on   Doc 1 Pg 1 Ln 1" Pos 5.72"

The copied text is easily reformatted to add emphasis.

File Edit View Layout Tools Font Graphics Window Help

Have you backed up your computer lately?

You typed so many letters and proposals today that your fingertips ache. Maybe you can escape the 5:00 p.m. rush if you dash out the door in the next five minutes, and print and mail all that stuff tomorrow. But wait! Did you back up?

Your business depends on the data in your computer. Can you afford to lose it? Last night's thunderstorm may be repeated tonight, and your poor PC may get zapped. Your dealer may bring you a loaner, but who will retype all those letters and proposals? YOU!

Have you backed up your computer lately? ———— Copied line

Roman-WP 14pt Bold (Type 1)   Doc 1 Pg 1 Ln 3.77" Pos 4.68"

Delete a Block

1. Select a block of text.

See preceding article "Selecting a Block."

2. Press Del or Backspace.

Troubleshooting

If you delete text by mistake, simply undelete it. See the following article "Using Undelete and Undo."

Selecting a block of text to be deleted.

File   Edit   View   Layout   Tools   Font   Graphics   Window   Help

September 17, 1993

Mr. David Schaffer
20931 Williamsburg Court
Point Albert, IN 46029

Dear Mr. Schaffer:

Thank you for talking with me by phone on Tuesday. Your time is valuable, and I appreciate your spending so much of it talking with me about our company and products. I'm particularly looking forward to hearing your comments about the new model XC9.

A copy of the marketing survey will be sent to you on Wednesday. Do you think you could get that back to me by early next week?

Although the XC9 will not be premiered until the fall of 1994, we are actively seeking suggestions from current customers for this new model. The improvements and new features suggested by owners of the XC7 were very helpful to us in producing the XC8. The Engineering Group is particularly

Block on   Doc 1 Pg 1 Ln 4.33" Pos 1"

The selected text has been deleted.

File   Edit   View   Layout   Tools   Font   Graphics   Window   Help

September 17, 1993

Mr. David Schaffer
20931 Williamsburg Court
Point Albert, IN 46029

Dear Mr. Schaffer:

Thank you for talking with me by phone on Tuesday. Your time is valuable, and I appreciate your spending so much of it talking with me about our company and products. I'm particularly looking forward to hearing your comments about the new model XC9.

Although the XC9 will not be premiered until the fall of 1994, we are actively seeking suggestions from current customers for this new model. The improvements and new features suggested by owners of the XC7 were very helpful to us in producing the XC8. The Engineering Group is particularly interested in any ideas that you may have about the replacement of petroleum-based lubricants with silicon-based lubricants in the friction-bearing parts of the new model. Obviously, we are concerned both about environmental impact

CG Times 14pt Bold Italic   Doc 1 Pg 1 Ln 3.66" Pos 1"

Move, Copy, and Delete Blocks

Using Undelete and Undo

Sometimes you'll make changes you wish you hadn't. Don't worry. If you delete text by mistake, you can undelete it. If you make some other change by mistake, you can undo the change.

Just as you can think of a thousand reasons for deleting text, you can think of an equal number of ways to make a mistake: deleting the wrong text, deleting too much text, accidentally pressing Del with a block selected, and so on. Whatever the reason, if you notice your mistake reasonably quickly, you can restore the deleted text.

What Happens To Deleted Text?

When you cut or copy a block of text, WordPerfect stores the text in memory in an electronic clipboard. When you delete text, the program does essentially the same thing, temporarily saving the text in memory. (WordPerfect stores deleted text in a different memory location than cut or copied text, so deleting and moving operations don't affect each other.)

As long as your deleted text stays in memory, you can undelete the text. WordPerfect reinserts the deleted text at the cursor position just as if you had intentionally cut and pasted the text.

WordPerfect, however, doesn't store your deleted text in memory forever. Instead, the program stores your last three deletions. When you delete a fourth piece of text, WordPerfect throws away your first deletion to make room for the new one; making a fifth deletion clears out your second one; and so on.

What Counts as a Deletion?

Does pressing Del three times count as three deletions? No. In fact, you can use all of the text deletion commands any number of times, in any combination, and WordPerfect counts them all as one deletion until you move the cursor, type a character, or choose a function.

Using Undo

Accidentally deleting text isn't the only mistake you can make in WordPerfect. You can just as easily make a formatting or editing change accidentally. In this case, there may be nothing to undelete, but you may be able to undo the procedure instead.

Where Undelete restores deleted text, Undo reverses a formatting change, which may include deleting text, but may also be typing text, changing margins, making text bold, and so on.

Also, while Undelete can restore your last three deletions, Undo can reverse only your last single change. As a result, unless you catch a mistake when you make it, you may not be able to undo a particular change because you have made several more recent changes.

Restore Deleted Text

1. Choose **E**dit, U**n**delete.

2. Do one of the following:

   Choose **R**estore to insert the deleted text in your document.

   Choose **P**revious deletion to view previously deleted text.

Undo an Action

Choose **E**dit, **U**ndo.

Troubleshooting

◆ If you undelete something by accident, you can Undo the undeletion. You can also reselect the undeleted text and redelete it.

◆ If you choose Undo by mistake or if WordPerfect reverses an action other than the one you wanted to undo, simply choose Undo again. The program reverses the reversal.

Shortcut Keys	
Undelete	Esc
Undo	Ctrl+Z

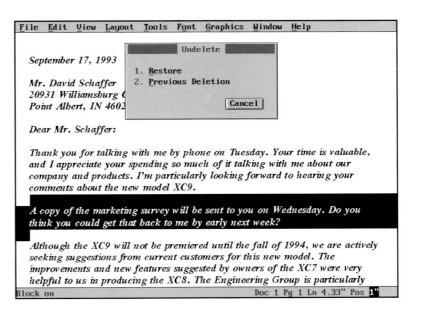

A paragraph was deleted accidentally and should be restored.

The Undelete feature can save a lot of retyping!

Typewriters are usually limited in the changes you can make to the appearance of the text. Word processors are different. You can add emphasis. Three of the most common emphases are bold, italic, and underline.

WordPerfect calls differences in text appearance *text attributes*. Just as you can create different kinds of emphasis when speaking, different text attributes give your text different emphases.

Picking the Right Emphasis

When you read a book, magazine, or newspaper, you usually see titles, headlines, and headings of all sorts printed in bold text. Bold text stands out from the normal text around it. For that reason, don't use bold within the body text of your document unless you want to give the impression of shouting.

Italicized text, on the other hand, stands out simply because it looks different, instead of heavier. Italic is a good choice to add emphasis to your body text. Italic is often used for foreign words not in common usage or for technical terms introduced in a document. You should also italicize book and magazine titles.

Although underlining was commonly used in the past, you should avoid it in most cases. Underlining is a typewriter's method of adding emphasis. Few professional publications ever use underlining. In modern usage, underlining looks unprofessional; use italic instead.

Underlining can be useful, however, for creating signature lines in documents or above the total in a column of numbers.

You also can combine attributes, adding italic within a bold heading or adding bold to a word in an italicized phrase. But don't overdo it.

> **TIP**
>
> Don't overuse text attributes; be subtle. Too much bold becomes meaningless, and your readers may tend to skip over bold words. Likewise, too many italic phrases or long passages of italic text can be hard to read.

Other Ideas

There are other ways to make the text stand out in a document. If you like to work with the look and feel of the document, you might be interested in these features:

◆ Font changes are another way to convey meaning to the reader. A business document should use a "serious" font. A decorative font might work well for an invitation.

◆ Font size is another way to add emphasis to a document. For instance, in a report you might want your document headings in a larger font than the body text.

◆ Bold, italic, and underline are the most common appearance changes, but WordPerfect offers other options. You can make text shadowed or outlined, for example. All these techniques are covered in the section "Formatting."

Make Text Bold, Italic, or Underline

1. Select a block of text.

2. Choose the Font menu.

3. Do one of the following:

    Choose **B**old.

    Choose **U**nderline.

    Choose **I**talic.

Troubleshooting

If you apply a text attribute by mistake or later decide that the attribute isn't appropriate, you can remove the attribute. Simply reselect the text and apply the attribute again.

Shortcut Keys

Bold	F6
Underline	F8
Italic	Ctrl+I

Bold text

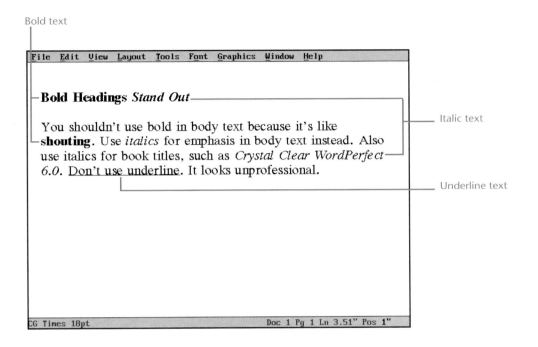

File   Edit   View   Layout   Tools   Font   Graphics   Window   Help

Bold Headings *Stand Out*

You shouldn't use bold in body text because it's like **shouting**. Use *italics* for emphasis in body text instead. Also use italics for book titles, such as *Crystal Clear WordPerfect 6.0*. Don't use underline. It looks unprofessional.

CG Times 18pt   Doc 1 Pg 1 Ln 3.51" Pos 1"

Italic text

Underline text

Indenting Text

Aligning your text enables your reader to more easily follow along with the document. For instance, indenting each paragraph provides a visual clue where each new paragraph starts.

To help your readers, you should always create a visual break between paragraphs so that the end of each paragraph and the beginning of the next are obvious.

Different Types of Indents

You can create several kinds of indented paragraphs:

◆ The most common is to simply indent the first line. This visual clue shows you where each paragraph starts.

◆ In some cases, such as in an outline, you may want to indent all lines from the left margin.

◆ When you quote long passages, you commonly indent the entire paragraph on both sides.

◆ If you create bibliographies, you may want to create hanging indents, where all lines except the first line are indented. WordPerfect creates hanging indents by combining a Left indent with a Back Tab, which shifts the first line back one tab setting.

Don't Use the Space Bar!

Some people who are used to typewriters press the space bar several times to indent paragraphs. Don't! In WordPerfect, a space is a character, and you should never use a space to indent. If you use tabs, you can easily change the indentation by changing the tab set. If you use spaces, you have to change every paragraph by hand.

Indent a Paragraph

1. Move the cursor to the beginning of the paragraph.

2. Choose **L**ayout, **A**lignment.

3. Do one of the following:

To indent from the left margin, choose **I**ndent →.

To indent from both margins, choose **In**dent → ←.

To create a hanging indent, choose **H**anging Indent.

Troubleshooting

◆ When you use Tab or Indent, WordPerfect inserts a hidden code in your document that you can delete like a normal character. To remove the code, move the cursor to the beginning of the paragraph and press Del or Backspace.

◆ You can also turn on Reveal Codes to delete these codes, which appear as [Lft Tab], [Lft Indent], [Lft/Rgt Indent], or [Back Tab].

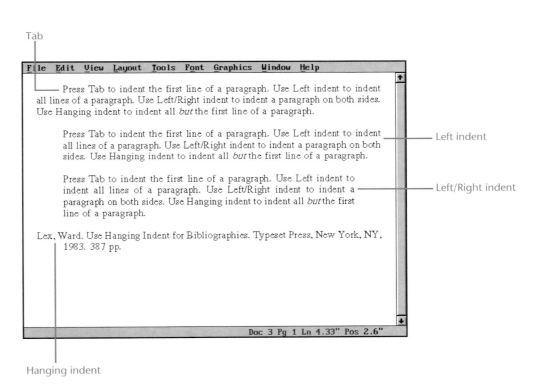

Tab

File Edit View Layout Tools Font Graphics Window Help

Press Tab to indent the first line of a paragraph. Use Left indent to indent all lines of a paragraph. Use Left/Right indent to indent a paragraph on both sides. Use Hanging indent to indent all *but* the first line of a paragraph.

Press Tab to indent the first line of a paragraph. Use Left indent to indent all lines of a paragraph. Use Left/Right indent to indent a paragraph on both sides. Use Hanging indent to indent all *but* the first line of a paragraph.   — Left indent

Press Tab to indent the first line of a paragraph. Use Left indent to indent all lines of a paragraph. Use Left/Right indent to indent a paragraph on both sides. Use Hanging indent to indent all *but* the first line of a paragraph.   — Left/Right indent

Lex, Ward. Use Hanging Indent for Bibliographies. Typeset Press, New York, NY, 1983. 387 pp.

Doc 3 Pg 1 Ln 4.33" Pos 2.6"

Hanging indent

Shortcut Keys	
Tab	Tab
Indent →	F4
Indent → ←	Shift+F4
Back Tab	Shift+Tab
Hanging Indent	F4, Shift+Tab

To call attention to a line, change the alignment.

Another way to set apart information on the page is to change the alignment. You might want to center headings, for example. Or right-justify address lines.

Aligning Text

Each of the alignment commands acts on a single line of text. If you want to change the alignment of whole paragraphs, use WordPerfect's justification commands (see the "Formatting Basics" section).

With each alignment command, you can insert the command and then type some text, or type the text and then insert a command to align that text.

If your cursor is at the left margin when you use the Center command, WordPerfect centers the following text between the margins. If you press Tab one or more times and then use the Center command, WordPerfect centers the following text on the cursor's tab position.

Similarly, you can use the Flush Right command to align all or part of a line. If your cursor is at the left margin when you use the command, WordPerfect aligns the entire line on the right margin. If your cursor is in the middle of a line, WordPerfect leaves the text to the left or the cursor in its current position, and only aligns the text to the right of the cursor.

TIP

Some people who are used to typewriters press the space bar several times to align text. Don't! In WordPerfect, a space is a character, and you should never use a space align text.

Using Decimal Tabs

The Decimal Tab command is a convenient, "quick and dirty" way to align a few numbers in a column. If you need to align more than a few rows or columns of numbers, you can use WordPerfect's Table feature (see the section "Tables").

You use a decimal tab just as you use a normal tab, but WordPerfect aligns numbers and text to the left of a decimal tab until you type a period or press Tab.

Align Text

1. If you want to align text you have already typed, move the cursor to the beginning of the line.

2. Choose **L**ayout, **A**lignment.

3. Do one of the following:

   To center the text, choose **C**enter.

   To right align the text, choose **F**lush Right.

   To decimal align the text, choose **D**ecimal Tab.

Troubleshooting

The alignment commands insert a hidden code into your document. To undo the formatting, delete the code. Press Alt+F3 to turn on Reveal Codes. Then delete the [Cntr on Mar], [Flsh Rgt], or [DEC TAB] code. Press Alt+F3 to turn off Reveal Codes. See the article "Looking At Reveal Codes" for more information on hidden codes.

Shortcut Keys

Center	Shift+F6
Flush Right	Alt+F6
Decimal Tab	Ctrl+F6

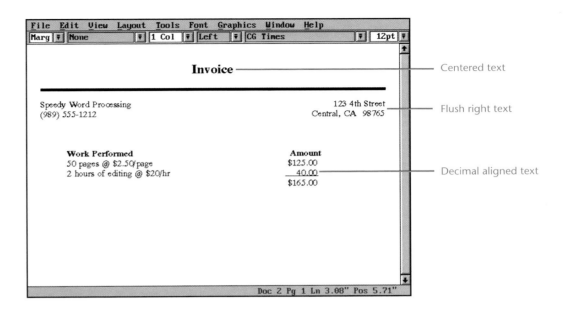

Centered text

Flush right text

Decimal aligned text

When you use WordPerfect, your documents may not always come out formatted in the way you intended. WordPerfect's Reveal Codes feature lets you "look under the hood" of a document to see what the problem may be.

When you apply formatting of any sort to a document—bold-face, indents, alignment, margin or tab sets, or other types of commands—WordPerfect inserts one or more hidden codes that instruct the program on the formatting options you've selected and what text that formatting needs to act on.

In Graphics or Page mode, you can see the results of your formatting selections as you work, but not the instructions themselves. Normally you don't want to be distracted by WordPerfect's formatting instructions when you're concentrating on writing. If you want to see what formatting codes you've used, you can turn on Reveal Codes.

The Reveal Codes Window

When you choose Reveal Codes, Word-Perfect splits the screen horizontally. Across the top of the screen, you see your document as normal. Across the bottom, you see a portion of the same document, but the text is interspersed with codes. Here's how to figure out the codes:

◆ Each code is displayed in bold text and surrounded by brackets. The codes are a sort of shorthand description of the for-matting instructions.

◆ Many of the codes, such as [Bold On] and [Font], are self-explanatory. If you can't figure out the meaning of a particular code, you can check WordPerfect's Appendix B.

◆ Some WordPerfect codes come in pairs. For every [Bold On] code at the beginning of a boldfaced word or phrase, a [Bold Off] code is always at the end. If you delete half of a code pair, WordPerfect automatically deletes the other half.

◆ When you move the cursor through the document window, WordPerfect high-lights the character to the right of the cursor in the Reveal Codes window. If that character is actually a code, Word-Perfect highlights the entire code.

◆ To save space on-screen, Reveal Codes doesn't always show you the full details of every code. When you change tab set-tings, WordPerfect stores the location of every tab, but in Reveal Codes, the code appears simply as [Tab Set]. If you high-light the [Tab Set] code, WordPerfect expands the code to show the individual tab settings.

Code Placement

If you select a block and make a formatting change, WordPerfect inserts a code at the beginning of the block to change the font and another at the end of the block to change the font back to its previous setting. In Reveal Codes, these codes appear as [+Font:Times] and [-Font:Helvetica].

If you just make the formatting change without selecting a block, WordPerfect inserts one code.

Turn On Reveal Codes

Choose **V**iew, Reveal **C**odes.

Troubleshooting

Follow the same procedure to turn off Reveal Codes that you use to turn it on (choose **V**iew, Reveal **C**odes).

Shortcut Key

Reveal Codes	Alt+F3 or F11

Why Look At Reveal Codes?

◆ You can see exactly what type of formatting has been applied to your document, whether on purpose or accidentally.

◆ You can delete codes to undo any formatting change. To delete, move the cursor to the code so that it's highlighted. Then press Del.

```
 File  Edit  View  Layout  Tools  Font  Graphics  Window  Help
                    This is Bold Text

                  This is Italic Text, centered

              Font change to Helvetica

              Revertible font change back to Times




                 {    ▲   ▲   ▲   ▲   ▲   ▲   ▲   ▲   ▲   ▲  ▲]▲   ▲   ▲   ▲
[Open Style:InitialCodes][Lft Mar][Rgt Mar][Tab Set:Rel; 0"L, every +0.5"][Lft T
ab][Bold On]This is Bold Text[Bold Off][HRt]
[Tab Set][Cntr on Mar][Italc On]This is Italic Text, centered[Italc Off][HRt]
[Font:Helvetica]Font change to Helvetica[HRt]
[+Font:Times Roman]Revertible font change back to Times[-Font:Helvetica]
Times Roman 18pt (Type 1)                        Doc 1 Pg 1 Ln 1" Pos 2"
```

— Reveal Codes

It's sometimes hard to find your place in a long document. You have to scan word after word after word after page after page. Use WordPerfect's Search feature to find text quickly.

The longer a document becomes, the harder it is for you to find things in it. You may know that you included several paragraphs on the Revolutionary War, but finding those paragraphs in a fifty-page manuscript may take some time. Or you may be editing a manuscript for someone who "helpfully" rearranged the printed text by using scissors and tape.

You can use WordPerfect's Search feature to find any word or short phrase. The program scans through your document looking for a match in the text.

If WordPerfect finds a match, the program moves the cursor to that location. If not, it briefly displays a Not Found dialog box.

Search Tips

Here are some search strategies:

♦ You must be careful when you type the text to search for. If you mistype a single letter, WordPerfect can't find the correct text in the document.

♦ If you use a particular word or phrase throughout a document and want to change it in all places, you can use WordPerfect's Replace feature to search for and change several versions of the word or phrase. See "Replacing Text and Codes" for help in using Replace.

Search Options

The Search dialog box contains several check boxes. By marking any check box, you can change the way WordPerfect searches:

♦ *Backward Search* tells WordPerfect to search backward to the beginning of the document instead of forward to the end of the document, which is the default.

♦ *Case Sensitive Search* tells WordPerfect to look for words with only an exact match of upper- or lowercase letters. Otherwise, WordPerfect finds any version of the word—with or without capitalization.

♦ *Find Whole Words Only* tells WordPerfect not to stop if it finds the word within a larger word. Otherwise, if you search for *kind*, for example, WordPerfect also stops at *kinder* or *unkind*.

♦ *Extended Search* tells WordPerfect to look for the word in headers, footers, footnotes, and other pieces of text that aren't part of the main document.

Searching with Wild-Card Characters

Sometimes you want to find several words that are similar but not identical. Instead of typing a specific word to search for, you can enter part of a word using a *wild-card* character.

A question mark (?) acts as a substitute for a single character. For example, the search string ?ake finds *bake, cake, fake, lake, make, rake, sake, take,* or *wake*.

An asterisk (*) acts as a substitute for any number of characters. For example, the search string r*d finds *red*, *rid*, *read*, *road*, *riled*, or any other word that begins with an *r* and ends in a *d*.

TIP If you search for a common word, WordPerfect may find a match every few paragraphs; try searching for a less common word or a short phrase that contains the word.

Searching for Codes

When you edit a document, you may often want to change its formatting as well as its text. Although you can scan a document on-screen or on a printout to see its text, finding formatting codes is more difficult. In the normal document window or a printed page, you can't see the codes at all, only the *results* of the codes. You can see the codes in Reveal Codes, but its window shows only a few lines at a time.

Just as you can search for a particular word or phrase in a document, you can also search for any formatting code. You may want to find a header or footer code, a particular font or font size, a margin or tab set, or any other code.

When you choose the Codes (F5) or Specific Codes (Shft+F5) buttons in the Search dialog box, you can select any formatting code from a list of all available codes and have WordPerfect add the code to the Search For text box.

You can search for any version of a code, such as any font change, or a specific version of a code, such as a change to the Swiss 721 Roman font.

TIP You can also use the Replace feature to search for and replace several instances of a formatting code. See the following article for help on using Replace.

more ▶

EDITING

Search for Text

1. Choose **E**dit, Sear**ch** to open the Search dialog box.

2. Type the text you want to find.

3. If you want to, select one or more check boxes to modify the search.

4. Choose Search (F2).

If WordPerfect finds a match, it moves the cursor to immediately after the found text.

Troubleshooting

◆ If the program doesn't find a match, it briefly displays a Not Found prompt. If you don't find a match, call up the Search dialog box and make sure that you spelled the word or phrase correctly. If not, correct the spelling and repeat the search.

◆ If you didn't make a mistake, try searching for a shorter version of the word or another related word you may have used.

Shortcut Keys

Search	F2
Backward Search	Shift+F2

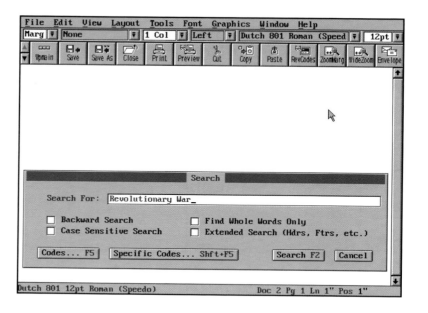

The Search dialog box can find text or codes.

To search for the same text again, press F2.

— The first instance of the search text

America has fought in many wars throughout its history, beginning with the French and Indian War, before we were even an independent nation. The Revolutionary War or War of Independence, created the United States of America. Soon after, we again fought Great Britain in the War of 1812. The American annexation of Texas led to Mexican War, and resulted in the acquisition of California and New Mexico. The Civil War, or War Between the States, tested the fabric of the nation. Many thought the Spanish-American War, which we fought to liberate Cuba from Spain, was created by William Randolph Hearst. World War I was thought, at the time, to be the War to End All Wars, but barely 20 years later World War II repeated the same tragedy. More recently America participated in the Korean War under UN auspices, and fought in the Vietnam War on the side of South Vietnam. The 1990s saw the Persian Gulf War, and with the collapse of the Soviet empire and the end of the Cold War, we can look forward to participating in countless ethnic skirmishes.

Search for a Code

1. Choose **E**dit, Searc**h**.

2. Do one of the following:

To find any instance of a code, choose Codes (F5) and then select an entry from the Search Codes dialog box.

To find a specific instance of a code, choose Specific Codes and select an entry from the Specific Codes dialog box. WordPerfect asks for the specific value of the code you want to find (such as font name or size, or a specific value for a margin or line spacing). Depending on the code, select the desired option from a list or type in a value.

3. If you want to, add additional codes or text to search for.

4. If you want to, select one or more check boxes to modify the search.

5. Choose Search (F2).

Troubleshooting

If you don't find a match, call up the Search dialog box and make sure that you used the right codes. If Search can't find a specific code, try searching for a generic code.

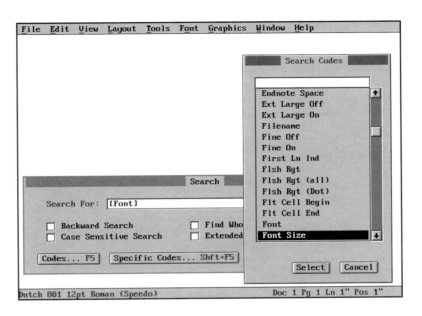

All of WordPerfect's codes are listed in the dialog box. You don't have to type a code name.

To find a font change, just choose the name of the font you want to find!

Shortcut Keys

Search	F2
Backward Search	Shift+F2

Sometimes you need to change all occurrences of a word or phrase to another. For instance, suppose that you created a long document and used the word "spokesman." You decide that "spokesperson" is a better term. You can search and replace the words.

Sometimes you need to make the same change in more than one place in a document. You may have misspelled a word throughout, for example, or decided to change a character's name in a work of fiction. You may also have decided to change your headings to a different font or to make some other formatting change. The Replace feature can save time in making these kinds of global changes.

How Replace Works

Replace is similar to Search in many ways. You enter the text and codes you want to find in the Search For text box in exactly the same manner, and you can use the same options to modify the way WordPerfect searches. With Replace, however, you can also enter text and codes in a Replace With text box. You can tell WordPerfect to search for Stephens, for example, and replace with Stevens.

When you select Replace, WordPerfect finds all occurrences of the information you're searching for. You can choose to automatically replace all occurences or go through each match and confirm each replacement.

Caution: Having WordPerfect automatically change every occurrence of your search information can be dangerous. If you replace a short, common word, the program may find that word within other words. Changing the to a through-out, for example, changes theory to aory.

Using Replace Options

Use these replacement options to control the replace:

◆ *Confirm Replacement* tells WordPerfect to stop at each match so you can verify whether you want each individual match to be replaced.

◆ *Backward Search* tells WordPerfect to search backward to the beginning of the document instead of forward to the end of the document, which is the default.

◆ *Case Sensitive Search* tells WordPerfect to look for words with only an exact match of upper- or lowercase letters. Otherwise, WordPerfect finds any version of the word—with or without capitalization.

◆ *Find Whole Words Only* tells WordPerfect not to stop if it finds the word within a larger word. Otherwise, if you search for *kind*, for example, WordPerfect also stops at *kinder* or *unkind*.

◆ *Extended Search* tells WordPerfect to look for the word in headers, footers, footnotes, and other pieces of text that aren't part of the main document.

◆ *Limit Number of Matches* enables you to limit the number of matches the program can replace. Check the **L**imit Number of Matches check box. WordPerfect displays a text box containing a default number of 1; you can change it to any number of replacements you prefer.

TIP

If you leave the Replace string blank, WordPerfect replaces the search string with <NOTHING>, which has the effect of deleting that text or stripping out those codes throughout the document.

Replace Text or Codes

1. Choose **E**dit, Rep**l**ace.

2. Enter any text or codes you want to change in the Search For text box.

3. Press Tab and enter the text or codes you want to replace within the Replace With text box.

4. If you want to, select one or more check boxes to modify the search.

5. Choose Replace (F2).

6. When WordPerfect stops on a match, do one of the following:

   Choose **Y**es to confirm the replacement.

   Choose **R**eplace All to have WordPerfect replace all occurences automatically.

   Choose **N**o to skip the replacement and move to the next occurrence.

Troubleshooting

If you make a mistake during a Replace operation, *immediately* choose **E**dit, **U**ndo (Ctrl+Z). If you don't catch the mistake until later, perform a Replace in the opposite manner, using the original search string as the Replace With string, and vice versa.

Shortcut Key

Replace	Alt+F2

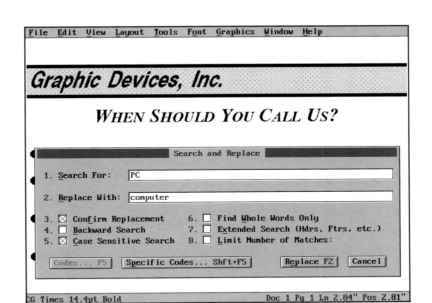

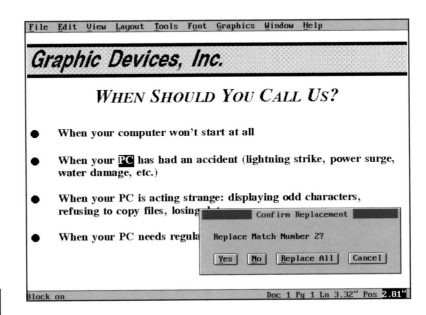

In this case, typing "PC" was faster than typing "computer." Search and Replace can save hours of typing — just use an abbreviation and then replace it!

You can replace all instances or check each instance before replacing. For example, you might not want to replace "PC-based" with "computer-based."

EDITING

When you finish working in a long document, you might want to mark the spot where you left off. Then you can quickly return to that spot.

When you finish reading a book for the night, you insert a bookmark to mark your place. The next day you can open the book at the bookmark and resume reading where you left off. With WordPerfect's Bookmark feature, you can do the same thing with a WordPerfect document.

A WordPerfect bookmark is a hidden [Bookmark] code inserted into a document at any location. Each bookmark must have a name, which you supply when you create the bookmark. You can insert as many bookmarks into a document as you like. For example, you can put a bookmark at the beginning of each section of a document. To move to any section, simply tell WordPerfect to find the bookmark for that section.

Note: If you have several documents open, WordPerfect can find bookmarks only in the active document.

Using the QuickMark
Each document can have one specialized bookmark called a *QuickMark*. By default, WordPerfect inserts a QuickMark at the cursor position every time you save a document and removes it from any prevoius location. The next time you retrieve the document, you can use the Ctrl+F shortcut key to jump to your last position in the document.

If you don't want WordPerfect to automatically insert a QuickMark whenever you save, uncheck the **S**ave QuickMark in Document on Save option in the Bookmark dialog box. Then you can set the location of the QuickMark yourself by using the Bookmark dialog box or the Ctrl+Q shortcut key.

Ideas for Bookmarks
If you select a block before you create a bookmark, WordPerfect puts paired [Bookmark] codes around the block. When you later want to return to that bookmark, the dialog box gives you the option to Find and **B**lock that particular block. If you choose that option, WordPerfect automatically selects the block.

To use this option, you can create a document containing form paragraphs you frequently have used in other documents. You then can quickly find and block a paragraph and then copy and paste the paragraph into another document.

You can also move a bookmark to a different location. To do so, move the cursor to the new location, call up the Bookmark dialog box, highlight the name of the bookmark you want to move, and choose **M**ove. WordPerfect deletes the bookmark from its original location and inserts it in the new location.

Create a Bookmark

1. Move the cursor to the desired location.

2. Choose **E**dit, Boo**k**mark.

3. Choose **C**reate.

4. Type a distinctive name.

5. Choose OK.

Find a Bookmark

1. Choose **E**dit, Boo**k**mark.

2. Highlight a bookmark name.

3. Choose **F**ind.

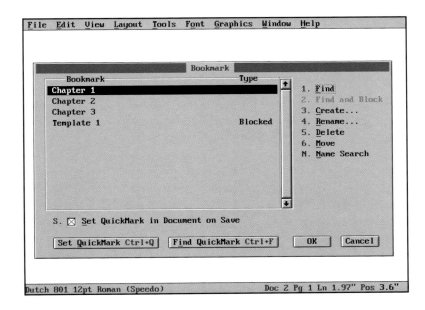

Don't you hate look-ing for your place in a document? You can put bookmarks any-where—and they can be called anything you like.

Troubleshooting

If you don't like the name you give a book-mark, you can call up the Bookmark dialog box and rename the bookmark. You can also highlight a bookmark in the dialog box and delete it. If you select the wrong book-mark to find, repeat the steps to find anoth-er bookmark.

Shortcut Keys

Bookmark	Shift+F12
Find QuickMark	Ctrl+F
Set QuickMark	Ctrl+Q

EDITING

If you accidentally type with your Caps Lock on, WordPerfect can convert your text back to lowercase.

When typing a document that someone else has handwritten, a good touch typist looks mostly at the pages, not at the screen. Combine this skill with turning the Caps Lock on and off, and it's easy to type several sentences in capital letters. When you make such a mistake in WordPerfect, you don't have to erase; you can just convert case.

You can convert the case of some text without having made a mistake. You may decide that a title looks better in all capitals or just the reverse; you may decide to turn a sentence you typed into a title. In any case, WordPerfect can intelligently convert any block of text to all uppercase letters, all lowercase letters, or lowercase letters with initial capitals. You must select a block of text before you convert case.

Case Conversion Rules

When you convert case, the results depend on your text's original case and the option you select:

◆ If you convert from lowercase to uppercase letters, WordPerfect converts every letter in the block to uppercase.

◆ If you convert from uppercase to lowercase letters, WordPerfect converts every letter in the block to lowercase (except the first letter in words that begin a sentence; for example, the first word in a paragraph or words following a period or other punctuation mark).

◆ If you convert from either case to initial caps, WordPerfect capitalizes only the first letter of each word, rendering the remainder in lowercase letters. Words such as *a*, *the*, *and*, and *to* are not capitalized, as is proper for book and magazine titles, unless they are the first word in the title.

Convert Case

1. Select a block of text.

2. Choose **E**dit, Con**v**ert Case.

3. Do one of the following:

   To convert to all uppercase letters, choose **U**ppercase.

   To convert to all lowercase letters, choose **L**owercase.

   To convert to lowercase letters with initial capitals, choose **I**nitial Caps.

Troubleshooting

If you select the wrong case conversion or aren't happy with the results, you can undo the change. You can also reselect the block of text and select a different case conversion.

Shortcut Key

Convert Case	Shift+F3 (only with a block selected)

Before:

UPPER TO LOWER

lower to upper

UPPER TO INITIAL CAPS

lower to initial caps

After:

Upper to lower

LOWER TO UPPER

Upper to Initial Caps

Lower to Initial Caps

Col 2 Doc 1 Pg 1 Ln 3.64" Pos 6.69"

If you're in a real hurry, try typing the whole document in lowercase. Then convert case while proofreading.

EDITING

Memos and letters usually contain the date. Rather than typing it, you can insert it quickly and automatically. You can do the same with the time and file names.

Sometimes you want to insert the date you created a document, and you *don't* want that date changed when you later retrieve the file. The date of a contract or agreement can be vital, for example, and you don't want a different date to appear if you print a second copy some time later. In this case, you can insert the current date as text.

Suppose that you write a letter on Monday but don't make the final corrections until Wednesday. Unless you remember to change the letter's date before you print, your letter probably has Monday's date. When you want to make sure that a letter or other document always prints with the current date, you can insert a date code. WordPerfect automatically updates this code whenever you retrieve or print a document.

Date or Time Format

You can insert a time instead of a date or insert both date and time by changing the date format. When you insert a date, by default WordPerfect inserts the month, day, and year, such as June 13, 1993. If you prefer another format, however, particularly if you want to include a time or day of the week instead of or in addition to a date, you can change the date format.

WordPerfect offers you a selection of common formats, illustrating how the current date and/or time appears in each format. You can select any format or edit a format until it's to your liking. If you later insert the date as code or text, WordPerfect inserts the information in the new format. You can insert several different date format codes in a document.

Inserting a File Name

When you create a letter or other document, including the name and location of the document's file on disk is a good idea. You may remember these details for a few days, but by the time you need to edit the document a month or two later, you may have forgotten. Just as you can insert the date as a code in a WordPerfect document, you can also insert its file name.

Because the file name is a code, you can insert the code before you save the file and give it a name. When you save or open the file, WordPerfect updates the code with the current information. You can have the code display only the document's file name or its *path* (location on disk) and file name.

To insert the file name, choose **L**ayout, **O**ther, Insert **F**ilename to access the Insert Filename dialog box. To insert just the file name, choose Insert **F**ilename. To list the file name and path, choose Insert **P**ath and Filename. Choose OK or Close to close all open dialog boxes.

Insert a Date

1. Move the cursor where you want the date to appear.

2. Choose **T**ools, **D**ate.

3. Do one of the following:

To insert a date code, choose **C**ode.

To insert the date as text, choose **T**ext.

Change the Date Format

1. Choose **T**ools, **D**ate.

2. Choose **F**ormat.

3. Specify a date or time format.

4. Choose OK.

Troubleshooting

The date or time inserted by WordPerfect is based on your computer's internal clock. If your computer's date or time is off, WordPerfect inserts the wrong information. If you use a date code, after you correct your computer's clock and retrieve the file, the code is also accurate. If you insert the date as text, you must delete and reinsert the information by hand.

Shortcut Key

Date	Shift+F5

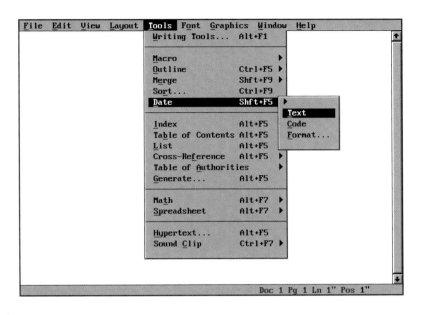

If the current date format is okay, just insert the date code.

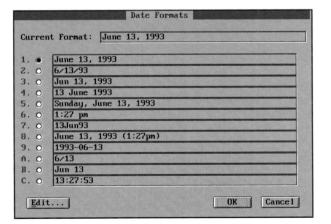

If you want a different date format, you can choose from this list.

EDITING

Even great spellers make typos. And if you're not a great speller, well... WordPerfect's Speller can help ensure that the words in your document are spelled correctly.

Whatever kinds of documents you create, you want them to make a good impression. No matter how beautiful your prose, how brilliant your arguments, or how great your mastery of the English language, you destroy your best efforts if your documents contain many spelling mistakes. Whether you're an excellent speller or a little shakier on the subject than you prefer to admit, you can still make typing mistakes.

How Speller Works

When you run the WordPerfect Speller, it compares the words in your document with its own dictionary file on disk. If Speller doesn't recognize a word, it stops, displays the word in context, and shows you several suggested words that are either spelled or pronounced similarly.

◆ If the word is indeed misspelled and the suggestions include the word you intended, you can select the desired word. The Speller corrects the word in the document and continues searching for words it doesn't recognize.

◆ If the list of suggestions doesn't contain the right word, you can edit the word yourself. Again, the Speller resumes when you're done.

◆ If a word the Speller doesn't recognize is correctly spelled, you can tell the Speller to skip that word once or to skip that word every other time it appears in the current document.

◆ You can tell the Speller to add the word to your *supplemental dictionary*, a small dictionary file containing words that aren't found in the main dictionary but which you use frequently. After you add a word to your supplemental dictionary, the Speller skips past the word when checking other documents. Your supplemental dictionary usually contains the personal and place names you use frequently in documents, as well as any specialized terminology.

Although the Speller's dictionary contains a large number of technical terms and obscure words, it doesn't contain most names and some specialized terminology. There is a tradeoff between the size of the dictionary and the speed with which the Speller can check your document.

Caution: The Speller only checks to see whether words are spelled correctly, not whether they're used correctly. If you use too *or* two *instead of* to, *the Speller doesn't catch the mistake. You can use Grammatik to detect many such grammatical errors. (See "Checking Grammar" for details.)*

Speller Options

You can choose how much of a document to spell-check, and what action to take when the Speller doesn't recognize a word:

◆ You can tell the Speller to check the current word, page, document, or the portion of the document from the cursor to the end. You can also select a block of text and then spell-check the block.

◆ If you know how a word sounds but not how it's spelled, you can choose **L**ook Up Word and enter an approximation of the word's spelling. Speller gives you a list of words that sound similar.

◆ If the Speller keeps stopping on numbers in your document, such as (2b), you can tell it to ignore numbers for the rest of the document.

◆ The Speller stops on words with irregular capitalization, such as *tHe*. You can tell it to ignore irregularly capitalized words for the rest of the document. If you frequently use irregularly capitalized words such as *pH*, you should add the words to your supplemental dictionary.

◆ If you're writing a letter with a foreign address or including a passage in a foreign language, you can tell Speller to ignore that part of the document. Block the passage you want ignored, choose Writing Tools (Alt+F1), and check the Disable Speller/Grammatik box.

◆ You can purchase foreign language Speller dictionaries from WordPerfect. You then can insert a language code in a document, and Speller automatically spell-checks a passage in a foreign language using the correct dictionary. Many other companies sell specialized dictionaries, such as legal or medical dictionaries, that you can add to your main dictionary.

Editing the Supplemental Dictionary

When you call up the Speller, instead of spell-checking a document, you can edit your supplemental dictionary. When you edit this dictionary directly, you can add new words for the Speller to skip and add words with automatic replacements or suggested alternates.

If you frequently mistype a word, such as *eht* or *hte* instead of *the*, you can add the misspellings with the correct word as a replacement, and the Speller automatically corrects the word during a spell check. If you mistype similar words, you can add the incorrect word with several alternate words that are possibly correct; when the Speller encounters the word, it then gives you the alternate words as choices to correct the word in context. You can also add words with specific or irregular capitalization, edit words already entered, or delete words you added by mistake.

more ▶

Check Spelling

1. Choose **T**ools, **W**riting Tools.

2. Choose **S**peller.

3. Indicate what you want to check: **W**ord, **P**age, **D**ocument, or **F**rom Cursor.

4. When the Speller stops on a misspelled word, do one of the following:

   Select a replacement word from the list of suggestions by typing the letter next to the word, or double-clicking the replacement word.

   Choose Edit **W**ord and make the correction yourself; press Enter or F7 when done.

5. When the Speller stops on a correct word, do one of the following:

   Choose Skip **O**nce.

   Choose **S**kip in This Document.

   Choose Add to Dic**t**ionary.

6. When the Speller prompts `Spell Check Completed`, choose OK.

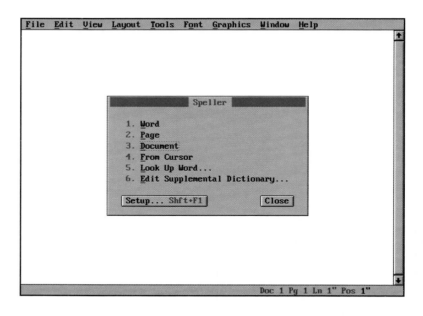

If you check from the cursor position, WordPerfect looks only at text through the rest of the document. The spell-check doesn't start at the beginning with this option.

Troubleshooting

If you correct a word with the wrong suggested alternate word, you have to change the word yourself. You can cancel the spell-check operation, correct the word, and resume spell-checking from the cursor position, or make a note of the word and search for it after the spell-check operation is finished. If you add a word to your supplemental dictionary by mistake, you can edit the dictionary and delete the word.

Shortcut Keys	
Writing Tools	Alt+F1
Speller	Ctrl+F2

Edit the Supplemental Dictionary

1. Choose **T**ools, **W**riting Tools, **S**peller.

2. Choose **E**dit Supplemental Dictionary.

3. Press the down arrow to highlight WP{WP}US.SUP, and choose **E**dit.

4. To add a word, choose **A**dd, then choose one of the following:

   Word/Phrase to **S**kip

   Word/Phrase with **R**eplacement

   Word/Phrase with **A**lternatives

5. To delete a word, highlight the word, then choose **D**elete.

6. To edit a word, highlight the word, then choose **E**dit, and correct the word's spelling.

7. When you're done, choose Close.

TIP

Always proofread important documents yourself even after WordPerfect checks spelling and grammar; even Grammatik can't detect the difference between "book" and "hook" in a sentence.

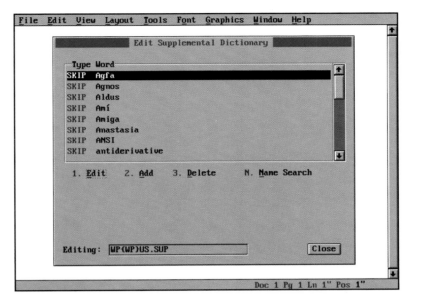

File   Edit   View   Layout   Tools   Font   Graphics   Window   Help

Edit Supplemental Dictionary

Type Word
SKIP Agfa
SKIP Agnos
SKIP Aldus
SKIP Amí
SKIP Amiga
SKIP Amastasia
SKIP ANSI
SKIP antiderivative

1. Edit   2. Add   3. Delete   N. Name Search

Editing: WP{WP}US.SUP   Close

Doc 1 Pg 1 Ln 1" Pos 1"

As this figure shows, the dictionaries contain quite a range of words!

Sometimes, only the *right* word works in a sentence, and you just can't think of it. When you can't think of the right word, WordPerfect's Thesaurus can help you find it.

Just as the Speller uses a dictionary on disk, the WordPerfect Thesaurus uses a thesaurus on disk to suggest alternate word choices. The Thesaurus can suggest *synonyms* (words with similar meanings) or *antonyms* (words with opposite meanings).

How the Thesaurus Works

To use the Thesaurus, you start with a look-up word whose meaning is similar to the word you're looking for. The Thesaurus then displays words that are related to the look-up word, grouped by part of speech and related meaning.

The word *right* can be an adjective, for example, with meanings such as accurate, ethical, appropriate, or straight: "It was the right thing to do." Right can also be a noun: "It's my right"—or a verb—"I must right that wrong." The Thesaurus lists synonyms for each, as well as antonyms such as *wrong*.

◆ If the list of suggestions contains the word you're looking for, the Thesaurus can replace the word in your document with the alternate.

◆ If the Thesaurus suggests a word that is closer to the meaning you're looking for, you can look up synonyms for *that* word and have the Thesaurus display them in the next column. You can continue to look from word to word in this manner.

> **TIP**
>
> If you think you're getting farther away from the word you're looking for, you can call up a history of the words you have looked up and return to an earlier word.

Thesaurus Limitations

The Thesaurus doesn't contain as many words as the Speller's dictionary, so it may not have suggestions for all words you may want to look up. Also, Thesaurus entries are mostly root words, so if you need a synonym for *wanting*, you get suggestions based on *want*. Because of this limitation, you may need to edit the suggestion after you replace the original word in your document.

Neither the Thesaurus nor the Speller lists definitions for alternate word choices. If you're unsure of the precise meaning of an alternate word, you may want to look it up in a dictionary.

> **TIP**
>
> Although the Thesaurus displays only three columns at a time, you can use the arrow keys or arrow buttons to scroll the columns left or right to see additional columns.

Look Up Words in the Thesaurus

1. Choose **T**ools, **W**riting Tools.

2. Choose **T**hesaurus.

WordPerfect lists synonyms and antonyms for the word containing the cursor.

3. Do one of the following:

To look up one of the suggested words, double-click the word or highlight the word and press Enter.

To look up another word not suggested, choose **L**ook Up and enter a word.

To replace the original word with an alternate, choose **R**eplace.

To close the dialog box without making a replacement, choose Cancel.

Troubleshooting

If you don't like a replacement word after you select it, you can Undo the replacement. You also can simply correct the word by hand or look up another choice in the Thesaurus.

Shortcut Key

Writing Tools	Alt+F1

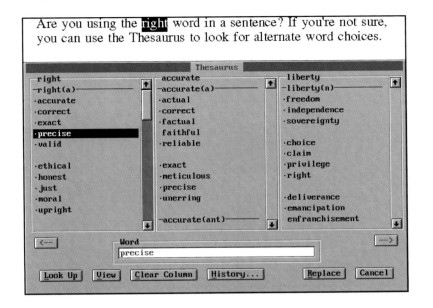

Are you using the ███ word in a sentence? If you're not sure, you can use the Thesaurus to look for alternate word choices.

The Thesaurus is really handy when you just can't think of quite the right word.

Even English majors can make grammatical mistakes; Grammatik helps you catch them.

No matter how strong your command of the English language is, you can still make stupid grammatical mistakes. You can use the wrong verb tense, make punctuation errors, or use a plural verb with a singular noun. You can also overuse a phrase or technique that is otherwise correct. *Grammatik* can catch these types of errors and dozens more.

What Is Grammatik?

Grammatik is a separate program included with WordPerfect and installed with the Speller and Thesaurus. Grammatik was developed by Reference Software, which was purchased by WordPerfect Corporation. As a result, Grammatik's interface is significantly different from the Speller and Thesaurus, and for that matter, from the rest of WordPerfect itself. Grammatik runs only in Text mode, for example, and has its own dictionary separate from the Speller's dictionary. You can call up Grammatik from within WordPerfect, however, just as you can call up the Speller or Thesaurus.

How Grammatik Works

Just as the Speller checks a document's spelling, Grammatik checks its grammar. When Grammatik finds a problem, it highlights the word or phrase, displays some advice about the nature of the problem, and suggests a possible replacement.

◆ Just as you can do with the Speller, you can let the program correct a problem, correct it yourself, or skip the problem.

◆ You can also tell Grammatik to ignore other problems of the same type in this document.

◆ If you want to correct the problem, at a later time, you can tell Grammatik to mark the problem in your document.

◆ You can select a writing style. Grammatik can check for dozens of different types of grammatical problems. A usage that is perfectly acceptable in a letter to a friend, however, may be completely inappropriate in a business proposal. As a result, Grammatik offers ten different writing styles, with three levels of formality, from which you can choose. You can also modify existing styles or create styles of your own.

Grammar Is a Complex Problem

Although the spelling of a word is either right or wrong, the proper use of grammar is much more complex and less precise, and for a computer program to recognize correct grammar is not an exact science.

Grammatik has to recognize nouns, verbs, adjectives, adverbs, pronouns, interjections, and conjunctions. It has to recognize when a word such as *right* is used as a noun, an adjective, or a verb. Unfortunately, English is one of the most irregular languages in the world, and Grammatik also has to know that the past tense of *bring* is *brought*.

As a result, Grammatik usually can't tell you whether a usage it has spotted is definitely improper; it can tell you only that a particular usage may not be proper in certain circumstances. On occasion, Grammatik itself is incorrect.

Check a Document's Grammar

1. Choose **T**ools, **W**riting Tools.

2. Choose **G**rammatik.

3. Choose **I**nteractive Check.

4. For each suggested problem, do one of the following:

   To skip the problem, press F10.

   To edit the text, press F9.

   To mark the problem to edit later, press F8.

   To replace the problem with Grammatik's suggestion, press F2.

   To replace the problem and move to the next problem, press F3.

   To add a word to Grammatik's dictionary, press F7.

   To ignore similar problems in the document, press F6.

   To ignore the specific word or phrase in the document, press F5.

   To have Grammatik parse your sentence, press F4.

5. After you finish checking your document, choose **Q**uit.

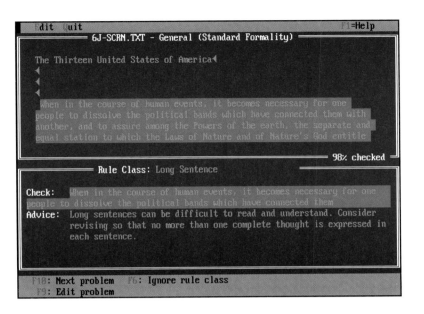

Grammatik helps even experienced writers by pointing out common errors.

Troubleshooting

Before returning your document to a WordPerfect document window, Grammatik allows you to abandon any changes you have made. After you return to WordPerfect, however, you can't undo changes made while in Grammatik. You may want to save a document before choosing Grammatik.

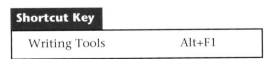

Shortcut Key	
Writing Tools	Alt+F1

Checking Grammar 57

The font you use for a document conveys an instant impression to the reader. For each of your documents, you should select a font that sets an appropriate mood or tone.

The appearance of a document is almost as important as its content, and a document's *font* or *typeface* is one of the most important parts of its appearance. If you receive a love letter printed in a typewriter-like type, you'll probably think it looks impersonal. If someone sends you a business proposal, you aren't impressed if its text looks flowery or frivolous. In each case, the font tells the reader what kind of information is contained in the text.

The font can also make other differences in how you use the text. You can make a document easier to read, for example, by choosing fonts that are large and bold for headings or captions. You can change the emphasis on a section of a document by using a different font for that section.

Making a Font Change

You can change the font for all of a document, or for only a selected block of text.

When you choose a different font, Word-Perfect inserts a font code at the cursor position and reformats any text that follows the code using the new font.

If you select a block of text and then change the font, however, WordPerfect inserts a pair of font codes around the block and only changes the font for the block.

Selecting a Font

The Font dialog box displays a list of all the fonts available in a drop-down list box. In Graphics mode or Page mode, when you highlight a font in the Font dialog box, WordPerfect shows you what the font looks like. You can also select a different font size and one or more text attributes at the same time. See "Changing the Font Size" and "Changing Font Appearance" for more information.

TIP You can also select a font by clicking the Ribbon's Font drop-down list box with your mouse.

What Is a Font?

Fonts have a history that goes back five hundred years to the invention of the printing press. There are many different kinds of fonts, and the appearance of fonts can vary widely. As a result, choosing the right font is an art and a science.

As far as WordPerfect is concerned, a *font* is information that describes the appearance of the letters of the alphabet, numbers, punctuation marks, and other printed characters. Fonts can be built into your printer, into font cartridges you plug into your printer, or in files on disk that WordPerfect can send to your printer.

Your printer has several built-in fonts. WordPerfect provides several more fonts that it can use, and you can also purchase additional font packages you can install for use by WordPerfect. The WordPerfect fonts can take significantly longer to print than your printer's built-in fonts but give you more flexibility in font appearance and size.

Fonts can vary widely in appearance. For example, look at a newspaper headline, then look at the article that goes with the headline. Not only are they a different size, but the appearance of each letter is different.

WordPerfect 6 comes with some basic fonts, including Dutch, Swiss, and Courier. These fonts are good, general-purpose scalable fonts you can use in a wide variety of documents, and in a font format that works with almost every printer. The program also comes with several decorative fonts, including Bodoni and Commercial Script. These fonts are useful for ornate titles and for documents such as fliers, posters, and invitations, but are hard to read as body text. To see some of WordPerfect's fonts, open and print the PRINTER.TST file, located in your WP60 directory.

Font Families

Many fonts are part of a *font family*. A font family is a group of related fonts, such as Dutch Roman, Dutch Bold, Dutch Italic, and Dutch Bold Italic. These fonts are all variations on the same basic design, but with slightly different appearances.

The Roman version of a font is the "normal" version. A different weight means a different thickness; Bold is the most common heavy weight, but some font families include a thinner Semibold or an even heavier Black. A font can also have a different style or change in appearance, such as Italic.

Some large font families, such as Adobe's Caslon, Garamond, and Minion, have a dozen or more related fonts of different weights and styles and include "expert" sets with small capitals, old-fashioned numbers, swash italics, and other special symbols.

The Dutch and Swiss font families that come with WordPerfect are very useful fonts, but they're extremely common. If you want your documents to look distinctive, you can purchase font packages in a wide range of styles, font formats, and prices.

Font Terminology

You should understand these terms when you choose fonts:

◆ A *serif font* is a font whose characters have *serifs*, the small bars or curls at the end of a main stroke. Dutch and Courier are common serif fonts. Most books and magazines use serif fonts for the main— or body—text.

more ▶

more ▶

Choosing the Right Size

Knowing how to select a font size doesn't tell you what size to choose. Your main guide should be readability. Here are some suggestions to consider when you're choosing a font size:

◆ Body text is commonly 10 to 12 points in size. Anything smaller than 10 points is "small print" and may be difficult for some people to read, and larger sizes take up more space without significant gains in readability.

◆ For ease of reading, your documents should average 10 to 12 words per line. If your lines have too many or too few words, you can change point size, adjust side margins, use text columns, or a combination of the three.

◆ You can make headings and titles stand out from the surrounding body text simply by choosing a larger size, although headings are usually also bold.

◆ Subheadings may be the same size as body text, but major headings can be much larger. Consider a size of 14 or 18 points for headings, and 24, 30, or 36 points for titles. You can also use successively larger relative size attributes, using Extra Large for titles, Very Large for main headings, and Large for subheadings.

◆ Don't be afraid to use really big fonts for special purposes. You can read 72-point type across a room, which is important for reading fliers.

Changing the Font **59**

- A *sans serif font* doesn't use serifs; its characters consist of simple lines and curves without embellishment. Swiss is a common sans serif font. Most newspaper headlines use sans serif fonts.

- A *monospaced font* has characters that are all the same width, like on a typewriter. Courier is the most common mono-spaced font.

- In a *proportional font*, the characters are different widths. Characters such as *i* and *l* are narrow while *w* and *m* are wide. Proportionally spaced fonts fit more characters into a line than monospaced fonts of the same size, and they look more professional. Dutch and Swiss are both proportional fonts.

- A *scalable font* (like those that come with WordPerfect) is a font whose overall size (height and width) can be changed. If you want your text to be larger, you simply choose a bigger size.

- A *bit-mapped font* is a font whose size is fixed. To make your text larger, you have to choose a different font file.

These terms describe several aspects of font design, and any font can combine several of them. For example, Dutch is a proportional, serif font; Swiss is a proportional, sans-serif font; and Courier is a monospaced, serif font.

Pitch and Point Size

The oldest computer font types are measured in characters per inch (cpi), also known as *pitch*. The most common sizes are 10 cpi and 12 cpi, corresponding to the pica and elite typewriter type sizes. Some of the more modern laser printers, such as the HP LaserJet series, still have Courier 10 cpi and 12 cpi built in. Fonts measured in cpi are fixed in size; if you want to change size, you actually must select a different, larger font.

Note: *12 cpi is a smaller size than 10 cpi because there are more characters per inch.*

Most modern computer fonts are measured in points, the measuring system used by typesetters for centuries. One point is 1/72 of an inch. The larger the point size, the larger the font; 12 points is an average size. If you use scalable fonts, you can select almost any point size. WordPerfect supports four major types of scalable fonts: Postscript Type 1, TrueType, Bitstream Speedo, and Intellifont. The Dutch, Swiss, and Courier fonts that come with WordPerfect 6 are scalable Speedo fonts. The Bodoni, Commercial Script, Helvetica, and Roman fonts that come with WordPerfect are Type 1 fonts. If a font is scalable, WordPerfect includes the font's type next to its name in the font list.

Font Suggestions

Consider these suggestions when selecting a font:

- Many fonts are appropriate for a wide variety of documents; don't use a different font for each document.

- Use the regular (Roman) version of a font for the main text of most documents; don't use bold or italic.

- Serif fonts are usually better choices for body text than sans serif fonts; the serifs help your eye decide what each character is, which makes text easier to read.

- Avoid using Courier and other mono-spaced fonts for important documents. They're designed for typewriters—and look it.

- Don't use more than two font families, such as Dutch and Swiss, in the same document. Too many font families tend to clash or look like a ransom note. Instead, use a different size, a bold weight, italic, or any combination of these elements for headings, titles, and so on.

- If you have many headings in a document, use styles to format the headings. You can put font, size, and appearance codes in a single style and then apply the style to each heading. See the section "Styles" for more information.

Change the Font

1. Place the cursor in the document where you want to change the font, or select a block of text to change.

2. Choose Font, Font. The Font dialog box opens.

3. Choose Font to display a list of available fonts.

4. Highlight a font in the list.

5. Choose OK.

Troubleshooting

If you select a font by mistake or just don't like the font you select, simply select a different font. You can also choose Reveal Codes (Alt+F3) and delete the Font code.

Shortcut Key

Font Dialog Box	Ctrl+F8

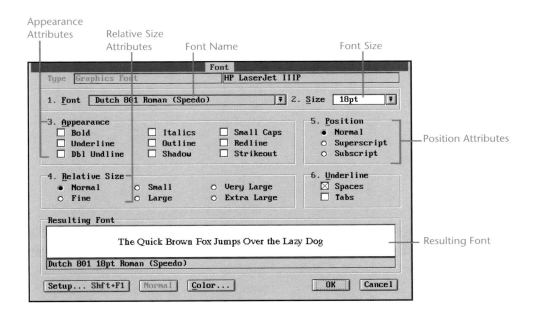

Appearance Attributes

Relative Size Attributes

Font Name

Font Size

Position Attributes

Resulting Font

You can see from this example how changing the font can dramatically change the look of the text.

Dutch is a proportionally spaced serif font. Dutch is a good choice for body text, although you can also use bold and large versions for headings. Dutch is a variant of Times.

Swiss is a proportionally spaced sans serif font. Swiss makes excellent headings, but long passages of Swiss may be hard to read. Swiss is a variant of Helvetica.

Courier is a monospaced serif font. Courier was designed for a typewriter and looks unprofessional.

Changing the Font Size

The font size you select gives your document a certain look and feel. Think about gigantic headlines. What do they convey? Think about itsy-bitsy tiny letters. What do they convey?

If you look at nearly any newspaper, magazine, or book, you see a variety of typefaces and various type sizes. Headings and titles are usually larger than body text. Banner headlines may be several inches high. Footnotes, on the other hand, are usually smaller than body text, and the fine print in some contracts or advertisements may be too small to read comfortably without a magnifying glass.

WordPerfect can print text of almost any size. The size you can print a given font, however, depends on your printer and the font type.

Changing the Font Size

You can change font size in WordPerfect in two ways: by using a font size code or by using relative size font attributes.

Font size codes act on a document much like changing the font itself. You can insert a font size code, which changes the size of all following text, or you can select a block of text and change the block's size.

When you choose a different font size, WordPerfect inserts a font size code at the cursor position and reformats any text that follows the code using the new font.

If you select a block of text and then change the font size, however, WordPerfect inserts a pair of font size codes around the block and only changes font size for the block. The code at the beginning of the block changes the selected text to the new font size, and the code at the end reverts the following text to the original size. See the article "Looking At Reveal Codes" for an explanation of revertible codes.

Selecting a Font Size

The Font dialog box displays a list of font sizes in a drop-down list box. If the current font is scalable, you can select any size listed or type any other size, even if it's not listed. If the current font is not scalable, only one size, or at most a small number of sizes, is listed; you can select only a listed size. You can also select a different font and one or more font appearance attributes at the same time.

In Graphics mode or Page mode, when you select a size or size attribute in the Font dialog box, WordPerfect shows you what the current font looks like at that size. See the articles "Changing the Font" and "Changing Font Appearance" for more information.

As you can with other font attributes, you can select a relative size attribute from the Font menu or from the Font dialog box. You can select only one relative size at a time.

Change the Font Size

1. Place the cursor in the document where you want to change font size, or select a block of text to change.

2. Choose Font, Font or click the Font button to open the Font dialog box.

3. Do one of the following:

   Choose **S**ize. Highlight a font size in the list or type another size in the Size text box.

   Choose a **R**elative Size attribute.

4. Choose OK.

Troubleshooting

If you select the wrong font size or size attribute, simply select a different size or attribute. You can also choose Reveal Codes (Alt+F3) and delete the font size code or attribute code.

Shortcut Key	
Font Dialog Box	Ctrl+F8

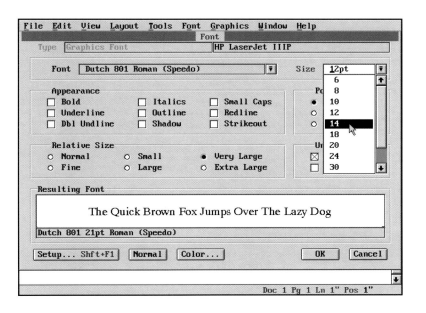

To specify a size, you can select from the list or type the value you want.

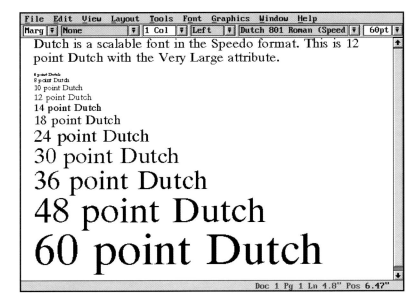

WordPerfect can show quite a range of font sizes in Graphics mode.

Just as you change the sound of your voice to give emphasis when you speak, you can change the appearance of your text to give emphasis to your documents.

The most common ways to change a font's appearance are to make the font bold or italic. But bold and italic are only two of WordPerfect's *appearance attributes*. WordPerfect offers nine appearance attributes in all. You can select the one you need.

Note: *Depending on your printer and the fonts you have available, you may not be able to use all the attributes, or the printed appearance of some attributes may not be quite what you expect.*

TIP

You can apply more than one appearance attribute to a block of text. You can mix bold with italic, outline with small caps, or even combine three or more attributes. If you combine several attributes, print a sample to see if the combined effect is pleasing.

WordPerfect Attributes

◆ *Bold*, *italic*, and *underline* have already been described in the "Changing the Font" section. You can also use double underline as an emphasized underline or to distinguish a grand total from a regular total in a column of numbers.

◆ *Outline* and *shadow* are special effects. Outline makes text appear as a hollow outline, and shadow prints an offset gray shadow slightly below text. Outline and shadow work best on large font sizes and may be most useful for posters and fliers.

◆ *Small caps* displays lowercase letters as uppercase letters of a smaller point size. You can use a mixture of normal and small caps as a design effect, or use small caps to make large groups of uppercase letters more readable. The uppercase letters of proportionally spaced fonts are much larger than lowercase letters, so acronyms such as AFL-CIO stand out awkwardly from the surrounding text. If you use small caps for an acronym such as AFL-CIO, the smaller capitals blend in more gracefully.

◆ *Strikeout* and *redline* show revisions to a document. Strikeout draws a line through text, clearly indicating that the text is to be deleted. Redline indicates that a word or phrase has been inserted into the document. Although redline appears as red on-screen, it can't print in red unless you have a color printer.

Superscript and Subscript

For technical word processing, you need superscripts and subscripts, whether to indicate measurements (ft^2) or formulas (H_2O). WordPerfect creates super- and subscripts through *position attributes*, which work like appearance and relative size attributes. When you apply a position attribute to a block, WordPerfect changes the font size of the block to 60 percent of the base font size and then raises or lowers the block from the line of text.

Selecting Appearance Attributes

You can apply appearance attributes to a block of text, or you can select an attribute, type the text, and then reselect the attribute to turn it off.

You can select appearance attributes one at a time from the Font menu, or you can select one or more appearance attributes at the same time in the Font dialog box.

In Graphics mode or Page mode, if you select appearance attributes in the Font dialog box, WordPerfect shows you what the current font looks like with that attribute, or combination of attributes, selected. You can also select a different font or font size at the same time. See "Changing the Font" for more information.

How WordPerfect Changes the Font

When you apply an appearance attribute to a block, WordPerfect places an *attribute on* code at the beginning of the block and an *attribute off* code at the end of the block. WordPerfect then changes the appearance of the text within the block by using one of several methods:

◆ First, if possible, the program changes to a related font. If you apply the bold attribute to the Dutch font, for example, WordPerfect uses the Dutch Bold font; for italic, WordPerfect switches to Dutch Italic, and if you combine the two attributes, WordPerfect uses Dutch Bold Italic. Most font packages intended for use as body text contain a regular (Roman), a bold, an italic, and a bold italic font.

◆ Second, if the font is not available, WordPerfect tells the printer to generate the attribute. For example, PostScript printers can generate outline and shadow effects automatically.

◆ Finally, if necessary, WordPerfect generates the attribute as a graphic.

more ▶

Relative Size versus Fixed Size

If you select a specific font size for a heading, changing the size of the body text doesn't affect the size of the heading. If you use a relative size for a heading, however, changing the size of the body text changes the heading size in proportion to the new size of the body text. Therefore, you need to specify a font size when you want the size of a block to remain fixed, regardless of the size of surrounding text; you also need to use relative size attributes when you want the size of a block to remain in proportion to the surrounding text.

You can also change size by using *relative size font attributes*, which are paired codes related to bold and italic. Just as bold and italic change the appearance of a block of text, relative size attributes change the size of a block of text relative to the current font size. Each relative size attribute changes the size of a block to a percentage of the current font size. By default, Fine is 60 percent, Small is 80 percent, Large is 120 percent, Very Large is 150 percent, and Extra Large is 200 percent.

Change the Font Appearance (Dialog Box)

1. Select a block of text.

2. Choose Font, Font.

3. Do one of the following:

   Click on an appearance attribute.

   Choose **A**ppearance, then type the mnemonic letter for an appearance attribute.

4. If desired, repeat step 3 to choose additional attributes.

5. Choose OK.

Troubleshooting

◆ If you select an attribute by mistake, select the same attribute to turn it off.

◆ You can also choose Reveal Codes (Alt+F3) and delete an attribute code.

Shortcut Keys

Bold	F6
Italic	Ctrl+I
Underline	F8
Normal	Ctrl+N
Font Dialog Box	Ctrl+F8

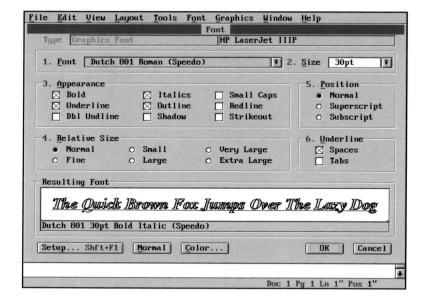

Notice that the sample text shows you in advance how your changes will affect the document.

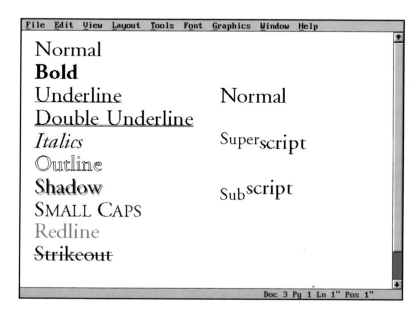

The font appearance options give you a wide variety of looks for your text.

Change the Font Appearance (Font Menu)

1. Select a block of text.

2. Choose Font to open the Font menu.

3. Choose the appearance attribute you want from the Font menu.

Troubleshooting

◆ If you select an attribute by mistake, select the same attribute to turn it off.

◆ You can also choose Reveal Codes (Alt+F3) and delete an attribute code.

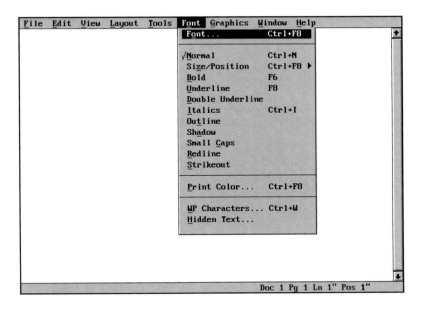

Shortcut Keys	
Bold	F6
Italic	Ctrl+I
Underline	F8
Normal	Ctrl+N
Font Dialog Box	Ctrl+F8

Many of the font appearance options can be selected directly from the Font menu.

The keyboard doesn't have enough room for every character you may want to use—even something as common as a cents sign (¢). But WordPerfect can insert thousands of special characters into your documents.

You can insert all kinds of special characters with the WordPerfect Characters feature. For legal work, you can use paragraph (¶), section (§), copyright (©), and registration (®) symbols. You can choose from many kinds of bullets (•). For a more professional-looking document, use true "curly" quotation marks (" "), en dashes (–), and em dashes (—).

Working in a foreign language? Insert foreign letters (è, ç, ñ). Scientific or technical work is much easier when you can insert Greek letters and other symbols (α, °, ±).

Character Sets and Numbers

WordPerfect groups the characters into 15 *character sets*. Each character set contains dozens or hundreds of related letters or symbols. To insert any character, you need to tell WordPerfect only the character set to which the character belongs and then the character's number within that character set. For example, a bullet (•) is character set 4, character number 0; or 4,0.

Your WordPerfect program directory contains a document named CHARACTR.DOC, which lists for each character the character set and number, the printed character itself, and a text description of the character. CHARMAP.TST is a shorter document that just contains the characters themselves.

TIP
If you know the character set and number of the character, use the Compose shortcut key.

Inserting a Special Character

Fortunately, you don't have to remember the numbers. WordPerfect displays a dialog box that shows the characters. (In Text mode, you can't see all the characters.) Because so many characters are available, the dialog box can show only one character set at a time. You may need to scroll the list box to see all the characters.

Mnemonic Shortcut Keys

WordPerfect provides mnemonic shortcuts for commonly used characters and symbols. To use these shortcuts, choose WP Characters or Compose and then type two characters (rather than numbers), without a comma in between.

To insert a bullet, for example, choose Compose and then type two asterisks. You can combine the accent marks and diacritics (such as umlaut (ü) and caret (ô)) with almost any vowel and many consonants.

The next page lists some common characters. Appendix A of the WordPerfect manual includes a more complete list.

Insert a Special Character

1. Choose F**o**nt, **W**P Characters.

2. Choose **S**et

3. Choose a character set from the drop-down list.

4. With the mouse, double-click on the character.

   With the keyboard, choose **C**haracters, then highlight a character and press Enter.

Troubleshooting

WordPerfect treats WordPerfect characters like any other letter, number, or punctuation mark. If you insert the wrong character, simply delete it and select another character.

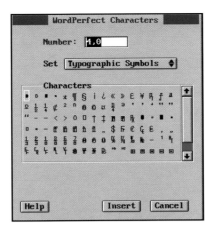

*To insert a character, you can either type the set and number, separated by a comma, in the **N**umber text box or select a character directly in the **C**haracters list box.*

Shortcut Keys	
WP Characters	Ctrl+W
Compose	Ctrl+A

Character	Description	Character	Description
**	(2 asterisks)	•	Bullet
*O	(asterisk, large O)	○	Hollow bullet
Pl	(P, vertical line)	¶	Paragraph
co	(small c, small o)	®	Copyright
c/	(c, slash)	¢	Cent
L-	(L, dash)	£	Pound
/2	(slash, 2)	½	One half
n-	(n, dash)	–	en dash
m-	(m, dash or 2 dashes)	—	em dash
>>	(2 greater thans)	»	Much greater than
>=	(greater than, equals)	≥	greater than or equal to
+ -	(plus, dash)	±	Plus or minus
??	(2 question marks)	¿	Spanish question mark
!!	(2 exclamation points)	¡	Spanish exclamation mark
n~	(n, tilde)	ñ	lowercase n with tilde
e'	(e, single quotationmark)	é	lowercase e with acute accent
e`	(e, left quotation mark)	è	lowercase e with grave accent
u"	(u, double quotation mark)	ü	lowercase u with umlaut
o^	(o, caret)	ô	lowercase o with caret
ss	(2 small s')	ß	German double s
c,	(c, comma)	ç	lowercase French cedilla

You can use tabs to align columns of numbers or to indent paragraphs or outlines.

If you've ever used a typewriter, you're probably familiar with tabs. Tabs align text a particular distance from the left edge of the paper, such as in columns of numbers. In WordPerfect, tabs are easy to set. What's more, you can change your tab setting in WordPerfect to change the alignment or indentation of text you've already typed.

Default Tabs

By default, WordPerfect sets tabs every $1/2$ inch, but you can insert a new tab at any point in a document. You can add or delete one tab or several tabs. You can delete all tabs or set tabs at a different repeating interval, such as every $1/4$ or $1/3$ inch.

Note: *Always clear existing tabs before inserting new repeating tabs.*

Absolute versus Relative Tabs

Tabs measure distance from the edge of the page (*absolute tabs*) or from the left margin (*relative tabs*). Absolute tabs are fixed; changing margins doesn't affect them. Relative tabs are flexible; if you change the margins, the tabs change with the left margin. You can't have a mix of absolute and relative tabs in one tab setting, but you can use absolute tabs in one part of a document and relative tabs in another. The default is relative.

Tab Codes

You can insert a tab set code anywhere in a document. WordPerfect changes the settings from that point until the end of the document or until it encounters another code of the same type. You can also select a block of text and apply a tab set to it.

> **TIP**
> You can create tables by setting tabs to align each column properly. If a table is large or complex, however, use WordPerfect's Table feature. See "Tables."

Adding Dot Leaders

A *dot leader* is a line of dots across a page that helps your eye connect a text description on the left with a number on the right. You can add a dot leader to any tab setting by selecting a tab, then choosing Dot Leader. (You may want to clear all tabs, then set one tab with a dot leader near the right margin.) In your document, when you press Tab, WordPerfect automatically adds the dots.

Left, Right, Center, or Decimal?

◆ A left tab is a "normal" tab; items align on their left edges.

◆ A right tab aligns items on their right edges.

◆ WordPerfect centers text around a center tab position.

◆ A decimal tab is similar to a right tab, but WordPerfect aligns with decimal points. You should *always* use decimal tabs to align numbers; never use spaces.

Set or Change Tabs

1. Place the cursor at the point in the document where you want to change the tab settings or select the block of text you want to change.

2. Choose **L**ayout, Ta**b** Set.

3. If desired, choose Absolute or Relative.

4. Do one or more of the following:

   To delete a tab, move the cursor under the tab and choose Clear **O**ne. To delete all tabs, choose Clear **A**ll.

   To set a tab, choose Set Tab and enter a measurement, double-click the position on the ruler or scroll to that position and press Enter.

   To set repeating tabs, choose Repeat Every and type a measurement.

   To change alignment, choose Left, Right, Center, or Decimal.

5. Choose OK or press F7 (Exit).

Troubleshooting

◆ Choose Cancel or press Esc to abandon your changes and return to your original settings. If you've already inserted the new tab set code, choose Undo or turn on Reveal Codes and delete the code.

Shortcut Key

| Tab Set | Ctrl+F11 |

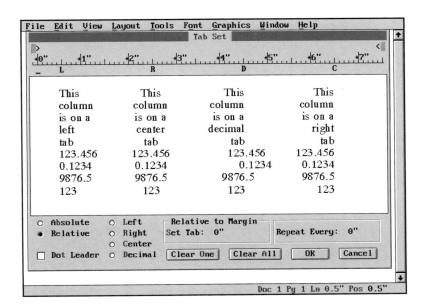

If you choose the right tab settings, typing a column of mixed numbers and text is really easy!

This figure shows a variety of tab options. (The text explains how the settings vary the look of the document.)

File   Edit   View   Layout   Tools   Font   Graphics   Window   Help

By default, WordPerfect sets tabs every one half inch. If you use tabs to indent your paragraphs, with most proportionally-spaced fonts, a half-inch tab set creates a large paragraph indent.

If you set tabs to every third of an inch, or even every quarter of an inch, the indentation is still quite noticeable, but creates a more pleasing effect.

VIII.   If you create an outline, you may need to adjust your tab settings to make room for your outline numbers.

You can set a tab with a dot leader . . . . like this
or without a dot leader   like this

Doc 1 Pg 1 Ln 1" Pos 1"

Do you want your right margin ragged (uneven) or even? Each gives your document a different look and feel. You can use Justification codes to change the alignment of your text.

When you type a paragraph on a typewriter, each line begins at the left margin; but due to differing word lengths, each line ends at a different spot near the right margin. Most books, magazines, and newspapers, however, are printed with both margins even. This effect is achieved with *justification*.

Types of Justification

Here are the different types of justification:

◆ Text with even left and right margins is said to be *justified*, or *full justified*. Most of your documents need to be primarily left justified or full justified to make long passages of text easy to read. Because full justification expands and compresses lines to fit exact margins, some lines may have large gaps between words, or words may appear to run together. These visual defects are magnified by larger font sizes and narrow text widths.

TIP Hyphenate long words to improve the appearance of full-justified text.

◆ Text with an even left margin and a ragged right margin is *left justified*, even though technically nothing is being adjusted. The spacing between words doesn't change, which looks more natural. The right margin may look ragged; fix it by hyphenating.

◆ Text with an even right margin and a ragged left margin is *right justified*. Right justification looks unnatural to most readers of English, although some languages such as Hebrew are read right to left and are normally right justified. You can use right justification as a design effect to justify small amounts of text, such as a heading or figure caption.

◆ Text aligned along its center is *center justified*. Center justification is excellent for centering multiline titles or for creating full-page fliers or posters with few words in a large point size.

◆ When you choose *Full, All Lines Justification*, WordPerfect forces *every* line of text to be justified on both margins, even lines with only two or three words. This justification option is useful as a design effect to spread out titles and headings but shouldn't be used on body text.

Justification Codes

Alignment codes act on only a single line of text, whereas justification codes change the justification for *all* text that follows, up to another justification code or the end of the document.

You can insert a justification code at any point in a document to change the justification of the following text. You can also select a block of text and change the justification of the block.

Change Justification

1. Place the cursor in the document where you want to change justification, or select a block of text.

2. Choose **L**ayout, **J**ustification.

3. Choose the desired justification setting: **L**eft, **C**enter, **R**ight, or **F**ull. To force all lines to full justification, choose Full, **A**ll Lines.

Troubleshooting

If you select the wrong type of justification, repeat the steps you used to change justification but select a different justification type. You can also use Reveal Codes to find and delete a justification code.

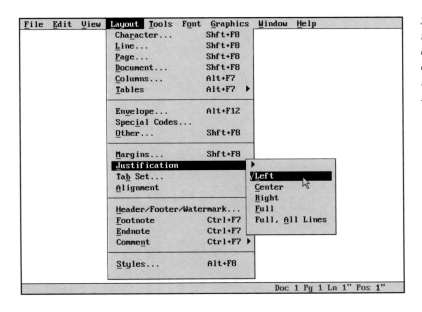

Specifying the justification is as quick as changing the menu command. If you don't like the result, just switch it back.

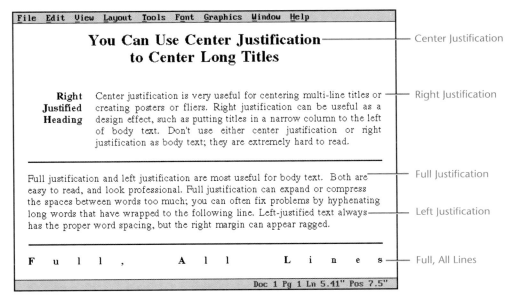

Changing Margins

The area where text is printed on the page is controlled by the margin settings. Margins are the frames around your text and graphics on each page.

Every printed page has margins—the empty border around any text and graphics. Margins help frame the text visually on the page and are often required for practical reasons as well. If your pages are bound, for example, without a margin you can't read any text where pages are close together.

WordPerfect starts text at the left margin and uses the right margin setting to decide where to wrap words to the following line. The program also uses the top margin to position the first line of text on a page and the bottom margin to decide when to start a line of text on the following page. Word-Perfect sets all four margins to 1 inch by default, but you can change the measurement for any or all margins at any time. The program inserts a separate code for each margin you change.

Margin Codes

As with other formatting codes, you can insert a code to change a margin for all following text, or select a block of text and change the left or right margin for just that block. You can't change the top or bottom margin for a block.

WordPerfect inserts left and right margin codes at the beginning of the current paragraph, and top and bottom margin codes at the top of the current page. If you change a block's margin, WordPerfect inserts a margin change code at the beginning of the

block and a revert margin code at the end of the block. See "Looking At Reveal Codes" for more information on revertible codes.

If you want to change the margins just for several paragraphs, you can use the paragraph margin adjustment codes to adjust the margins of those paragraphs without affecting the margins of the entire document. See "Indenting" for more information.

Choosing the Right Margins

◆ Your text should always look balanced on the page. If you create a short letter or memo that fills only a portion of the page, increase the size of all your margins to at least 1.5 inches.

◆ Your margins don't need to be symmetrical. In particular, the left margin is commonly set to a larger value, although you can experiment with changing any margin to achieve a particular effect.

◆ Although page numbers appear to print within your top or bottom margins, they don't. When you use WordPerfect's automatic page numbers or a running header or footer, the program prints that information where the first or last line of text normally prints and subtracts a line or two of text from each page. If you want your page numbers, headers, or footers to appear to print *in* the margin, change the appropriate top or bottom margin setting to a smaller value, roughly between $1/2$ and $2/3$ inch.

Change Margins

1. Place the cursor in the document where you want to change margins, or select a block of text to change.

2. Choose **L**ayout, **M**argins.

3. Choose the desired margin setting: **L**eft Margin, **R**ight Margin, **T**op Margin, or **B**ottom Margin.

4. Type a value. You don't need to type a double quote ("); WordPerfect adds it for you. Again, you can enter a fraction or a decimal value.

5. Press Enter or press Tab to change the next margin setting.

6. Choose OK.

Troubleshooting

If you catch a mistake while you're still in the Margin Format dialog box, you can type a new value for any margin setting or choose Cancel to abandon your changes and return to the previous setting. If you have already inserted a code, you can choose Undo or turn on Reveal Codes and delete the margin code.

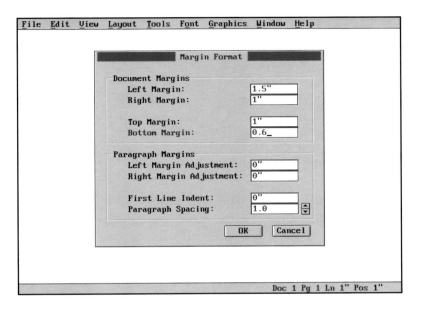

You can specify left and right margins that are different—for example, if you plan to use a plastic binder to hold the document.

*WordPerfect shows both right and left margins. If the text runs off the screen, change the zoom level with the **V**iew **Z**oom command.*

Most documents have 1 inch left and right margins, which provides a nice balance of text on the page. If you are writing a short letter, however, you may want to make your margins wider to keep the text in proportion.

When you change your left and right margins, the length of each line of text changes in proportion. If you make your margins wider, your lines of text become narrower.

If you make your margins narrower, your lines of text become wider. Changing the top and bottom margin has the same effect on the number of lines per page.

You can change the amount of space between lines or paragraphs to improve readability, to enhance a design, or simply to create space to write comments on a printed copy.

As the name implies, *line spacing* is simply the space between the lines of your text. If you look at any printed page, you can see that adjacent lines of text don't actually touch; between each line is a small amount of white space.

Where line spacing changes the spacing between all lines, paragraph spacing changes only the spacing between paragraphs. Because, by definition, a hard return ends a paragraph, when you change paragraph spacing, WordPerfect adds (or removes) space after every hard return that follows the paragraph spacing code.

Changing Line Spacing

You can change spacing on a typewriter; single space, double space, and space-and-a-half are the common settings. Single-spaced text is usually six lines to the inch. Double-spaced text adds a full blank line between lines of text, resulting in three lines per inch, and space-and-a-half adds half a line between, resulting in four lines per inch.

Although you can use equivalent line spacing values of 1.0, 1.5, and 2.0 in Word-Perfect, the program calculates the actual distance between lines based on font point size. The amount of white space between lines changes in proportion to the point size, so single-spaced lines of 10-point type are slightly closer together than single-spaced lines of 12-point type.

By default, WordPerfect sets line spacing to 1.0, but you can change that measurement at any time. WordPerfect doesn't limit you to those few line spacing values either. You can type in nearly any value, out to several decimal places. A value of 1.1 makes your lines print 10 percent farther apart, 0.5 prints your lines half as far apart, and 3.0 prints your lines three times farther apart.

Changing Paragraph Spacing

When you change line spacing, WordPerfect changes the spacing between all lines that follow—or at least until it encounters another line spacing code. But what if you want to change only the space between paragraphs? You can add an extra single line space by pressing Enter twice at the end of each paragraph, thus inserting two hard returns. If you want to add an extra half space between paragraphs, though, you have to insert one hard return, change line spacing to 0.5, insert the second hard return, and then change line spacing back to 1.0 for the following paragraph. In either case, if you later decided to change the spacing between all paragraphs, you have to work your way laboriously through the document, changing spacing one paragraph at a time. Instead, you can change the paragraph spacing.

Combining Line and Paragraph Spacing

In practice, the paragraph spacing value acts as a multiplier of the line spacing value. If your line spacing value is 1.0 and your paragraph spacing value is 2.0, you get double spacing between paragraphs. If you change your line spacing to 1.5, you then get triple spacing between paragraphs. On the other hand, with a line spacing of 2.0 and a paragraph spacing of 0.5, you get single spacing between paragraphs (a combination you would never use in practice). WordPerfect sets paragraph spacing to 1.0 by default, but you can change that measurement at any time.

Line Spacing Codes

As with other formatting codes, you can change line spacing from the location of the cursor down, or select a block of text and change the line spacing for just the block. WordPerfect inserts line spacing codes at the beginning of the current paragraph. If you change a block's spacing, WordPerfect inserts a spacing change code at the beginning of the block and a revert spacing code at the end of the block. See "Looking at Reveal Codes" for more information on revertible codes.

TIP

If you want to proofread a printed copy of a document, you can insert a line spacing code set to 2.0 or larger at the beginning of a document before printing. To finalize the document, change the value back to 1.0.

Paragraph Spacing Codes

You can insert a code to change the spacing for all following paragraphs, or you can select a block and change the paragraph spacing for just the block. WordPerfect inserts paragraph spacing codes at the beginning of the current paragraph. If you change a block's paragraph spacing, WordPerfect inserts a change paragraph spacing code at the beginning of the block and a revert code at the end of the block. See "Looking At Reveal Codes" for more information on revertible codes.

TIP

Paragraph spacing is only one method to separate paragraphs visually. Another equally common method is to indent paragraphs. You can combine the two easily. With single-spaced text, for example, paragraph spacing of 1.5 and indents of $1/4$ inch or $1/3$ inch make an attractive combination. See "Indenting Paragraphs" for help on indenting paragraphs.

more ▶

FORMATTING

Change Line Spacing

1. Place the cursor in the document where you want to change line spacing, or select a block of text.

2. Choose **L**ayout, **L**ine.

3. Do one of the following:

Choose Line **S**pacing and then enter a value.

Click the increment buttons to raise or lower the value.

4. Choose OK.

Troubleshooting

◆ If you catch a mistake while you're still in the Line Format dialog box, you can type in a new value or choose Cancel to abandon your change.

◆ If you have already inserted a line spacing code, you can choose Undo or turn on Reveal Codes and delete the margin code.

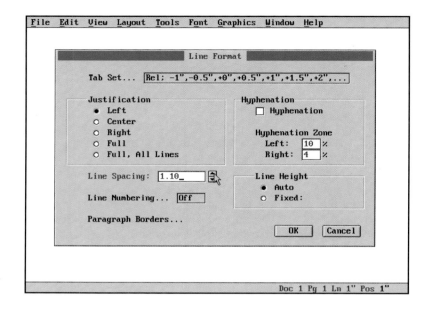

Many teachers specify double spacing as the required format for term papers. Use this dialog box to set the spacing as you need it.

Notice how the change in spacing varies the look of the document. Experiment with spacing in flyers, brochures, and so on for different effects.

Change Paragraph Spacing

1. Place the cursor in the document where you want to change paragraph spacing, or select a block of text to change.

2. Choose **L**ayout, **M**argins.

3. Do one of the following:

Choose **P**aragraph Spacing and then enter a value.

Click the increment buttons to raise or lower the paragraph spacing value.

4. Choose OK.

Troubleshooting

◆ If you want to change a paragraph spacing value, move your cursor to the paragraph in which you previously changed paragraph spacing and repeat the steps, selecting a different value.

◆ You can also turn on Reveal Codes and delete the [Para Spacing] code.

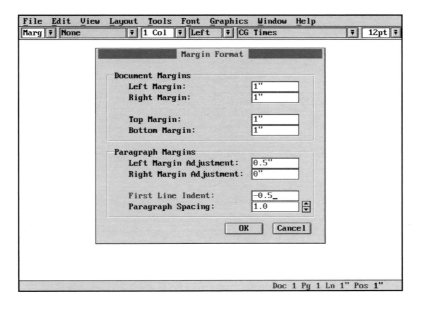

Depending on the format of your document paragraphs, you may want spacing of all paragraphs to be uniform.

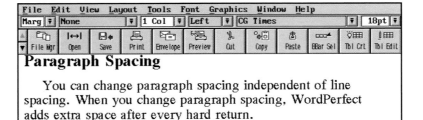

Paragraph Spacing

You can change paragraph spacing independent of line spacing. When you change paragraph spacing, WordPerfect adds extra space after every hard return.

The paragraph spacing value acts as a multiplier of the line spacing value. With line spacing set at 1.0, a paragraph spacing value of 1.5 adds an extra half space between paragraphs. With line spacing set at 2.0, paragraph spacing of 1.5 results in a triple space between paragraphs.

You can change paragraph spacing in combination with paragraph indents to visually separate paragraphs.

Although you can insert extra hard returns between paragraphs, changing the paragraph spacing saves time.

Documents should always display a visual break between paragraphs so that the end of each paragraph and the beginning of the next are obvious. One of the most common methods is to indent paragraphs.

You can indent a single paragraph using one of WordPerfect's Tab and Indent codes (see "Indenting Text"); however, if you want to indent every paragraph of a document in the same manner, you must insert one or more of these codes for every paragraph. If you later decide to change the way your paragraphs are indented, you must go through your document paragraph by paragraph, inserting or deleting codes. Instead, you can change the indentation of all paragraphs by inserting margin adjustment codes.

You can adjust three values for your paragraphs: left margin adjustment, right margin adjustment, and first line indent.

Margin Adjustment Codes

You can adjust paragraph margins for all following text, or you can select a block of text and adjust the paragraph margins for just the block. WordPerfect inserts margin format codes at the beginning of the current paragraph. If you change a block's margin, WordPerfect inserts a change code at the beginning of the block and a revert code at the end of the block.

Understanding Margin Adjustment

Margin adjustment settings are relative to your document's left and right margin. Selecting a left margin adjustment value of 0.5" indents each line of all paragraphs $1/2$ inch from the left margin. If you later change the left margin, adjusted paragraphs move with the margin.

The first line indent setting, on the other hand, changes only the first line of following paragraphs. If you type a document in block format, with no indentation of any sort, and then insert a first line indent code with a value of 0.5" at the beginning of the document, WordPerfect indents the first line of all following paragraphs by $1/2$ inch.

Margin Adjustment Tips

Keep the following thoughts in mind when you specify the margin adjustment settings:

◆ A first line indent of $1/2$ inch is often much too large for proportionally spaced fonts such as Dutch or Swiss, particularly at sizes smaller than 12 points. Try indenting by $1/3$ inch or even $1/4$ inch.

◆ You can create a hanging indent by combining a left margin adjustment with a negative first line indent. If you select a left margin adjustment of 0.5" and a first line indent of –0.5", WordPerfect indents the entire paragraph and then reverse indents the first line by the same amount.

◆ If you want to indent paragraphs in several ways throughout a document, place the paragraph adjustment codes in paragraph styles. You can then change a paragraph's indentation by applying a single style code to the paragraph.

Adjust Paragraph Margins

1. Place the cursor in the document where you want to adjust margins, or select a block of text to change.

2. Choose **L**ayout, **M**argins.

3. Choose the setting you want to change: L**e**ft Margin Adjustment, **R**ight Margin Adjustment, or **F**irst Line Indent.

4. Type a value; you can use decimals or fractions.

5. Press Enter or press Tab to change the next setting.

6. Choose OK.

Troubleshooting

◆ If you discover a mistake while still in the Margin Format dialog box, you can choose the setting again and enter a different value, or choose Cancel to abandon any changes and return to the document.

◆ If you want to change your margin adjustment at a later time, move the cursor to the original location, then repeat the steps above, entering a different value. You can also turn on Reveal Codes and delete the [Lft Mar Adj], [Rgt Mar Adj], or [First Ln Ind] codes.

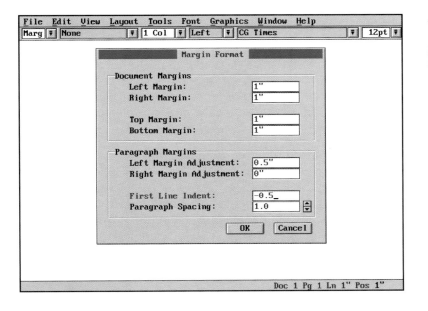

If the margin is off "by a fraction," feel free to make adjustments in fractions!

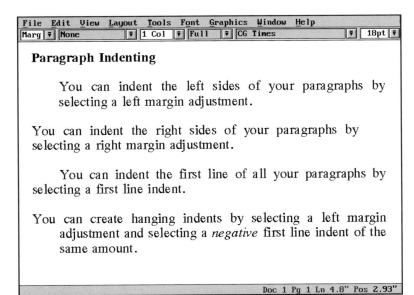

A hanging indent is particularly useful for bibliography entries and bulleted lists.

If you create long documents, add page numbers so that your reader can keep track of the pages.

If you look at any book, magazine, or newspaper, you find numbered pages. Page numbers tell you where you are in a document and help you find specific pages quickly and easily. If you drop a 20-page report, for example, putting the pages back in order takes much longer if they don't have page numbers.

When you use WordPerfect's automatic page numbering, your document is printed with the correct page numbers. You can add or delete text at will; when you reprint the document, the numbers still come out correctly because page numbers are tied to the pages themselves, rather than to the information on any given page.

Page Number Locations

WordPerfect can print page numbers in any of six standard locations, with several variations:

You can instruct the program to print numbers at the top or bottom of each page, positioned at the left margin, centered between margins, or at the right margin. These positions are most useful if you expect people to read a document printed on one side of each page.

If you intend to print or reproduce your document on both sides of the page, WordPerfect can print page numbers in opposing corners, top or bottom. WordPerfect's settings for two-sided documents place the numbers for odd pages in the upper or lower right corner and the numbers for even pages in the upper or lower left corner, so the numbers are always at the outside edge of the page.

The Page Number Position dialog box lets you choose between all the preceding options. The diagrams on the right side of the dialog box illustrate where page numbers appear if you choose the corresponding number on the left.

TIP

In any two-sided document, when you look at two facing pages, the odd-numbered page should always be on the right.

Where Do the Numbers Print?

Although you may expect WordPerfect to print page numbers within your top or bottom margins, the program doesn't work that way. Instead, WordPerfect prints page numbers at the top of the page where the first line of text normally prints or at the bottom of the page where the last line of text normally prints. As a result, the amount of text that prints on each page is a line or two shorter.

TIP

If you want your text to remain the same but have your page numbers print higher or lower on the page, change the top or bottom margin setting to a smaller value, usually to between $1/2$ and $2/3$ inch.

Viewing Page Numbers

After you turn on page numbering, you can't see the page numbers on-screen in Text mode or Graphics mode. You must select Page mode or use Print Preview to see the numbers with your document's text. See "Changing the View" for help in changing View mode and "Previewing a Document" for help in using Print Preview.

TIP

If you want to combine other information with page numbers, such as a chapter title or some other text, use a header or footer instead. Headers and footers can contain text, graphics such as a logo, and page numbering codes. You can also choose the Insert Formatted Page Number option from within a header or footer to include a page number with more elaborate formatting. See the following article for help in using headers and footers.

more ▶

Changing Page Numbering Options

In addition to selecting the placement, you can also change other page numbering options:

◆ *Starting page number.* If your document is actually part of a longer document, you can start numbering at any number—10, 32, 263, or any other appropriate number. Alternatively, if you have a title page and other introductory material, you can also start page numbering over again at 1 for your body text.

◆ *Numbering Method.* Many books contain an introductory section with pages numbered with Roman numerals. WordPerfect lets you change the numbering method to upper- or lowercase Roman numerals, upper- or lowercase letters, or simple numbers.

◆ *Secondary Page Number.* You can actually maintain two page numbering sequences. For example, some magazines number the pages of each issue separately but also use a cumulative page count for all issues in a volume. Secondary page numbers act exactly like "normal" page numbers.

◆ *Chapter and Volume.* If your document is divided into chapters, volumes, or other sections, WordPerfect can automatically include the current chapter or volume number in your page numbering, such as A-4. Chapter and volume are essentially the same; however, they enable you to maintain two different numbering schemes for document sections, much like "normal" and secondary page numbers. You must tell WordPerfect where each section starts, though.

◆ *Page Number Format.* By default, WordPerfect prints page numbers using the selected numbering method. You can embellish the page number with text or include secondary page numbers, chapter, or volume number. You can make the numbers appear as Page 3, - 3 -, Volume 2, Issue 4, Page 3, or other combinations.

◆ *Insert Formatted Page Number.* WordPerfect normally prints page numbers at the top or bottom of the page. If you choose Insert Formatted Page Number, WordPerfect inserts a code in your document that causes the current page number to appear in your text.

Number Pages Automatically

1. Move the cursor to the top of the page on which you want to start page numbering, before any text.

2. Choose **L**ayout, **P**age to open the Page Format dialog box.

3. Choose Page **N**umbering to open the Page Numbering dialog box.

4. Choose Page Number **P**osition to open the Page Number Position dialog box.

5. Choose a position or choose **N**one to turn off page numbering.

6. Choose OK to close each open dialog box.

Troubleshooting

If you don't like the page number position you select, repeat the steps and select a different position, or you can choose None to remove page numbers. You can also turn on Reveal Codes and delete the [Pg Num Pos] code. When you turn on page numbering, WordPerfect inserts the code at the top of the current page.

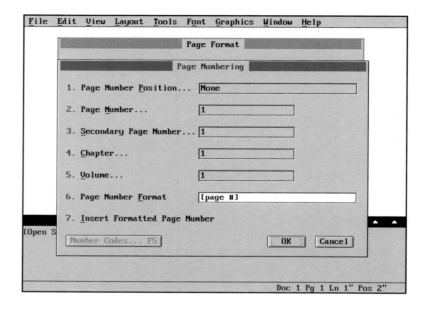

The page numbering feature makes reading long printed documents much easier.

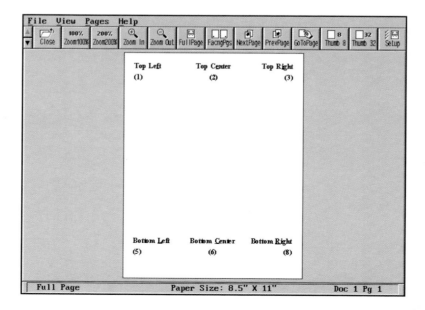

If you want one page number to include text, use a header or footer instead.

Change Page Numbering Options

1. Choose **L**ayout, **P**age.

2. Choose Page **N**umbering.

3. Do one of the following:

   To change the starting page number, choose Page **N**umber, New **N**umber, and enter the desired page number.

   To change the numbering method, choose Page **N**umber, Numbering **M**ethod, and choose an option.

   To change the secondary page number, choose **S**econdary Page Number, New **N**umber, and enter the desired page number.

   To use chapter and volume numbers, choose **C**hapter or **V**olume, **I**ncrement Number.

   To change the page number format, choose Page Number **F**ormat, then add any text or symbols you like on either side of the [page #] code. To include **S**econdary Page Number, **C**hapter Number, or **V**olume Number, choose Number Codes (F5), then select one of the preceding options.

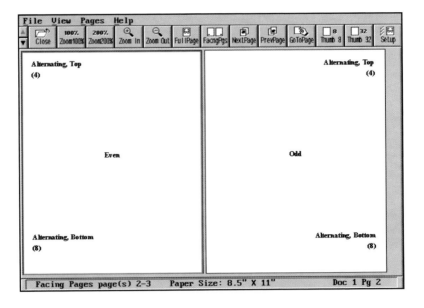

You can choose a numbering method for secondary page numbers, if desired.

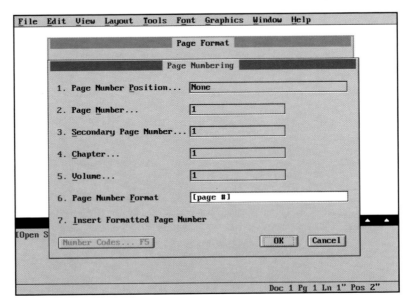

If you don't like the new option, follow the same steps and change back to the original setting.

FORMATTING

For long documents or articles, you may want certain information (article name, your name, date) to print on every page. To do so with WordPerfect, you create a header or a footer.

At the top or bottom of each page, many books and magazines print the current page number and information such as the author's name, the title of the current chapter or article, the name of the book or magazine, the current date, or the volume and issue number. When you write a letter or memo longer than one page, it's customary to identify subsequent pages with a page number and the name of the person you're writing to and the date. Like page numbers, this information repeats from page to page, regardless of the contents of individual pages.

Repeating information at the top of a page is a *header* and at the bottom of a page is a *footer*. Don't confuse these terms with "heading" or "footnote."

How Headers and Footers Work

Just as WordPerfect can print page numbers automatically at the top or bottom of each page, the program can also print headers and footers on each page. The contents and position of headers and footers aren't affected by changes to the document. In Word-Perfect, a header or a footer is actually a small document all to itself, usually one or two lines long but capable of holding up to a page's worth of information. (If you want a header to repeat on every page, you cannot make the header longer than a page.) As you do with any document, you must decide what text to put in a header or footer, how to align or justify it, and so on.

On any given page, WordPerfect allows you to have as many as two headers, two footers, and automatic page numbers. The headers are referred to as Header A and Header B, to distinguish one from the other, and the footers are likewise Footer A and Footer B. You can create Header B, however, without creating Header A.

Header and Footer Positions

When you create a header or footer, Word-Perfect gives you some options about placement. Any header or footer can appear on all pages, on odd-numbered pages, or on even-numbered pages. If you're creating a two-sided publication, you can print Header A on odd pages and Header B on even pages. You can also print one or both on all pages.

TIP

If Header A and Header B print on the same page, you must make sure that the information in one doesn't overlap information in the other (or automatic page numbers, if present) when you print; otherwise, WordPerfect cheerfully prints one on top of the other. To avoid this situation, you can align one header on the left margin and the other on the right margin, or you can put the information in Header B on a different line from Header A.

WordPerfect prints headers at the top of the page, where the first line of text normally prints, and footers at the bottom of the page, where the last line of text normally prints. As a result, the amount of text that prints on each page is a line or two shorter.

> **TIP**
> If you want your text to remain the same but have your headers or footers print higher or lower on the page, change the top or bottom margin setting to a smaller value, to roughly between $1/2$ and $2/3$ inch.

Creating and Changing Headers and Footers

If you want a header or footer to print only on a certain number of pages, such as the current chapter of a long document, you can use one of two methods. First, turn off the header or footer at the end of the chapter. Alternatively, replace the header by inserting a new header or footer at the start of the next chapter. Your document then can have one Header B containing the title of the overall publication, for example, and multiple Header A's, each containing the title of the current chapter or section.

Keep in mind that when you edit the contents of a header or footer, if your document has several instances of the same header or footer letter, the program searches backward through the document to find the header or footer to edit.

To edit the header or footer, choose Layout, Header/Footer/Watermark, Headers or Footers, A or B, Edit. Then make any changes.

If you want to delete a header or footer after you create it, move the cursor to the paragraph in which you created the header or footer and choose **L**ayout, **H**eader/Footer/ Watermark, **H**eaders or **F**ooters, **A** or **B**, O**ff**.

You can turn on Reveal Codes and delete the [Header A] code or other header or footer code. WordPerfect places header and footer codes at the beginning of the current paragraph.

> **TIP**
> If you want to move the location of the page number to the bottom center of the page, instead of suppressing the number entirely, don't choose the Page Numbering option. Instead, choose Print Page Number at **B**ottom Center.

Viewing the Header or Footer

After you create a header or footer, you cannot see it on-screen in Text mode or Graphics mode. You must select Page mode or use Print Preview to see the header or footer with your document's text. See "Changing the View" for help in changing views and "Previewing a Document" for help in using Print Preview.

Suppressing Headers and Footers

On some pages—for instance, title pages— you probably don't want the header or printer to print. You can suppress these page elements on any given page and at the same time change the page numbering location to bottom center.

> **TIP**
> You aren't limited to using the Suppress feature on the first page of a document. You can suppress page elements on any individual page or several different pages. Each suppress code can suppress many page elements but suppresses only those elements on the current page.

more ▶

FORMATTING

Create a Header or Footer

1. Move the cursor to the top of the page on which you want to start the header or footer, before any text.

2. Choose **L**ayout, **H**eader/Footer/Watermark.

3. Choose **H**eaders or **F**ooters.

4. Choose **A** or **B**.

5. Choose the frequency for the header/footer to appear: **A**ll Pages, E**v**en Pages, or **O**dd Pages.

6. Choose **C**reate.

7. Insert any text, graphics, or formatting codes you want.

8. If you want to include an automatic page number, press Ctrl+P.

9. When you're satisfied, press F7.

Troubleshooting

If you decide not to use your header or footer while in the process of creating it, press Esc and then choose **D**iscard Changes and Exit from the small dialog box that appears.

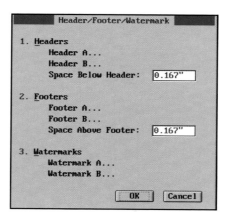

Remember that headers and footers are visible only in Page Mode or Print Preview.

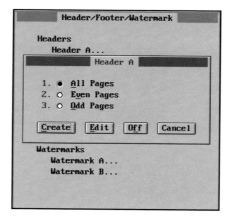

After you specify that you want to create a header or footer, you indicate where you want it to appear.

Suppress a Header or Footer

1. Move the cursor to the page on which you want to suppress page elements.

2. Choose **L**ayout, **P**age.

3. Choose S**u**ppress.

4. Do one of the following:

   Mark one or more check boxes for the headers, footers, watermarks, or page numbers you want to suppress by clicking the option with your mouse or by typing the option's mnemonic letter.

   Choose **S**uppress All to mark all page elements to be suppressed.

5. Choose OK or Close to close all open dialog boxes.

Troubleshooting

◆ You can also turn on Reveal Codes and delete the [Header A] code or other header or footer code.

◆ If you decide that you want to suppress different page elements, move the cursor to the desired page and then repeat the steps, marking or unmarking the appropriate check boxes. If you unmark all boxes, WordPerfect removes the suppress code. You can also turn on Reveal Codes and delete the [Suppress] code. Word-Perfect places suppress codes at the top of the current page.

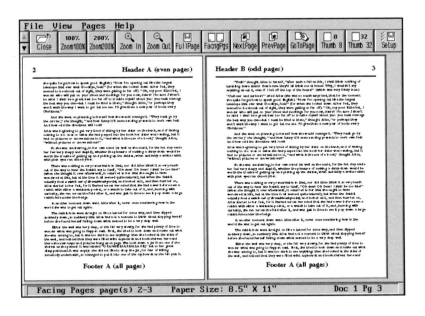

Notice that you can have different combinations of headers and footers.

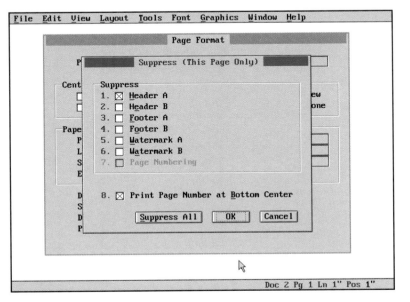

You can suppress any or all of the current headers, footers, and watermarks.

FORMATTING

Confidential. Do not copy. For internal use only. When you need to mark a document for special treatment, you don't have to stamp every page; WordPerfect "stamps" documents automatically with a watermark.

A real watermark is a faint logo impressed on fine quality paper. In WordPerfect, a *watermark* is a faint graphic or piece of text printed "behind" the text of your document. In fact, Word-Perfect prints the two together, but it prints only a faint image of the watermark.

Watermarks Compared to Headers and Footers

In many respects, watermarks act like headers and footers. Any page can have up to two watermarks—Watermark A and Watermark B—and you can print any watermark on all pages, odd-numbered pages, or even-numbered pages. Watermarks differ from headers and footers in one crucial aspect, however. Where a header or footer "pushes aside" your document's text to make room for itself, a watermark is printed as a layer underneath the document text.

Ideas for Watermarks

A watermark is actually a small document all to itself. You can put virtually any information in a watermark, including text and graphics images. Whether you use text or a graphic in a watermark, WordPerfect displays the watermark's contents grayed out.

If you want to use text as a watermark, use a large point size, such as 60 or 72 point, and you may want to center your text. You can also retrieve any graphic image into a watermark. WordPerfect includes several sample images designed to be used as watermarks. You can find them in your graphics subdirectory, with names such as WATER4.WPG. See "Lines and Boxes" for help in working with graphic images.

TIP

After you create a watermark, you cannot see it on-screen in *any* view mode. You must use Print Preview to see the watermark with your document's text. See "Previewing a Document" for help in using Print Preview.

Creating and Changing Watermarks

You can edit or turn off a watermark just as you can a header or footer. You can also replace the watermark by inserting a new watermark on a later page. When you edit the contents of a watermark, keep in mind that if your document has several instances of the same watermark letter, the program searches backward through the document to find the watermark to edit.

TIP

To suppress the watermark on a page, see the preceding article. This article includes the steps to suppress a header, footer, or watermark.

Create a Watermark

1. Move the cursor to the top of the page on which you want to start the watermark, before any text.

2. Choose **L**ayout, **H**eader/Footer/Watermark.

3. Choose **W**atermarks.

4. Choose **A** or **B**.

5. Choose the frequency for the watermark: **A**ll Pages, E**v**en Pages, or **O**dd Pages.

6. Choose **C**reate.

7. Insert any text, graphics, or formatting codes you want.

8. When you're satisfied, press F7.

Troubleshooting

If you want to edit a watermark after you create it, move the cursor to the paragraph in which you created the watermark. Choose Layout, Header/Footer/Watermark, Watermarks, A or B, **E**dit. To delete the item, choose O**ff** (or delete the code in Reveal Codes).

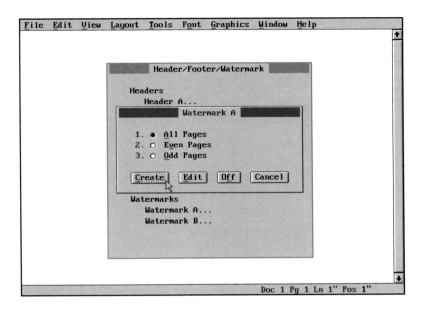

The watermark options are the same as those for headers and footers.

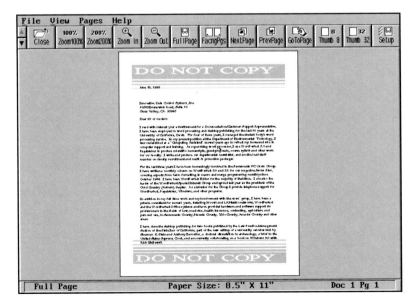

Print preview of watermark.

Paragraph and Page Borders

If you want to give a document a distinctive appearance, add a graphic border around one or more individual paragraphs or entire pages. You can also add a shaded background.

When you create a page border, WordPerfect automatically draws a rectangular border around your entire page, including headers, footers, and page numbers.

Paragraph borders act much the same as page borders, but do not surround page numbers, headers, or footers.

Note: Both types of borders have the same line, fill, and customization options, and except for the titles, the dialog boxes that create the two types of borders are identical.

Page Borders

WordPerfect automatically selects a single line 0.13-inch thick to create a page border, but you can select a different line appearance from a list of line styles, including double, dotted, dashed, thick, thin, and more. At the same time, you can select a fill style. Most fill styles are uniform gray shades of different densities, although you can also select a "button fill," which uses light and dark shading on the edges to simulate a pushbutton. You can also customize a page border with a drop shadow, rounded corners, a gradient fill, color (if your printer supports it), or other options. See "Using Line Styles" for more information.

Paragraph Borders

When you create a paragraph border, WordPerfect automatically draws a rectangular border around all paragraphs that follow. If you turn on paragraph borders at the beginning of one paragraph, for example, and turn off borders after the following paragraph, the two paragraphs are enclosed in a single rectangle. Because WordPerfect automatically places paragraph border codes at the beginning of the current paragraph, you should press Enter to insert a hard return before you turn off paragraph borders.

You also can block several paragraphs and then turn on a paragraph border. In this case, WordPerfect creates paired paragraph border codes, which turn on the border at the beginning of the block and then off again at the end of the block. Because these codes are paired, if you delete one of the pair, WordPerfect automatically deletes the other.

If you don't turn off paragraph borders, WordPerfect draws a border around each entire page that follows *except* for headers, footers, and page numbers, which are outside the borders.

Add a Paragraph Border

1. Move the cursor to where you want borders to begin, or select a block of text.

2. Choose **L**ayout, **L**ine, Paragraph **B**orders.

3. If you want to, do one or more of the following:

   Choose **B**order Style and select a style from the list box.

   Choose **F**ill Style and select a style from the list box.

   Choose **C**ustomize to create a drop shadow, rounded corners, gradient fill, or other options.

4. Choose OK to close all open dialog boxes.

Troubleshooting

◆ If you don't like the line or fill style you selected for a border, place the cursor in the first page or paragraph with a border and then repeat the steps and select different styles.

◆ You can also turn on Reveal Codes and delete the [Para Border] code. WordPerfect places paragraph border codes at the beginning of the current paragraph.

more ▶

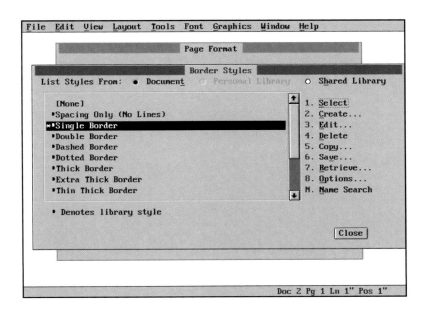

You can choose from a variety of border styles. Keep in mind that the border should look good visually with the fill style you use.

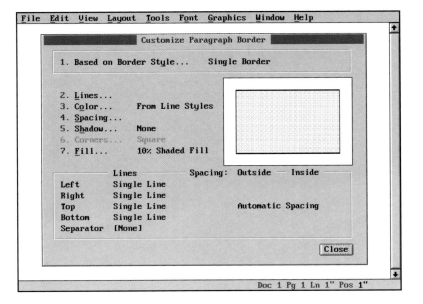

If you're not sure what fill style you want, peruse all the options and watch the example box until you see something you like.

FORMATTING

Paragraph and Page Borders **93**

Add a Page Border

1. Move the cursor to where you want borders to begin, or select a block of text.

2. Choose **L**ayout, **P**age, Page **B**orders.

3. If you want to, do one or more of the following:

   Choose **B**order Style and select a style from the list box.

   Choose **F**ill Style and select a style from the list box.

   Choose **C**ustomize to create a drop shadow, rounded corners, gradient fill, or other options.

4. Choose OK to close all open dialog boxes.

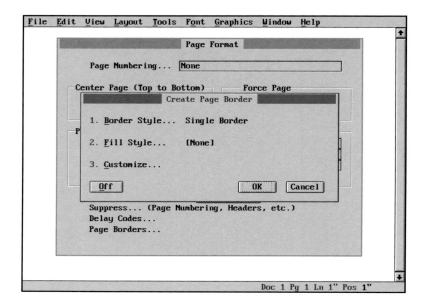

Remember that you don't have to use all of these visual elements. Try for a pleasing effect.

Troubleshooting

◆ If you don't like the line or fill style you selected for a border, place the cursor in the first page or paragraph with a border and then repeat the steps and select different styles.

◆ You can also turn on Reveal Codes and delete the [Pg Border] code. WordPerfect places page border codes at the top of the current page.

◆ After you turn on page borders, Word-Perfect puts a border around all subsequent pages until you turn borders off. To turn off page borders, repeat steps 1 and 2 and then choose **O**ff.

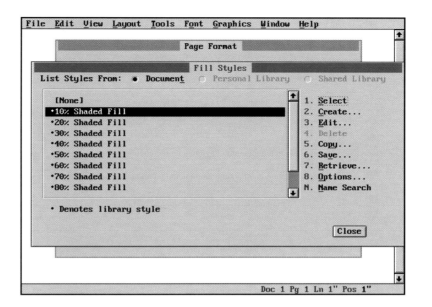

The percentage of fill indicates the amount of color versus white. A 10% red fill, for example, may appear a light pink.

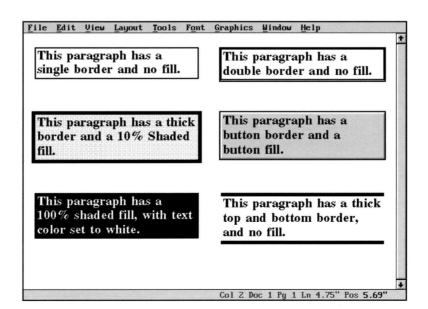

Some fill and text combinations don't work well. Avoid using a dark fill unless the paragraph contains no text at all.

Paragraph and Page Borders   95

Headings should stay with the text that follows. Otherwise, readers won't know how to connect headings and text. With WordPerfect, you can avoid this situation and other "bad" page breaks.

WordPerfect calculates page endings similar to the way it does line endings. When WordPerfect has fit on a page all the lines it can, the program inserts a soft page break code and starts the following line on the next page. There are some times when you need more control over page breaks.

Ways to Control Page Breaks

With WordPerfect you can control these situations:

◆ Some text, such as the beginning of a new chapter or section, should always start at the top of a new page.

◆ What WordPerfect sees as a one-line paragraph at the bottom of a page may actually be a heading that introduces the text at the top of the next page.

◆ You may have a short block of text, such as a small table, that you don't want split by a page break. WordPerfect includes codes designed to deal specifically with all these possibilities.

Hard Page Breaks

If you want to stop WordPerfect from putting additional lines on a particular page, you can insert a hard page break. Any information that follows a hard page break automatically starts at the top of the next page. Just as you press Enter to insert a hard return, you press Ctrl+Enter to insert a hard page break.

Conditional End of Page

If a one-line heading prints on the bottom of a page, you may be tempted to add an extra hard return above the heading to push it onto the following page so that it prints with the text it introduces. You may even be tempted to use a hard page break to force the heading to the top of the next page. If you later add or delete a few lines, however, the extra hard return may leave an extra blank line in the middle of a page, and the hard page break may leave part or all of a page blank. You then need to edit the placement of the heading again to restore the proper paragraph spacing.

Unfortunately, WordPerfect cannot decide which one-line paragraphs are headings and which are not; you must instruct the program when you want a particular line kept with the following text. You can do that by placing a *conditional end of page* code at the beginning of the heading. This code tells WordPerfect to keep the next X number of lines together; if a page break would ordinarily fall within those lines, the program moves the entire X lines to the top of the next page, just as it does with a one-line orphan. With single-spaced text, keep three or four lines of text together; with double-spaced text, keep six or eight lines together.

If you later edit your document and the heading falls in the middle of a page, the code remains dormant, and your original paragraph spacing is preserved.

Block Protect

You may have a short table or other block of text that you don't want split by a page break. If you use a conditional end of page code to protect a four-line table and then you add another line to the table, the last line of the table may still be separated by a page break. Instead, put *block protect* codes around the table or block of text. These paired codes tell WordPerfect not to allow a page break between them. If you later add text within the block, the entire block is still protected.

You can't use block protect on more than a full page of text, of course, and in practice you should use it only on fairly short blocks. Otherwise, you may wind up with a very large blank space at the bottom of the previous page.

TIP

Put a block of text into a graphics box; if the box doesn't fit at the bottom of a page, WordPerfect bumps the box to the top of the following page and moves the following text back to fill in the gap on the previous page. See "Lines and Boxes" for more information.

Widows and Orphans

Sometimes, the last line of a paragraph doesn't fit on a page and prints by itself on the top of the next page, or only the first line of a paragraph fits at the bottom of a page. These straggling lines (called *widows* and *orphans*) don't look good on a printed page.

Widows and orphans are annoying. You can easily add an extra hard return to push the start of a paragraph onto the following page, but how do you pull a line that doesn't fit onto the bottom of the previous page? You can change the bottom margin for the previous page, but then the page lengths of your document are uneven. Further, if you add or delete several lines from a document when editing it, the widow or orphan may move to the middle of a page and cease to be a problem—except that you then have to take out any formatting you have inserted to deal with the widow or orphan "by hand"—and you may have several new widows or orphans to deal with at other page breaks.

You can solve all your widow and orphan problems by using WordPerfect's Widow/Orphan Protect feature. When you turn on this feature, the program automatically fixes widows and orphans for you. If the first line of a paragraph ordinarily prints at the bottom of a page, WordPerfect simply moves the soft page break in front of that paragraph, leaving the previous page one line short. Likewise, if the last line of a paragraph ordinarily prints by itself at the top of the next page, WordPerfect again moves the soft page break back one line so that the last two lines of the paragraph print on the next page. If the paragraph in question is only three lines long, WordPerfect can't split the paragraph without leaving another widow or orphan, so the program moves all three lines to the next page. By default, WordPerfect doesn't protect against widows and orphans. If you use Widow/Orphan Protect, you should put the code at the beginning of your document or in your Initial Codes Style (see "Open Styles" for information on initial codes).

more ▶

Control Page Breaks

1. Choose **L**ayout, **O**ther.

2. Do one of the following:

Choose **W**idow/Orphan Protect.

Choose **C**onditional End of Page. Enter the number of lines to keep together.

Choose **B**lock Protect.

3. Choose OK.

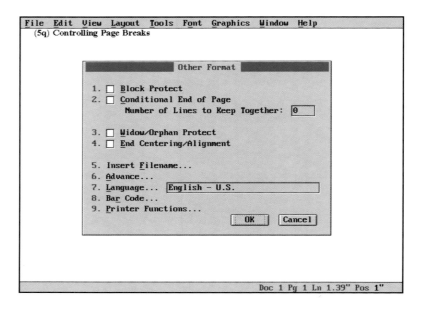

If you don't control the page breaks, remember that WordPerfect will. Because the program has limited judgment, you should specify the breaks you want.

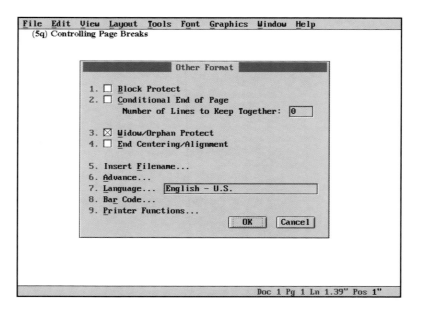

Widows and orphans are often a problem for tables or graphics introduced or followed by a single line of text. Use the conditional end of page to prevent this problem.

Troubleshooting

◆ You can delete a hard page break just as you can any other character, if necessary. To remove a block protect or a conditional end of page, turn on Reveal Codes and delete the [Block Pro On], [Block Pro Off], or [Condl EOP] code.

◆ If you insert a conditional end of page and WordPerfect doesn't move the text to the next page, delete the code, then insert a new code specifying a larger number of lines to keep together.

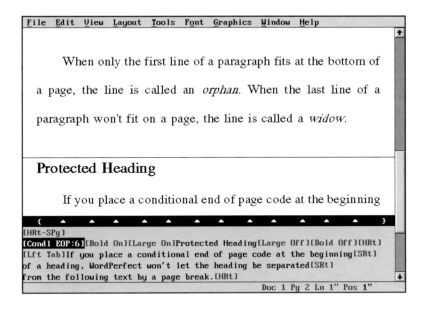

Don't forget that Reveal Codes may show you what's going on if a printed line won't behave properly. Look for codes like these.

Using a mouse, you can change your selections for justification, font, font size, and several other options with a few clicks on the Ribbon.

The Ribbon, one of WordPerfect's screen tools, contains six drop-down lists with special options—mainly for formatting. In addition to justification, font, and font size, you can also use the Ribbon to select paragraph styles, zoom in or out, and turn newspaper columns on or off.

Note: You can use the Ribbon only if you have a mouse.

To use the Ribbon, you click on one of the drop-down list box arrows with the mouse. A list of options appears. You then double-click on one of the options to select it from the list.

Zooming the View

To get a close-up look at a document or a bird's-eye view, you can zoom in or out. You can zoom to varying percentages of full size, to the margins of your document, or to the full page width or height.

◆ Theoretically, *100%* is full size. The size and resolution of your monitor affect how large the characters are actually displayed. At *50%* zoom, WordPerfect displays characters at one-half of full size. At *200%* zoom, WordPerfect displays characters at twice full size.

◆ *Marg (Margin Width)*. WordPerfect displays the full width of your text with roughly 1/4 inch of white space on either side, making full use of the screen without cutting off characters at either edge.

◆ *Wide (Page Width)*. WordPerfect displays the full width of your page on-screen, including your side margins. This setting leaves a great deal of wasted space on each side of the screen.

◆ *Full (Full Page)*. WordPerfect displays the full height of your page on-screen. In Page mode, this view includes top and bottom margins. Text is usually too small to read, but you can see the overall layout of a full page and then edit where necessary (unlike Print Preview, in which you can zoom out but not edit).

Note: The Margin Width setting displays the full width of each line and is the easiest to read. The 100% setting usually displays the characters in a somewhat smaller size but, as a result, can display more lines on-screen.

Choosing a Paragraph Style

Paragraph styles may be WordPerfect's most powerful formatting tool. You can place any formatting codes in a paragraph style—font, margins, tabs, paragraph spacing. When you select a paragraph style from the second drop-down list in the Ribbon, WordPerfect automatically applies those codes to the entire current paragraph, no matter how short or long.

WordPerfect's outline levels are controlled by paragraph styles. If you select a different paragraph style, you can change the outline level. Until you create paragraph styles of your own, the styles visible in the Ribbon's drop-down paragraph style list are all outline styles. If you select Level 1, you start an outline. The Ribbon doesn't list open styles or character styles; you must select these styles from the main Style List. See the section "Styles" for more information on creating styles.

Setting Up Text Columns

You can turn on newspaper columns quickly and easily by using the Ribbon. When you click on the third drop-down list button, a list appears that lets you select from 2 to 24 columns. When you make a selection, WordPerfect inserts a column definition code at the beginning of the current paragraph, and all following text is formatted into columns.

TIP If you want to turn off columns again, select 1 Col.

Formatting columns through the Ribbon has limitations. You cannot select parallel columns through the Ribbon, and you cannot change the distance between columns, which is ½ inch by default. To make those choices, you must use the Text Columns dialog box. See the section "Columns" for details.

Specifying Justification

Whether you want to center a heading, right justify an address, or make some body text left or full justified, you can change justification quickly by clicking on the fourth drop-down list in the Ribbon.

If you select a block of text before making a selection, WordPerfect changes only the format of the block. If you don't select a block, WordPerfect reformats all subsequent text.

Selecting a Font and Font Size

Using the last two drop-down lists in the Ribbon, you can choose any of the fonts and font sizes available in the Font dialog box. As with justification, you can select a block of text and change the font or size for just the block, or simply insert a code to reformat all subsequent text.

more ▶

Use the Ribbon

1. To turn on the Ribbon, choose **V**iew, **R**ibbon.

2. To change the Zoom selection, click on the first drop-down list button, and double-click on a Zoom option.

3. If you want to change the formatting of a specific block of text by using any of the remaining Ribbon features, select a block of text. Otherwise, choose an insertion point where you want the formatting change to take effect.

4. To change the paragraph style, click on the second drop-down list button, and double-click on a style name.

5. To change the number of columns, click on the third drop-down list button, and double-click on a number of columns. Selecting one column turns columns off.

6. To change the justification, click on the fourth drop-down list button, and double-click on a justification option.

7. To change the font, click on the fifth drop-down list button, and double-click on a font name.

8. To change the font size, click on the last drop-down list button; then double-click on a font size, or type a different size.

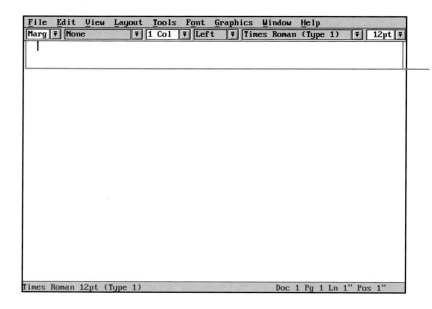

The WordPerfect Ribbon.

Notice that the Ribbon occupies very little space. It's worth losing the space on-screen in exchange for so many functions that are easily accessed.

Troubleshooting

If you make the wrong selection from one of the Ribbon's drop-down lists, you can choose Undo or drop down the list again and make another selection.

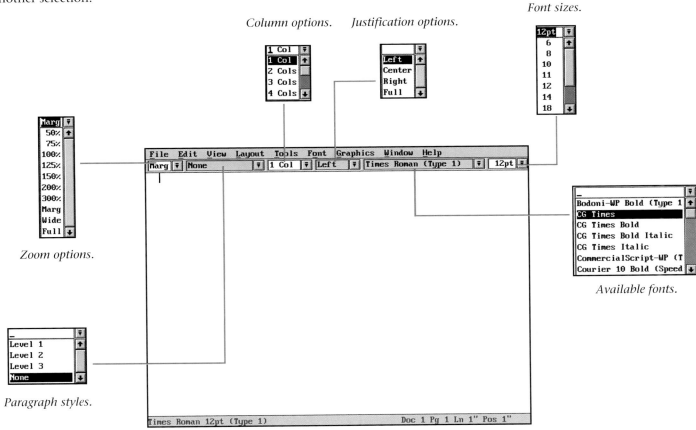

Column options.

Justification options.

Font sizes.

Zoom options.

Available fonts.

Paragraph styles.

FORMATTING

Part Two

Section 4—Files

Files is an important concept in WordPerfect. As you type in WordPerfect, the letters aren't committed to paper; they are displayed on-screen and stored in the computer's memory. Memory is a temporary electronic blackboard where the computer stores information it is working on. To keep a copy of your document, you must save it. Saving your document means to take the information in memory and record it on a disk. After you save a document, you can return to it later—minutes or years later—and your information is just as you left it.

This section covers the all file-related tasks such as how to save a document, open a document, preview a document, and print a document, just to name a few.

WordPerfect includes several tools for helping you manage your files and subdirectories. The most important tool is the File Manager. By using the File Manager, you can look at the contents of any file and then open or retrieve it. You can copy or move a file, rename it, or delete it. You also can mark several files or even a complete directory and then copy, move, or delete them all.

The information in a WordPerfect document is valuable; it represents your time and creative energy. You should always safeguard your documents by saving them as files on a computer disk.

While you work in WordPerfect, the program keeps the information that represents your document in RAM (your computer's temporary working memory). When you turn off your computer, any information in your computer's memory is lost. If you lose power or if your computer locks up while you're working on a WordPerfect document, any information you haven't saved is gone. That's why you should save a copy to your hard disk or a floppy disk.

Your computer's hard disk and floppy disk drives represent permanent file storage. Although you can delete or destroy computer files (just as you can destroy paper files), a file on a computer disk lasts for years (barring accident).

What Happens When You Save?

The first time you save a document, you must assign a name. WordPerfect creates a file on disk and copies the document's information from memory to the disk. As you add to your document, you can continue to use the Save command to update the file on disk with the additions or changes you have made.

TIP Saving a document doesn't remove the document from screen or from memory. When you finish with a document, choose Close.

Naming Files

When you save a file, you must use a "legal" name. DOS (the disk operating system) imposes certain restrictions on file names: A file name can be from one to eight characters long and can have an optional extension of one to three characters. A period separates the two parts. Here's an example:

FILENAME.EXT

Saving a Document with a New Name

Occasionally you may want to keep the disk version intact but still save the on-screen version. Maybe you want two copies of the same document, for example. Or perhaps you have experimented with the on-screen version and want to keep the disk version in case the experimental version goes awry. In this case, choose Save As.

When you choose Save As, you're prompted for a new file name. WordPerfect saves the document on-screen with the new name, creating a second file. Any further changes you make are saved to the second file and not to the original file.

Closing a Document

If you are finished working on the document, save it and then close it. You should also close all documents when you exit WordPerfect.

Each time you open a document window, WordPerfect assigns part of your computer's working memory to hold the information in that window. If you're finished working on the document, close it to free up the memory it's using.

WordPerfect always keeps track of whether you have modified a document you're working with. If you close an unmodified document, WordPerfect simply clears the screen and frees up any memory the document was using. If you have added or deleted a single character in your document, though, or changed the formatting in any way, when you close a document, WordPerfect prompts

`Save Changes to C:\FILENAME?`

If you choose **N**o, WordPerfect removes the document from memory without saving any changes. If you choose **Y**es, the program performs a Save. Choose Cancel to keep the document in memory and continue to edit.

> **TIP**
> If you want to abandon changes you have made to a document, close it. When prompted, choose **N**o.

File Naming Rules

◆ Many programs suggest or enforce a particular extension for their own files, such as XLS for an Excel spreadsheet or PM5 for a PageMaker 5 publication. The extension identifies which program created the file.

◆ You certainly can use an extension such as WP6 to identify your WordPerfect 6 files. But you also can use more meaningful extensions such as LTR to identify letters, or you can use numerical extensions such as CHAPTER.12 or VERSION.3 to identify files in sequence or revision numbers.

◆ Try to use a descriptive name that will still mean something to you six months from now.

◆ You can't use the characters * + = [ ] : ; " < > ? / \ ¦ , or a space in a file name. If you use an illegal character, WordPerfect warns `Illegal drive/path specification!`, and lets you change the file's name before saving.

◆ If you use the name of a file that already exists, WordPerfect asks if you want to replace the existing file. If you choose **Y**es, the program deletes the older file and saves the current document. If you choose **N**o, the program lets you enter a different name.

more ▶

Saving and Closing a Document

Save a Document the First Time

1. Choose **F**ile, **S**ave.

2. Type a new file name.

3. Press Enter or choose OK.

Save a Document Again

Choose **F**ile, **S**ave.

Troubleshooting

◆ After you name the file, when you choose **S**ave, the program doesn't prompt you before overwriting the previous version of the file. If you accidentally overwrite the previous version, you can only get the deleted file back by using a program such as the Norton Utilities or PC Tools.

◆ To guard against accidentally overwriting older versions, you can use WordPerfect's original backup feature, which automatically makes a backup of the previous version when you use save. See "Working with a Timed Backup."

◆ If you type the wrong name when saving a file, close the file, then use the File Manager to rename the file to the proper name. See "Starting the File Manager."

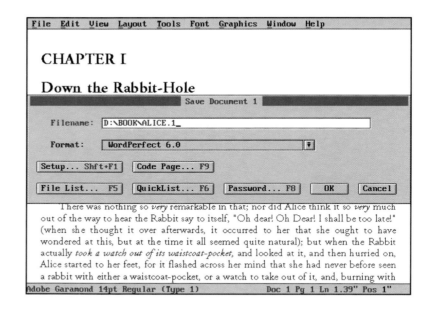

Shortcut Keys

Save	Ctrl+F12
Save	F10

Save a Document with a New Name

1. Choose **F**ile, Save **A**s.

2. Type a new file name or edit the existing name.

3. Press Enter or choose OK.

Close a Document

Choose **F**ile, **C**lose.

Troubleshooting

◆ If you close a document by mistake, you can quickly reopen the file. Choose **F**ile, **O**pen, then press the down arrow to highlight the last file closed, and press Enter.

◆ If you accidentally close a document without saving any changes, you may be able to open a timed backup file to recover most of the lost information. See "Working with a Timed Backup."

◆ To guard against accidentally overwriting older versions, you can use WordPerfect's original backup feature, which automatically makes a backup of the previous version when you use save. See "Working with a Timed Backup."

◆ If you type the wrong name when saving a file, close the file, then use the File Manager to rename the file to the proper name. See the article "Starting the File Manager."

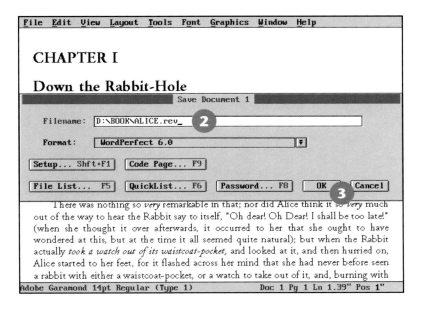

Saving a file with a new name.

Shortcut Keys

Save	Ctrl+F12
Save	F10

FILES

When you save an electronic file, you can go back to it—to make changes, to print it, to use it again. To work on the file again, you open it.

When you start the program, WordPerfect automatically opens Document 1; you see a blank document window. You can start typing away if you want to create a new document. If you want to work on a document you've already started, you need to open it.

When you open a document, WordPerfect displays it in its own document window. You can have more than one document open at a time (see the article "Arranging Open Documents").

> **TIP**
> If you can't remember the name of your file, you can choose the File Manager button in the Open or Retrieve dialog box to see a list of available files. See "Starting the File Manager" for information on using the File Manager.

Creating a New Document

When you start WordPerfect, the program automatically opens Document 1. It's a new, empty document, and you can begin typing immediately. You can create another blank document at any time.

Suppose that while you're in the middle of one document, you get a phone call and want to take some notes in WordPerfect. To get an empty screen, you can close all your open documents, which leaves you with an empty Document 1 again. Or you can just open a new document.

> **TIP**
> When the Open or Retrieve dialog box appears, you can display the names of the last four documents you have edited. Press the down-arrow key or click the drop-down list button to the right of the Filename text box; then select one of the files.

The New Document Window

When you choose New, WordPerfect opens a new document window and switches to it. The program assigns the new document to the next available document window number. If you already have three documents open, for example, the status line for a new document may read Doc 4 Ln 1" Pos 1".

A new document window is like any other document window; it's merely empty. You can start typing immediately. You can also retrieve other documents into the window or switch between the new window and other open windows to copy information.

Open a Document

1. Choose **F**ile, **O**pen.

2. Type the name of the document you want to edit.

3. Press Enter.

Create a New Document

Choose **F**ile, **N**ew.

Troubleshooting

◆ If you open the wrong document, choose **F**ile, **C**lose to remove the document from the screen, then repeat the following steps to open another document. If you retrieve the wrong file into an open document, use Undo to remove the added text, then retrieve the desired file.

◆ If you choose New by mistake, use the Close command to close the document window.

Shortcut Key	
Open	Shift+F10

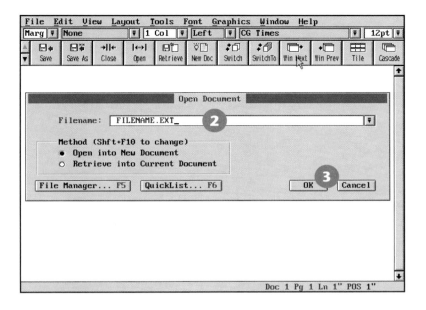

Type the name of the file you want to open.

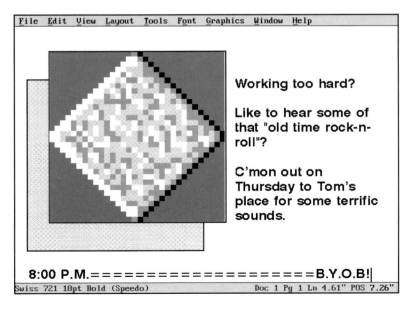

The document is now open on-screen, ready to edit.

FILES

Combining two documents is easy with WordPerfect. No cutting or pasting. No retyping. Just insert one document within the other.

Suppose that you're working with someone else on a project. That person is writing the first half of the report; you're writing the second. Do you have to retype the first half? Do you have to paste them together? Not with WordPerfect. With WordPerfect, you can combine the documents.

Or suppose that a document you did a month ago fits perfectly in the document you're working on now. You can combine the two.

What Happens When You Retrieve a Document?

WordPerfect follows these rules when retrieving documents:

♦ WordPerfect inserts a retrieved document at the cursor position in the current document window.

♦ When you retrieve a document, WordPerfect inserts all of the retrieved document.

♦ Retrieving a document into the current document window doesn't affect the original version of the retrieved file on disk. The on-screen document is saved to a different file.

♦ If you combine documents unintentionally and can't use Undo to reverse the procedure, you can close the document without saving changes and then immediately open the file again. You lose any changes you make between saving the file and retrieving improperly, however. If you can't undo and you have already saved, you have to block and delete the entire inserted document.

Inserting Only Part of a Document

If you want only part of a second document, you can retrieve the document and then delete the portions you don't need. Or you may find it easier to open the second document into a new window and then cut or copy the information from one document window to the other. See the articles "Switching between Documents" and "Move, Copy, and Delete Blocks" for more information.

Open or Retrieve

Open and Retrieve are similar commands. Retrieve always combines a document on disk with whatever is in the current document window. Open, on the other hand, never combines two documents but instead opens a new document window if the current window is occupied.

If you choose Open or Retrieve but, while the dialog box is on-screen, decide that you actually want the other command, you can switch between the two commands. Simply press the shortcut key (Shift+F10) or click the Open or Retrieve radio buttons.

When you call up the dialog box using the shortcut key, the default action is Open; press the shortcut key again to choose Retrieve.

Combine Documents

1. Move the cursor in your document to the location where you want to insert the retrieved file.

2. Choose **F**ile, **R**etrieve.

3. Type the name of the file you want to retrieve.

4. Press Enter or click OK.

Troubleshooting

If you retrieve the wrong file, retrieve a file to the wrong location, or accidentally retrieve a file in the first place, choose **E**dit **U**ndo to undo the insertion.

Shortcut Key	
Retrieve	Shift+F10

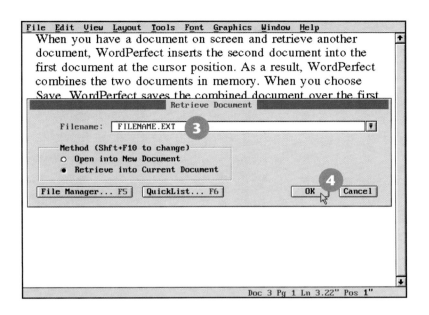

Type the name of the document.

The second document is inserted.

Just like you may have several papers on your desk, WordPerfect lets you have several documents open. You can switch around between the documents.

Your work is busy, busy, busy. You might be working on three or four things at once. WordPerfect lets you work the way you're used to. It enables you to open several documents at once. You might need to copy information from one document to another. Or you might be working on two documents at once.

Although you're not likely to open nine documents at a time, you can do so in WordPerfect 6. Even if you have only two or three documents open, you need to be able to navigate between your open documents.

Switch, Next, Previous, and Switch To

When you have only two documents open, choose the Switch command. When you have three documents open, Switch is less useful. Use Next or Previous. If you have more than three, use the Switch To command.

Cutting and Pasting between Documents

You can copy or move information between two open documents as easily as you can copy or move between two locations in the same document. Suppose that you're editing Document 1, and you want to copy a paragraph or two from a file on disk. First, open the disk file into Document 2 and then switch to that document. Select a block of text and copy or cut the block.

Then switch back to Document 1 and move the cursor to where you want to insert the block. When you choose Paste, WordPerfect inserts the block of text from the second document. You can switch back and forth between the two files, copying as much information as you like.

Keeping Track of Documents

When you can have nine open documents, WordPerfect obviously needs some way to keep track of them. Here's how WordPerfect does it.

◆ WordPerfect refers to open documents by document window number. The program can't work from only the document name because you don't name a document until the first time you save it. Also, you can create several new documents and type in them before you save.

◆ By default, the program displays each document full-screen, which means that while you're working in Document 2, you can't see Document 1, and vice versa. If you want to display several documents on-screen at the same time, see the article "Arranging Open Documents."

◆ Document window numbers don't necessarily refer to the order in which you opened several documents; the numbers are simply locations. If you have two documents open and you close Document 1, even though only one document remains open, that document remains in Document 2. The next time you open a file, WordPerfect puts the new file in the first available document window, which is Document 1.

Switch to the Previous or Next Document

1. Choose **W**indow.

2. Do one of the following:

   To switch to the document you were editing previously, choose **S**witch.

   To switch to the next (open) document number, choose **N**ext.

   To switch to the previous (open) document number, choose **P**revious.

Switching to a Particular Document

1. Choose Window.

2. Choose S**w**itch To.

3. Choose the number that corresponds to the document you want.

Troubleshooting

If you switch to the wrong document, you can use any of the switching commands to switch again.

Shortcut Keys	
Switch	Shift+F3
Switch To	F3 or Home, 0
Document #	Home, # (1-9)

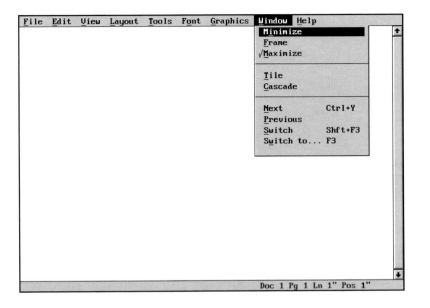

*Choose **S**witch, **N**ext, or **P**revious.*

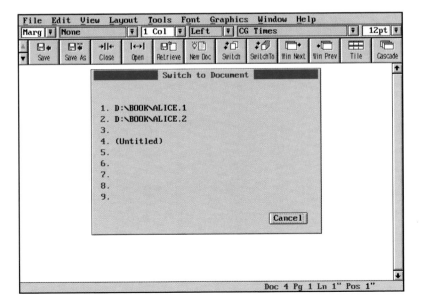

Choose the number of the document window you want.

FILES

Having lots of documents on-screen may not be that helpful if you can't see each of the documents. WordPerfect provides several ways to view all open documents.

WordPerfect automatically displays your documents full-screen. (A full-screen window is *maximized*.) When you open more than one document, you can see only the document you're currently editing. The current document is the *active* document; all other documents are *inactive,* even though they're open.

Suppose, however, that you want to see several documents on-screen at the same time. You may want to compare two different versions of the same file or refer to information in another file. WordPerfect lets you do just that.

Tile and Cascade

When you choose Tile, WordPerfect arranges all your open documents so that you can see as much of each document as possible. The more windows you have open, the less you can see of each document. Each tiled window is displayed in a frame.

Across the top of each framed window is a title bar that contains the document's window number and name. WordPerfect displays the title bar of an active window in dark blue and the title bars of inactive windows in gray (although these colors may change if you choose a different color scheme).

Depending on the number of documents you have open when you choose Tile, the windows may not all be the same size. If, for example, you tile three windows, one window occupies the top half of the screen, and the other two windows split the bottom half of the screen down the middle.

When you choose Cascade, WordPerfect arranges all your open document windows so that they overlap each other. You see the contents of only the window on top, but you can also see the title bars of all the other windows. Cascaded windows are generally larger than tiled windows, but you can't see as much of each window at the same time.

Switching between Documents

Whether you tile or cascade your document windows, you can switch between them easily by clicking any open window or title bar. Clicking the title bar of a cascaded window brings that window to the front. You also can still switch between windows by using the switch commands.

When you switch between several framed windows, the color of the active title bar always reminds you which document is active. The cursor appears in that window as well.

Arrange Windows

1. Choose **W**indow.

2. Do one of the following:

   To arrange several open windows on-screen, choose **T**ile.

   To arrange your open windows so that they overlap, choose **C**ascade.

Troubleshooting

If you choose the wrong windowing option, you can repeat the following steps to choose a different option. If you want to go back to a full-screen view of a window, switch to that window and choose **W**indow, **M**aximize.

Shortcut Key	
Window Controls	Ctrl+F3, W

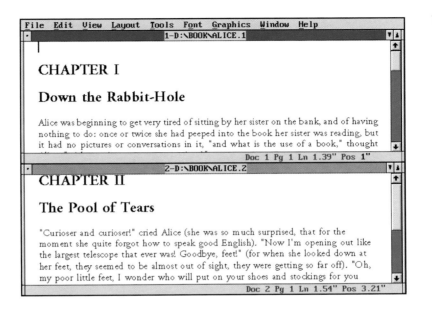

Tiled documents.

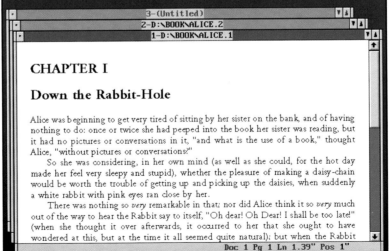

Cascaded documents.

When you arrange documents so that more than one is displayed, you can change the size and location of the open windows.

WordPerfect automatically displays your documents full-screen. (A full-screen window is *maximized*.) If you display more than one document, each document appears in a window, bordered by a frame. You can use this frame to move and resize the windows.

Changing the Window Size

◆ Change a framed window's width or height by dragging in or out on the frame's left or right side or bottom. You can also drag one of the four corners of the frame to change the window's width and height at the same time.

◆ Move a framed window by dragging the title bar.

◆ To the left of the title bar is a small close button with a dot in the middle. Clicking this button is equivalent to choosing Close.

◆ To the right of the title bar is a small minimize button with a small triangle pointing down. Clicking the minimize button reduces the window to a small rectangle, taking up the least amount of space possible without actually closing the window.

◆ To the right of the title bar—next to the minimize button—is a small maximize button with a small triangle pointing up. Clicking the maximize button restores the window to full-screen.

TIP

You can also move or resize windows by using commands available in the Window dialog box. Press Ctrl+F3, then choose Window.

Move, Resize, or Close a Framed Window

1. To move a window, drag its title bar with your mouse.

2. To resize a window, drag a frame edge or corner.

3. To close a window, click the button in the window's upper left corner.

4. To minimize or maximize a window, click the down or up triangle, respectively, in the window's upper right corner.

Troubleshooting

As long as a window is framed, you can use any of the commands to change its size or position. If you maximize a window by mistake, choose **Window, F**rame to return the window to its previous appearance.

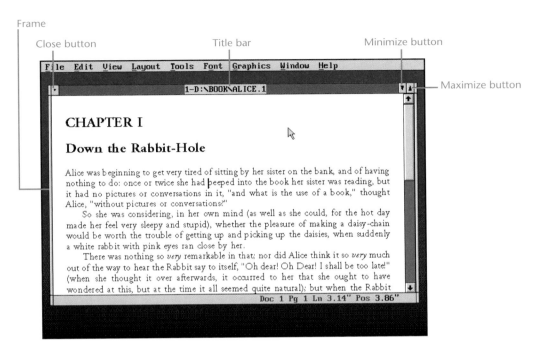

Frame · Close button · Title bar · Minimize button · Maximize button

Shortcut Key	
Window Controls	Ctrl+F3, W

FILES

Before you print, preview your document on-screen.

Few things are more frustrating than printing a document and seeing an obvious, glaring mistake on the printed page. Although the whole point of using a word processor is to be able to make changes and reprint a document, you don't want to do so more often than necessary. Reprinting takes time. Paper and other printer supplies cost money—only a few cents per page, perhaps—but over time, enough wasted pages add up to a fair amount of wasted time, money, and resources.

You can catch many mistakes by previewing a document before you print.

The Preview Window
Here's how Print Preview works:

- ◆ Print Preview is a Graphics mode window that displays every element of a document: your text, in the correct fonts and with bold and italic correctly displayed; any graphics lines or graphics images; and page elements such as headers and footers, page numbers, and footnotes.

- ◆ With Print Preview, you can zoom in to see an enlarged view of one small part of a page or zoom out to see *thumbnail* views of as many as 32 pages simultaneously.

- ◆ You can't edit your document in Print Preview; you must return to the normal document window to make any changes.

- ◆ Print Preview has its own Button Bar, a small group of pull-down menus, and its own status line.

- ◆ The view you see when you choose Print Preview depends on the view you last used.

- ◆ When you display more than one page in Print Preview, WordPerfect outlines your current page in red.

Preview a Document

1. Choose **F**ile, Print Pre**v**iew.

2. Choose View.

3. Choose one of the following:

To view one page at a time, choose **F**ull Page.

To view facing pages, choose Fa**c**ing Pages.

To view text at full size, choose **1**00%.

To view text at twice full size, choose **2**00%.

To increase the text size 25%, choose Zoom **I**n.

To decrease the text size 25%, choose Zoom **O**ut.

To view small images of several pages, choose **T**humbnails, then choose **1**, **2**, **4**, **8**, or **3**2.

4. When finished, choose **F**ile, **C**lose.

Troubleshooting

Creating a preview of multiple pages can take WordPerfect some time. If you want to interrupt the program and switch to a different view, press Alt+V to choose the view menu, then choose a different view option.

Zoom In (250%).

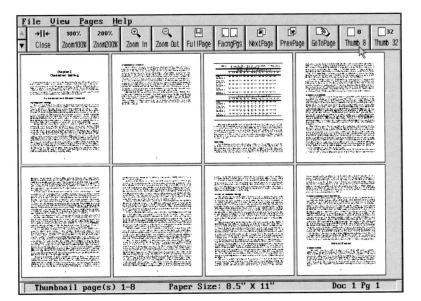

Thumbnails (8 pages).

FILES

All of your creative efforts are summed up in the final printed document.

ou might think that computers will lead to the paperless office. But really computers just make creating paper work easier. You still print paper copies of most of the things you do on a computer. For instance, with a word processor such as WordPerfect, the real goal is to send the letter, make copies of the report, distribute the memo. The real goal is still a printed document.

> **TIP**
> Preview first! Before you print, preview the document so that you can catch any formatting or text problems.

Installing a Printer

When you install WordPerfect, the installation program requires you to specify the type of printer you use. (WordPerfect then copies the appropriate file, called a printer driver, to your hard disk.) The type of printer you have will determine how your printed copy will look. The printer driver you select not only tells WordPerfect how to control your printer, it also tells the program which fonts and other features your printer has available.

Printing

When you choose Print in WordPerfect, the only thing you need to decide is which pages to print. By default, the program prints your entire document, but you can just as easily print the current page or several specific pages. You can also select a block of text and print only that block.

> **TIP**
> If you use more than one printer, you can install additional printers. If you add or change printers, you can run the installation program again to install new printers. (See the articles in the section "Customizing" for help in selecting printer drivers and installing new printer drivers.)

In addition, you can tell WordPerfect to print another document while the first document is still printing. Each time you give a print command, WordPerfect adds the print job to its print queue and prints each queue entry in turn. If you want to cancel a print job or change the order of print job entries in the print queue, see the article "Controlling the Printer."

When you issue a print command, WordPerfect returns to the current document window. You can continue to work while the program prints in the background. You can even close the document without affecting the print operation.

Because WordPerfect is using part of your computer to print while letting you work, you may find that the program operates more slowly while printing, but you can still get work done.

Although you can continue to work, don't exit WordPerfect while a document is printing. If you try to, the program gives you the option of canceling the print job or exiting.

Print a Document

1. Choose **F**ile, **P**rint.

2. Do one of the following:

   To print the full document, leave the default set at **F**ull Document.

   To print the current page, choose **P**age.

   To print specific pages, choose **M**ultiple Pages; in the dialog box that appears, choose **P**age/Label Range and then enter the specific page numbers (such as **4,6-9**) and choose OK.

3. Choose the P**r**int button.

Troubleshooting

If you need to cancel a print job, choose **F**ile, **P**rint, **C**ontrol Printer, **C**ancel Job. See the article "Controlling the Printer."

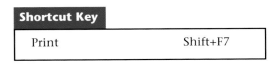

Shortcut Key	
Print	Shift+F7

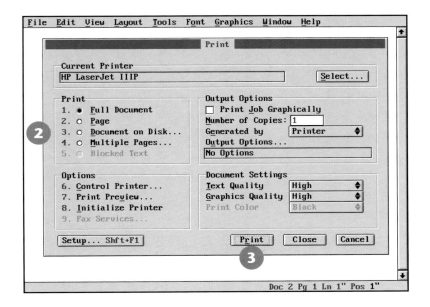

The Print dialog box.

File   Edit   View   Layout   Tools   Font   Graphics   Window   Help

Print

Current Printer
HP LaserJet IIIP   [Select...]

Print
1. ● Full Document
2. ○ Page
3. ○ Document on Disk...
4. ○ Multiple Pages...
5. ○ Blocked Text

Output Options
☐ Print Job Graphically
Number of Copies: [1]
Generated by   [Printer ▲▼]
Output Options...
[No Options]

Options
6. Control Printer...
7. Print Preview...
8. Initialize Printer
9. Fax Services...

Document Settings
Text Quality   [High ▲▼]
Graphics Quality [High ▲▼]
Print Color   [Black ▲▼]

[Setup... Shft+F1]   [Print] [Close] [Cancel]

Doc 2 Pg 1 Ln 1" Pos 1"

FILES

You may or may not clear off your desk when you're done working. With a computer, you should exit all the programs (like WordPerfect) when you're finished.

When you exit, the program checks to see if you have any files open and prompts you to close them. The program also performs some internal housecleaning: deleting some temporary files before shutting itself down.

Caution: Never turn off your computer while WordPerfect is running; you can lose data!

You can exit WordPerfect by using either of two commands: Exit or Exit WP. Exit WP is the most convenient.

Exit WP

The Exit WP command always exits the program, no matter how many documents you have open. When you choose Exit WP, the program displays a dialog box listing all your open documents by name, with a check box next to each document. WordPerfect saves any document whose check box is marked. (If a document has been modified, its check box is already marked.) You can mark or unmark any or all documents before you choose Save and Exit.

Exit

The Exit command combines the features of saving a file, closing a document window, and exiting the program. Exit lets you save and close one document at a time. For each open file, you'll see a dialog box that asks

```
Save D:\BOOK\ALICE.2?
Document has been modified
```

(You'll see the name of your actual file—not ALICE.2.)

◆ Choose Yes to save the document.

◆ Choose Save As to save the document with a new name.

◆ Choose No to abandon the document.

◆ Choose Cancel to return to WordPerfect and the document.

You must repeat the command for each open document. After you save (or abandon) the last document, you're asked whether you want to exit WordPerfect.

This way of exiting is long but is included because it maintains some consistency with how Exit works in previous WordPerfect versions.

Save First!

Even though WordPerfect will prompt you to save all open documents, it's a good habit to save them anyway before you close. You might have exit on your mind and not think to save the documents. It's easy to fly right through all the prompts.

Better safe, than sorry. Save all your files. Then exit.

Saving and closing files are covered in the article "Saving and Closing a Document."

Exit WordPerfect

1. Choose **F**ile, E**x**it WP.

2. Mark the check boxes for any documents you want to save.

3. Choose **S**ave and Exit.

Troubleshooting

If you turn your computer off without exiting WordPerfect, any changes you make to open documents since saving are lost. The next time you load the program, WordPerfect may prompt Backup File Exists. This prompt tells you that the program saved a backup copy of a document, and you may be able to recover your lost data. See the next article for help in retrieving backup files.

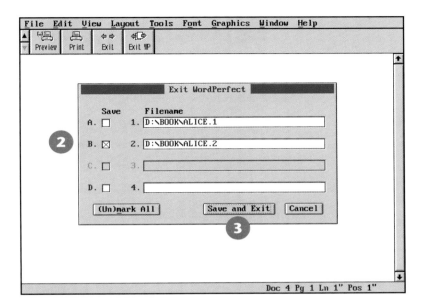

The Exit WordPerfect dialog box.

Shortcut Keys

Edit	F7
Exit WP	Home, F7

FILES

WordPerfect protects against accidents (power outs or system crashes) with its timed backup feature.

Never turn off your computer while WordPerfect is running. Doing so doesn't physically hurt your computer or the program, but if you haven't saved your documents recently—or at all—you lose any changes you have made.

Unfortunately, accidents happen. The power may go out or your computer may lock up while you're running WordPerfect. Whatever the reason, even if you haven't saved recently, your documents may not be gone.

> **TIP**
> By default, the program backs up every 10 minutes, although you can change the frequency to any interval you desire. The more frequently WordPerfect makes backups, the fewer changes you can lose. On slow machines, however, timed backups of long documents can interrupt your work for several seconds, so frequent backups can become annoying. See the section "Customizing" for help on changing your Timed Backup settings.

How Backup Works

When WordPerfect is running, it automatically saves a complete backup copy of the document in each open document window on a periodic basis. When you exit the program properly, WordPerfect deletes these backup copies. If, however, you lose power or shut off the computer without exiting, the backup files remain.

Each time you start WordPerfect, the program automatically looks for any timed backup files on disk. If it finds them, the program knows that you weren't able to exit properly for some reason, and it displays a dialog box with the warning `Backup File Exists!`.

The dialog box displays the name of a backup file, which always is named WP{WPC}.BK1, WP{WPC}.BK2, and so on, up to BK9. These names bear no relation to the names of the documents you may have been editing. Instead, the number in each backup file name extension refers to the document window number the file has backed up.

> **TIP**
> If you have several documents open, WordPerfect prompts you on how to dispose of each timed backup file individually. You can rename a backup file, open it, or delete it.

You Still Need To Save!

Even though WordPerfect makes timed backups, you should still save your documents frequently. It's important to realize that WordPerfect deletes the backups whenever you exit properly. If you exit without ever saving a document, WordPerfect also deletes the equivalent backup file, and your document is gone.

Handle a Backup File

1. If WordPerfect displays the Backup File Exists warning, do one of the following:

   To rename the backup file, choose **R**ename.

   To immediately open the backup file, choose **O**pen.

   To delete the backup file, choose **D**elete.

2. If necessary, repeat for each backup file.

Troubleshooting

If you choose to delete a backup file, the backup information cannot be recovered by WordPerfect. You can use a utility program such as The Norton Utilities or PC Tools to recover deleted files. If you choose to rename a backup file, and its information turns out to be useless, you can safely close and delete the file.

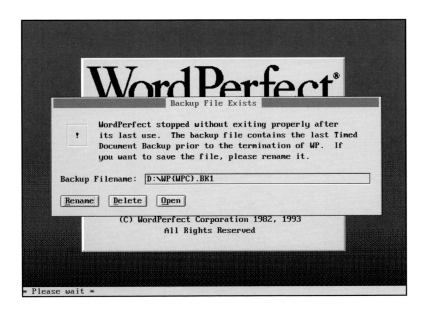

Tell WordPerfect what to do with the backup file.

FILES

You can use the File Manager to display a list of files and directories. After they're displayed, you can open, delete, copy, and perform other actions on the files.

You usually can remember the name you give a file shortly after saving it, but can you remember the file's name a week later? A month later? Using the File Manager, you don't have to remember what you called a file because you can look at a list of all files in the current directory.

Selecting the Directory

When you call up the File Manager, WordPerfect displays the Specify File Manager List dialog box, which gives you several options. If you want to look at a different drive or directory, you can type the path to that location in the Directory text box. If you want to look at the current directory, simply press Enter or choose OK.

Sorting Files

By default, the File Manager displays files sorted alphabetically. If you can't remember a file's name but have some idea of when you saved it, its size, or its file name extension, you can choose **S**ort by to change the sorting criterion. You can sort by extension so that all files with the same extension are listed together, by the date and time each file was last saved or by the size of the files. You can also choose to sort the files in descending instead of ascending order.

The File Manager Display

Here's what the File Manager displays:

◆ The File Manager displays the contents of the current directory in a list box down the left side of the screen. The file list can contain files and directories.

◆ Each file name is followed by the file's size in bytes and the date and time the file was last saved.

◆ The File Manager always displays directory names at the top of the list and identifies them by <Dir> in place of a file size.

◆ At the bottom of the screen, the File Manager also lists the total number of files in the directory, how many of those files you have marked to perform some action, the amount of free space on the current disk drive, and the combined size of the files in the directory.

Note: If you mark files, the File Manager changes the last entry to list the combined size of the files you have marked.

Selecting Files

You can also change *which* files are displayed in the File Manager. If you want to display just certain files (for instance, just files with the extension LTR), you can do so.

When WordPerfect displays the Specify File Manager List dialog box again, it displays *.* (which means all files). These asterisks are wild-card symbols, each of which stands for one or more letters or numbers—any file name and any extension. You can use the wild cards to display the types of files you want. For instance, to display all LTR files, type ***.LTR**. To display all files that start with CH, type **CH*.***.

Start File Manager

1. Choose **F**ile, **F**ile Manager.

2. If you want to look at a different directory, type the path to that directory.

3. Choose OK or press Enter.

Troubleshooting

If you call up the File Manager by mistake, choose Close or press Esc to return to the document window.

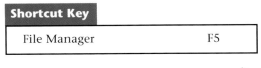

Shortcut Key

File Manager   F5

more ▶

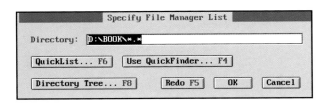

```
┌──────── Specify File Manager List ────────┐
│                                            │
│  Directory:  D:\BOOK\*.*                   │
│                                            │
│  [ QuickList... F6 ]  [ Use QuickFinder... F4 ] │
│                                            │
│  [ Directory Tree... F8 ]  [ Redo F5 ] [ OK ] [ Cancel ] │
└────────────────────────────────────────────┘
```

Looking at a different directory.

Directories   Files   Size in Bytes   Date and time last saved

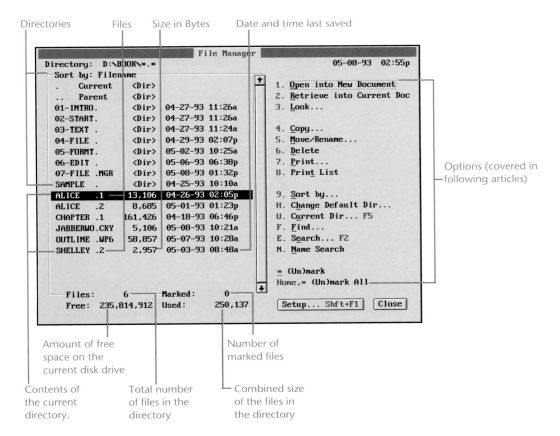

Options (covered in following articles)

Amount of free space on the current disk drive

Contents of the current directory.

Total number of files in the directory

Number of marked files

Combined size of the files in the directory

FILES

Sorting Files

1. Start the File Manager.

See the preceding page if you need help with this step.

2. Choose Sort by.

3. Choose Sort List by.

4. Choose a sort order:

Filename

Extension

Date/Time

Size

5. If you want to sort by descending order, choose the Descending Sort option.

6. Choose OK or press Enter to return to the File Manager.

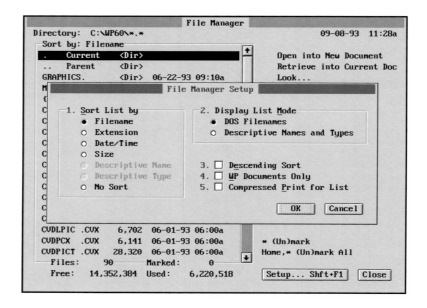

Select how you want to sort the files.

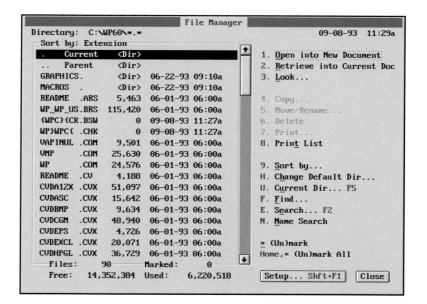

The files sorted by extension.

Selecting Which Files Are Displayed

1. Start the File Manager.

2. Choose Current Dir.

3. Type the files you want to display, using wildcard.

   For instance, type ***.DOC** to display all **[DOC]** files that end with a DOC extension.

4. Press Enter.

Troubleshooting

To change back to a full directory list, choose Current Dir, type *.*, and press Enter.

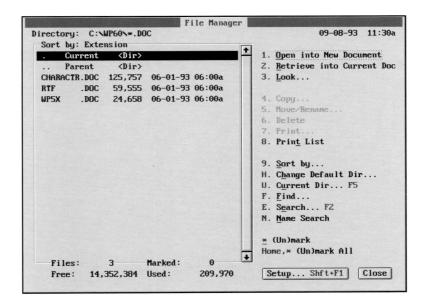

Files with a DOC extension.

If you don't know the name of the file you want to open, start File Manager. Then select your file from the file list.

If you know the name of a file on disk, you can choose **O**pen to open a file into a new document window. When you don't know the name of a file, however, you can look for the file in the File Manager and then open the file from there.

The File Manager lists all the files in the current directory in alphabetical order. Each entry displays the file name, the size of the file in bytes, and the date and time the file was last saved to disk. You can highlight any file, and then choose Look, Open, or Retrieve.

Looking At a File

If the file list contains several files that might be the file you're looking for, use the Look option. When you highlight a file and choose **L**ook, the File Manager displays the beginning of the file on-screen, using a generic screen font and displaying minimal formatting.

The Look window can display the contents of WordPerfect documents, text files, documents created by other word processing programs that WordPerfect can import, and graphics images that can be imported. If the file isn't in a format WordPerfect can import, the Look window displays gibberish.

◆ You can't edit the file in the Look window.

◆ You can scroll through the file to see whether it contains some information you're looking for.

◆ To see the next file in the list, choose **N**ext, or choose **P**revious to see the previous file.

◆ If this file is the one you want, choose **O**pen.

Opening the File

To open a file, highlight it. Then choose **O**pen into New Document (or just press Enter). Opening a file automatically closes the File Manager and returns to the document window.

If you want to combine files (insert text from one document into the document on-screen), highlight the file you want to insert and then choose **R**etrieve into Current Doc.

Marking Files

If you want to open several files simultaneously, you can mark each file with an asterisk (*). When you choose **O**pen, Word-Perfect opens each marked file into its own document window. If no files are marked, you can press Home, * to mark all files. If one or more files are marked, pressing Home, * unmarks all files.

Open a File

1. Start the File Manager.

2. Highlight a file name.

You can scroll through the list of files by using the up- or down-arrow keys to highlight a file name.

You can click a file name with your mouse or click the scroll arrows to highlight a file name.

To jump to a different part of the list, choose **N**ame Search and then type the first few letters of a file name. To locate SMITH.9, for example, choose **N**ame Search and type **smi**. The File Manager jumps to the first file name beginning with those letters.

3. Do one of the following:

To look at a file, choose **L**ook.

To open a file, choose **O**pen into New Document.

To retrieve a file, choose **R**etrieve into Current Doc.

Troubleshooting

If you open a file by mistake, simply close the file.

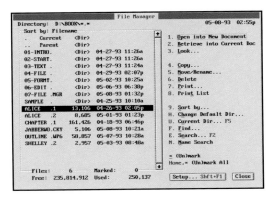

Highlight the file name.

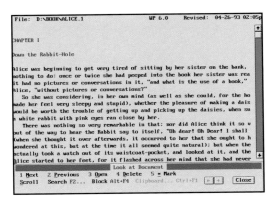

A look at the file.

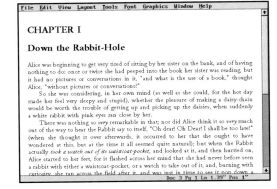

The file is opened.

FILES

The File Manager is designed to manage files. Among other actions, you can copy a file, move it to a different location, delete it, or rename it.

WordPerfect's File Manager makes working with files easy. Without this built-in tool, you'd have to use the DOS command prompt or another program to do file management tasks such as deleting or renaming a file. The File Manager makes file management easy because you can select the files you want from a list.

Copying Files

You may want to edit a copy of a document so that you don't change the original version. You might want to make a copy onto a floppy disk to act as a backup in case something happens to the original or to give to someone else. Using the File Manager, you can make the copy and put it in the same directory (the file has to have a new name) or in a different directory (the file can have the same name).

Moving and Renaming Files

If you organize your files in directories, you may need to move your files around. To do so, use the Move/Rename command. If you're not satisfied with the name you assigned a file when you saved it, you can also use Move/Rename to assign a different name.

Deleting Files

You should delete files you no longer need so you don't clutter up your hard disk. When you delete a file, the File Manager first prompts to make sure that you want to delete information. If you confirm the deletion, the File Manager removes the file name from the directory listing.

Always be very careful when deleting files. Once you delete a file, WordPerfect cannot recover the information. You may want to copy or move old documents to a floppy disk rather than deleting them altogether.

Caution: If you're not sure what a file contains, don't delete it! Use the File Manager's Look command to see its contents. Also, don't delete files in the WP60 or WPC60DOS directories; these directories contain the WordPerfect program files, and deleting the wrong files can disable the program. Appendix M of the WordPerfect manual lists the meaning of all the program files.

Marking Files

You can mark one or more files with an asterisk (*) and then copy, move, or delete them as a group. When you choose **C**opy or **M**ove/Rename, WordPerfect asks for a directory name and then makes a copy of each marked file in that directory (and removes the original, if you choose **M**ove). When you choose **D**elete, the File Manager makes you confirm that you want to delete multiple files, then prompts you a second time with the message Multiple files will be deleted and makes you confirm again before proceeding. This valuable safeguard prevents you from accidentally deleting large amounts of information.

You can't rename marked files.

Copy a File

1. Start the File Manager.

2. Highlight a file.

3. Choose **C**opy.

4. If you want to copy the file to another directory and keep the same name, type a new directory. If you want to make a copy in the same directory, type a file name for the copy.

5. Choose OK or press Enter.

Move a File

1. Start the File Manager.

2. Highlight a file.

3. Choose **M**ove/Rename.

4. Type a new directory.

5. Choose OK or press Enter.

Troubleshooting

If you copy or move a file to the wrong destination, you can change the directory to the new location and then move the file to its intended destination. See the article "Changing Directories" for help on changing the directory.

more ▶

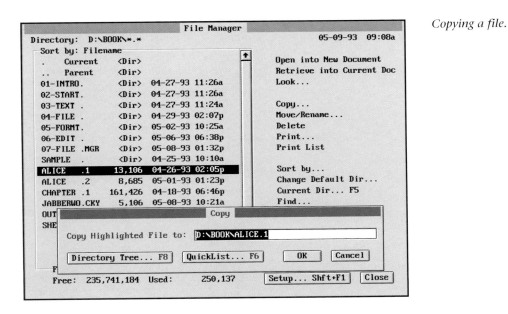

Copying a file.

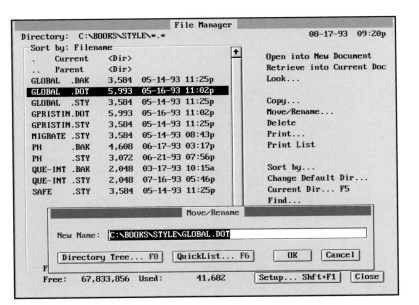

Moving a file.

Copy, Move, Delete, and Rename 135

Rename a File

1. Start the File Manager.

2. Highlight a file.

3. Choose **M**ove/Rename.

4. Type a new file name.

5. Choose OK or press Enter.

Delete a File

1. Start the File Manager.

2. Highlight a file.

3. Choose **D**elete.

4. Confirm the deletion by choosing **Y**es.

   The default is **N**o.

Troubleshooting

◆ If you rename a file incorrectly, simply rename it again.

◆ If you delete a file accidentally, the File Manager can't recover the file. You can often use a program such as the Norton Utilities or PC Tools to recover a deleted file, but only if no other file has been saved over the file's location on disk.

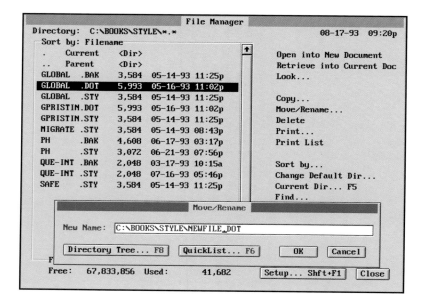

Renaming a file.

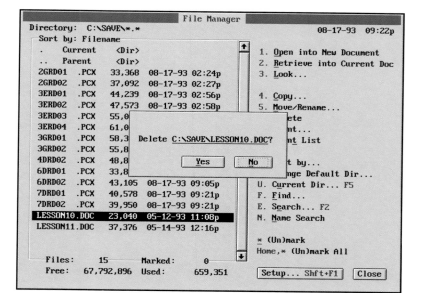

Deleting a file.

Work with Multiple Files

1. Start the File Manager.

2. Mark each file you want by highlighting the file and pressing *. To select all files, press Home+*.

3. Do one of the following:

   Choose Copy and then type a new directory for the files.

   Choose Move/Rename and type a new directory for the files.

   Choose Delete. When prompted to confirm the deletion, choose Yes.

4. Choose OK or press Enter.

Troubleshooting

If no files are marked, you can press Home, * to mark all files. If one or more files are marked, pressing Home, * unmarks all files.

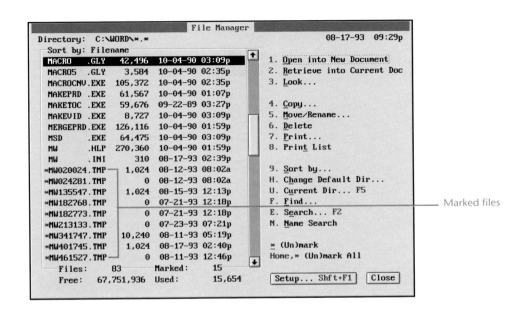

Marked files

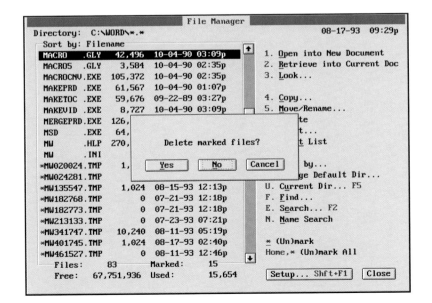

Deleting marked files.

When you create many files, you should always organize the files into directories. You can create directories with the File Manager.

When you group related files in directories, each directory name gives some meaning to the files in the directory. For example, instead of having 20 files named SMITH.1, SMITH.2, and so on, that deal with a client named SMITH, you can create a SMITH directory and name the files PROPOSAL.1, BUDGET.93, and other more specific names.

Directory Rules

You can create only one directory and one directory level at a time. If the NEW directory doesn't exist, you cannot directly create C:\SMITH\NEW\NEWER. You have to create NEW first and then create NEWER as a subdirectory of NEW.

Directory names have the same limitations as file names. They can be up to eight characters long, with an optional period and three-letter extension. To make it quicker and easier to change directories, use the shortest directory names possible. For example, use LTR instead of LETTER.

Organizing Your Directories

How you organize your files isn't really important as long as you stick to a consistent scheme.

◆ You can organize files by type (LETTERS, RESUMES, PROPOSAL).

◆ You can organize files by person or project (SMITH, JONES, and so on).

◆ You can use any other organizational scheme that makes sense to you.

What You Can Do with the New Directory

After you create a new directory, that new directory is not yet displayed. You can change to that directory, making it the default directory, or you can copy or move files to the new directory. See "Changing Directories" and "Copy, Move, Delete, and Rename."

Create a New Directory

1. Call up the File Manager.

2. Choose **Ch**ange Default Dir.

3. Type a new directory path.

4. Press Enter.

5. Type **y** when prompted whether you want to create the directory.

Troubleshooting

To change to this directory, see the next page.

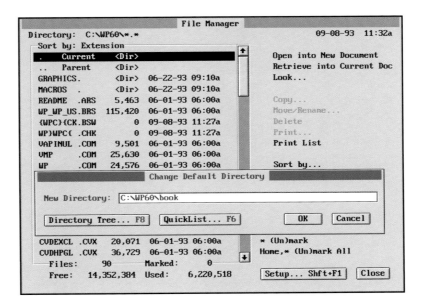

Typing the directory name.

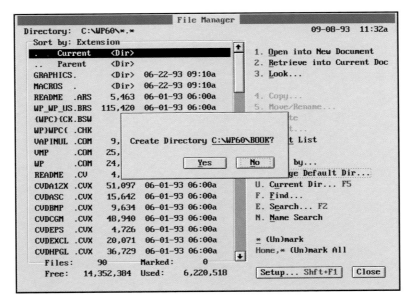

Confirming the new directory.

To display files in another directory, change the directory.

As you work in WordPerfect, one directory is always your default directory. If you want to save or open files in another directory, you must change to that directory.

You can change the default directory so that WordPerfect uses that directory each time you save or open a file. Or if you simply want to display files in another directory (without changing the default), you can do that, too.

Browsing Directories

To display files in another directory—without changing directories—first display the File Manager. The top two entries in the file list represent directories. The `. Current <Dir>` entry represents the current directory, and the `.. Parent <Dir>` entry represents the directory that contains the current directory. Other directories within the current directory are listed next. `<Dir>` is displayed next to the directory name.

◆ To display another directory, highlight the name and press Enter.

◆ If the directory is not displayed in the current list, you can move to a different branch of the directory tree. Highlight the `.. Parent <Dir>` entry and press Enter to display the files and subdirectories within that directory.

◆ You also can choose **Cu**rrent Dir, type a directory name, and press Enter to display a directory.

Note: Displaying another directory doesn't change the default directory.

Changing the Default Directory

If you want WordPerfect to use the directory for all file operations, use the Change Default Dir option. The default directory is often called the current directory as well.

◆ When you save a document for the first time, WordPerfect saves it to the default directory, unless you type a different directory name in front of the file name.

◆ When you use the **F**ile **O**pen or **R**etrieve commands, WordPerfect assumes that the file you want is in the default directory, unless you type a different directory name in front of the file name.

◆ When you start the File Manager, WordPerfect first displays the Specify File Manager List dialog box, which contains the current (default) directory. You can type a different directory to display a list of its files, or simply press Enter to display the files in the current directory.

◆ You can change the default directory at any time and as often as you like. Whenever you start a new project, you should change the default directory to the location of the files you need to use.

◆ Each time you start WordPerfect, the program sets the default directory to the location of the Documents directory specified in the Setup, Location of Files dialog box. See "Customizing" for help in setting locations of files.

Display a Different Directory

1. Highlight the directory in the file list.

2. Press Enter.

Change the Default Directory

1. Call up the File Manager.

2. Choose **Ch**ange Default Dir.

3. Type a new directory path.

4. Press Enter to display the Specify File Manager List dialog box.

5. Press Enter to redisplay the File Manager with the new default directory file list.

Troubleshooting

If you type the name of a directory that doesn't exist, the File Manager asks if you want to create that directory. If you don't, press Enter or choose **N**o. You can browse through the directories to find the one you want, then choose **Ch**ange Default Dir to select that directory.

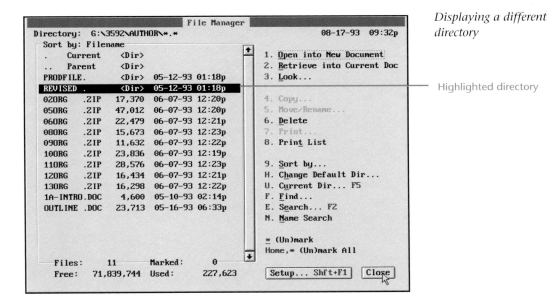

Displaying a different directory

Highlighted directory

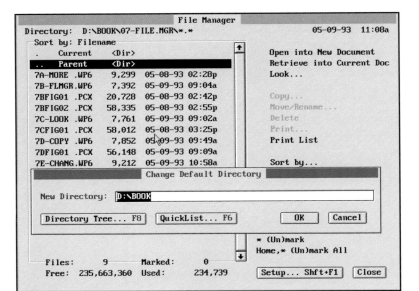

Changing the default directory.

FILES

If you can't find a file just by looking at its name, use the Find option to search through the contents of the file.

Occasionally, you may be convinced that you saved a file in a particular directory, but after using the File Manager to view the files in that directory, you still don't see any file names that seem to contain the right document. If you can think of a name or word that might be in the file but not in most other files in the directory, the File Manager may be able to locate the file for you.

The File Manager can search through the contents of each file in a directory and provide you with a short list of files that contain the word you searched. You can then look at these files individually.

TIP

Searching through the entire contents of each document is the most thorough kind of search and, therefore, also takes the longest time. If you're reasonably sure that the word you're looking for occurs in the first page of the document, you can narrow the search and thereby speed it up considerably.

Find Options

Here are several ways you can use the Find option to refine the search:

◆ After you have searched through the files once, you can have the File Manager narrow the list even further by searching for a different word.

◆ You can instruct the File Manager to search through the entire contents of each document, through only the first page of each document, or through the document summary of each document.

◆ If the File Manager's search doesn't help you find a document in the current directory, you can change to a different directory and search that directory.

Find a File

1. Call up the File Manager.

2. Choose **F**ind.

3. Do one of the following:

To search through each entire document in the directory, choose **E**ntire Document.

To search only the first page of each document in the directory, choose First **P**age.

4. Type a word that the File Manager should search for.

5. Press Enter or choose OK.

Troubleshooting

If the File Manager can't find a document with a particular word or finds too many documents with that particular word, try searching for another word to narrow the search.

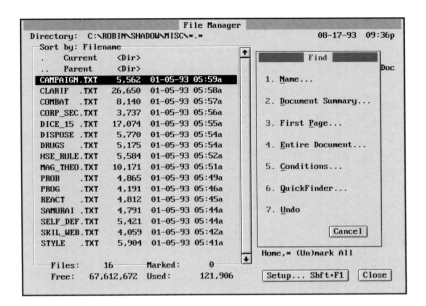

The File Manager.

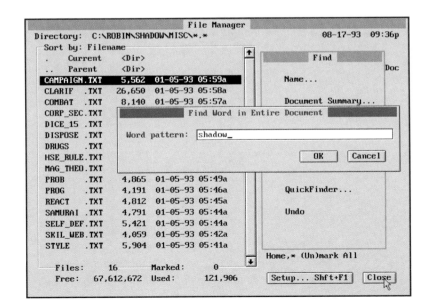

WordPerfect will search for the specified word through all the files in the directory.

You can use the File Manager's QuickList to create a list of the directories that you use most frequently. You can use that list whenever you select a directory to change to or view.

The more documents you create, the more directories you have to organize those documents. You may have a working directory, where you store files until you decide how to categorize them. You may have several directories for currently active projects and many more directories for projects that are finished or inactive. You also may have directories for graphics, source files that you use frequently, or any other type of information.

You can organize these directories into the QuickList.

What's the QuickList?

The *QuickList* is a list of the directories that you use most often. Instead of showing you actual directory paths such as C:\WORK\LTR, the QuickList displays text descriptions of your selected subdirectories, such as Letters and Memos. Each description is tied to a specific directory path.

When you install WordPerfect, the program creates a default QuickList that contains entries for documents, backup files, graphics files, macros, and other types of files listed in the Setup Location of Files dialog box. You can add, delete, or edit QuickList entries at any time.

Editing the QuickList

Each QuickList entry consists of a description and a directory or file name. The description is what you see when you use the QuickList, and the directory or file name is what the QuickList uses to change the directory for you.

For the description, you can enter any text that describes the contents of the directory or file name. For the directory, you must enter a legal DOS path. If your main work directory is C:\WORK, for example, the description can be Work Directory or Working Files, but the directory entry must specify C:\WORK.

> **TIP**
>
> You can use the QuickList whenever you choose a directory to look at or change to. When you start the File Manager and see the Specify File Manager List box, you can display the QuickList instead of typing a directory name.
>
> You can also use the QuickList to choose a directory in File Manager.

Making Other Changes

After you create a QuickList entry, you can edit the entry again at any time. In the QuickList dialog box, highlight the entry and choose **E**dit. You can then change the entry's description, the directory path, or both.

If you never use a particular QuickList entry, you should delete the entry. In the QuickList dialog box, highlight the entry and choose **D**elete. WordPerfect displays the description and directory path of the entry, and makes you confirm the deletion.

Change the Directory Using the QuickList

1. In the File Manager, choose **Ch**ange Default Dir.

2. Choose the QuickList button or press F6.

3. Highlight a QuickList entry.

4. Choose **S**elect or press Enter.

Add a QuickList Entry

1. Choose **F**ile, **F**ile Manager.

2. Choose the Quicklist button.

3. Choose **C**reate.

4. Enter a description for the entry.

5. Enter a directory path for the entry.

6. Choose OK.

7. Choose Close.

Troubleshooting

◆ If you choose the wrong QuickList description, you can repeat the steps to select a different entry.

◆ If you make a mistake in a QuickList entry's directory path, you get an error message when you select that entry in the QuickList. Edit the entry and correct the directory name.

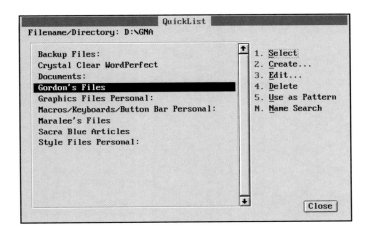

You can change a directory with the QuickList.

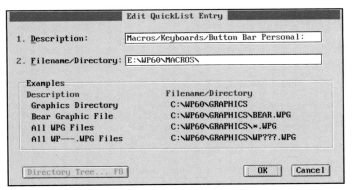

You can create a QuickList entry.

Shortcut Key

QuickList	F6

Part Three

Section 5—Styles

When you create a document, you usually want a document's format to be consistent throughout. Your main headings should all be in the same font, the same font size, and aligned the same. At the same time, you want to use as few steps as possible to format each document and to be able to change a document's format quickly and easily when necessary. You can accomplish these goals by using styles.

Section 6—Columns

Many newspapers, magazines, and newsletters print their text in several columns. Magazines and newsletters usually use two or three columns, and newspapers often use six or eight columns. You can use WordPerfect's Text Columns feature to format your documents in multiple columns.

Section 7—Tables

Using tabs to create columns of text or numbers is creating tables the hard way. Instead, you can use WordPerfect's Tables feature whenever you want to arrange information in columns and rows. You can create a professional-looking table in seconds, with virtually no effort.

Section 8—Lines and Boxes

Adding an image or simply highlighting a heading or title with a graphics line can make the difference between an ordinary-looking document and one that catches your eye. With WordPerfect, you now can place graphics anywhere in a document.

If you use the same set of formatting changes (bold, indented, 14-point type), don't make the changes each time. Instead, create and use a character style.

You often use character styles where you normally apply one or more font attributes. Unlike font attributes, however, character styles can contain many different types of codes, and they are always linked to a style definition.

Benefits of Styles

When you apply a bold or italic font attribute to a block of text, the codes are *static*: you can delete them or add new attribute codes, but you cannot change them. When you apply a character style to a block of text, editing the style definition changes the appearance of the block of text and of every other block of text formatted with the same style.

Using a style also improves consistency. If you use a style for all your headings, for example, you ensure that they are all formatted the same way.

Creating New Styles

Each document has a list of available styles. When you first use WordPerfect 6, those styles are samples provided by the program, but you can create styles for your own needs, save your styles, and use them on other documents.

Suppose that you want to make the first character or the first word of some paragraphs stand out. You can use a style containing the bold and extra large font attributes.

To add a style to your list, call up the list of available styles and choose **C**reate. Each style must have a name, a type, and the actual codes that make up the style. You also can add an optional description that WordPerfect displays in the Style List dialog box next to the style's name, to help remind you or others what the particular style does.

After you go through the initial steps to name the style, you must choose Style **C**ontents to insert the desired format codes. To create the "big and bold" style, for example, select the bold and extra large font attributes from the Font menu or Font dialog box. The codes appear in the Style Contents dialog box just as they appear in Reveal Codes.

Creating a Style from Existing Formatting

If have already formatted some text, you can also tell WordPerfect to create a style that includes the current formatting codes. Simply place the cursor within the formatted text before creating the style, and when you name the style, check the box to **C**reate From Current Paragraph. WordPerfect then copies the current font, size, and color, as well as any line and paragraph formatting. You can then edit the style contents to delete codes that you may not want in the style (such as font color) and add any other codes that you like.

TIP

You aren't limited to fonts and font attribute codes. You can put almost any format code into a character style. You can also include text in a style. If you need to create a list of questions and answers, for example, you could create a Question style that includes the text "(Q)," followed by an indent, and a similar style for the answers.

Editing Styles

After you apply a style throughout a document, you may decide that you don't like something about its appearance. The Big&Bold style may be *too* big, for example, or you may want to select a display font, such as Bodoni.

To edit the style, highlight the style name in the Style List, choose **E**dit, and then choose Style **C**ontents. You then can add or delete any format codes you like.

When you exit and close all the dialog boxes, WordPerfect automatically reformats the text where you have used the Big&Bold style in the document.

Using a Style

Once you create a style, you can use this style in your document or in other documents.

If you know in advance that you want to use the Big&Bold style in your document, at the beginning of each section you can turn on the style, type a letter or word, and then turn off the style.

If you don't decide to use the style until after you've entered the document's text, at the beginning of each section you can simply select a block of text and turn on the style.

Displaying Style Codes

When you apply a character style to some text, you can see the results of the style immediately in the document window, and you can also see the style codes in the Reveal Codes window. Unless you highlight a character style code, it appears in Reveal Codes as [Char Style On:*stylename*] or [Char Style Off:*stylename*]. If you highlight the code, WordPerfect expands the code to reveal all the individual codes within the style.

more ▶

Create a Character Style

1. Choose **L**ayout, **S**tyles.

2. Choose **C**reate.

3. Enter a short name for the style.

4. If you want to, choose **D**escription and then enter a longer description of the style.

5. Choose Style **T**ype and choose **C**haracter Style.

6. If you want WordPerfect to copy the current formatting, choose **C**reate From Current Character.

7. Choose OK.

8. Choose Style **C**ontents.

9. Insert any formatting codes you want, using the function keys or pull-down menus. You can also delete codes that you don't want included in the style.

10. Press F7 when you're done adding codes.

11. Choose OK to return to the Style List dialog box.

12. Choose Close to return to the document window.

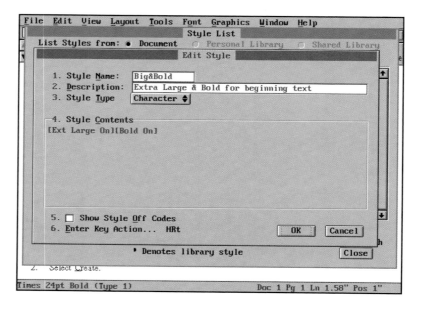

Creating a style is so easy that you can do it for any occasion. Do you write often to a nearsighted friend? Create a style with a large bold typeface and indented margins to make your letters easy to read.

Troubleshooting

◆ If you insert the wrong code into a style definition, simply delete the code just as you delete any code in Reveal Codes.

◆ If you don't discover a mistake until later, you can edit the style.

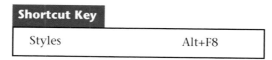

Shortcut Key	
Styles	Alt+F8

Apply a Character Style

1. Select a block of text.

2. Choose **L**ayout, **S**tyles.

3. Highlight the character style you want to use.

4. Choose **S**elect.

Troubleshooting

If you select the wrong character style, turn on Reveal Codes and delete one of the paired style codes.

Shortcut Key

| Styles | Alt+F8 |

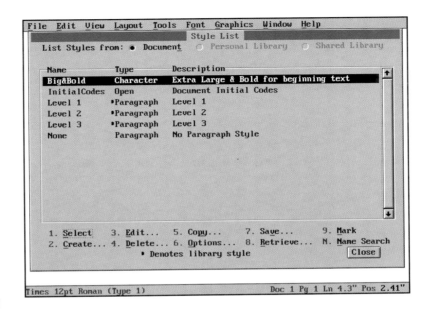

Specifying the Big&Bold style for use in a document is as easy as a click.

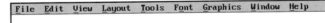

WordPerfect really does the coding to create this great look. All you do is apply the style.

Open styles are ideal for setting the initial formatting of a document and for creating letterheads.

Character styles are useful when you want to change the format of a specific block of text but don't want to affect any following text. An open style, however, can change the format of all text that follows it.

Changing the InitialCodes Style

Every WordPerfect document begins with an open style created by the program. In Reveal Codes, the style shows as [Open Style:InitialCodes]. You can't delete this style, but you can edit it, adding any codes you want, just as you would any other style.

Because the InitialCodes style appears at the beginning of a document, any codes in it act on the entire document (although you can always change formatting later in the document).

You can change the contents of the InitialCodes style for the current document or for all new documents you create. When you start using WordPerfect, the Initial Codes style in each of your documents is empty. You can edit the style in each individual document.

If you want to change all new documents, you can call up InitialCodes Setup and add those codes. Thereafter, each new document you create automatically contains those codes in its InitialCodes style. See the section "Customizing" for help in setting up your InitialCodes style.

Creating an Open Style

If you regularly create two types of documents with different formatting, you can create a second InitialCodes style with a slightly different name for the second document type. Then, every time you want to create a document of that type, simply insert the style at the beginning of a document, immediately after WordPerfect's InitialCodes style. Because your open style comes after WordPerfect's, your codes override the original initial codes.

Note: If you use paired codes within an open style, however, they act on text that you type as part of the style. These codes won't affect any text following the style code in a document.

See "Creating a Style Library" for help in saving and reusing styles in different documents.

> **TIP**
>
> Because styles can contain text and codes, you can create a very complex and distinctive letterhead and save it as a style. When you insert your letterhead style at the beginning of a letter or memo, WordPerfect prints your letterhead at the same time it prints the rest of the page.

Create a Style with Cut and Paste

When you create or edit the contents of a style, you can't see the appearance of the style's codes and text until you return to a document and use the style in the document. As a result, creating a letterhead style in the Style Contents dialog box can be a long process of trial and error. You can, however, use Cut and Paste with style definitions just as you do between two documents.

Instead of creating an entire letterhead style in the Style Contents dialog box, create it in a normal document and then adjust the text and format codes until you're satisfied with their appearance. Then block and copy all the text and codes, create a new open style, and paste the block into Style Contents.

> **TIP**
>
> You need to save your letterhead style in a style library so that you can use it with other documents. See "Creating a Style Library" for help.

more ▶

Open Styles 153

Create an Open Style

1. Choose **L**ayout, **S**tyles.

2. Choose **C**reate.

3. Enter a short name for the style.

4. Choose Style **T**ype and choose **O**pen Style.

5. Choose OK.

6. If you want to, choose **D**escription and then enter a longer description of the style.

7. Choose Style **C**ontents.

8. Insert any formatting codes you want, using the function keys or pull-down menus. You can also delete codes that you don't want included in the style.

9. Press F7 when you're done adding codes.

10. Choose OK to return to the Style List dialog box.

11. Choose Close to return to the document window.

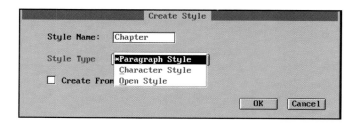

Style names don't have to be dull. Maybe "Charming" suits your fancy better than "Swiss Light."

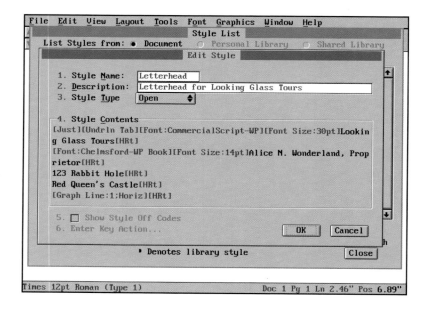

Notice that the style can include text. This feature makes open styles really useful for memo forms, fax documents, and so on.

Apply an Open Style

1. Choose **L**ayout, **S**tyles.

2. Highlight an open style.

3. Choose **S**elect.

Troubleshooting

If an open style doesn't change a document's format in the manner you expect, edit the style definition to change its contents, or delete the style definition and create a new one. If you insert the wrong open style in a document, turn on Reveal Codes and delete the style.

Shortcut Key	
Styles	Alt+F8

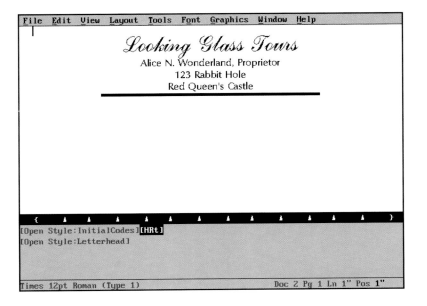

The letterhead style here includes multiple typefaces and point sizes, as well as plenty of text and a graphic line.

Paragraph styles have an infinite number of uses: headings, quotations, hanging indents, outlines, and more. When you want to format two or more paragraphs in the same way, create a paragraph style.

If you need to format paragraphs with a hanging indent for a bibliography, you can create a hanging indent paragraph style. If you need to quote extensively, you can create a quotation style that indents a paragraph from the left and right margins. Paragraph styles are also ideal for creating headings, and WordPerfect uses them when you create outlines.

Paragraph vs. Character vs. Open Styles

Paragraph styles are the most versatile type of WordPerfect style. Whereas a character style formats a block of text like paired attribute codes, and an open style formats any following text like a single (if complex) formatting code, a paragraph style formats an entire paragraph—no matter how long or short the paragraph is and no matter what text and codes the paragraph contains.

You normally use character styles on short blocks of text, whereas by definition you use paragraph styles on entire paragraphs. As a result, paragraph styles more often contain codes such as margin changes, indents, tab sets, line and paragraph spacing, and justification.

Creating a Paragraph Style

You create a paragraph style just as you create a character or open style. You can insert all the codes in the Style Contents dialog box, or you can base the style on the format of the current paragraph.

Changing the Enter Key Action

When you press Enter at the end of a paragraph to which a paragraph style has been applied, WordPerfect automatically turns the style off. You can tell WordPerfect to take additional actions by changing the Enter Key Action option in the Edit Style dialog box.

Instead of simply turning the style off when you press Enter, you can tell WordPerfect to turn the style off and then immediately turn it back on, to format the following paragraph with the same style. You can also tell WordPerfect to turn the style off, but to link to a *different* style for the following paragraph.

If you're typing a bibliography, for example, you can create a style that contains hanging indent codes and that turns itself off and then on again automatically. Each time you press Enter at the end of a reference, WordPerfect formats the following paragraph as another reference.

Alternatively, if you create a document in which a heading is always followed by a subheading, you can tell WordPerfect to link the heading to the subheading. When you press Enter at the end of the heading, WordPerfect automatically turns off the heading style and turns on the subheading style.

Paragraph Style Codes

No matter where your cursor is in a paragraph, when you select a paragraph style, WordPerfect inserts the paragraph style code at the beginning of the paragraph and automatically turns off the style when you end the paragraph with a hard return. In Reveal Codes, the hard return looks like a normal [HRt] until you highlight the code, at which point WordPerfect expands the code to resemble [Para Style End:;[HRt].

TIP

When you use paragraph styles, you never need to worry about selecting a block of text or about affecting text beyond the end of the paragraph.

Switching and Removing Paragraph Styles

Each paragraph can have only one paragraph style; if you select a second style, WordPerfect replaces the first paragraph style code with the second. As a result, you can reformat a paragraph completely by simply selecting a different paragraph style.

To remove a paragraph style, select None from the Style List. WordPerfect removes the style codes and returns the paragraph to its original formatting.

Paragraph Styles and Headings

Because any text that ends in a hard return is treated by WordPerfect as a paragraph, you can format most headings and titles quickly and easily by using paragraph styles. You can create a selection of heading styles for different heading levels and then simply select the appropriate style to format a heading at a given level.

If a subheading is embedded in a longer paragraph and takes up only part of the first line of the paragraph, you should use a character style to format the subheading. A paragraph style formats the entire paragraph, not just the subheading.

Outline Styles

WordPerfect provides a large number of sample paragraph styles that you can select at any time. All of WordPerfect's default paragraph styles are tied to outlines, and each style automatically identifies a paragraph as belonging to a particular outline level. If you change the outline level, WordPerfect automatically changes the paragraph style. By selecting a different outline style, you can format your document with simple headings—headings with Roman numerals or paragraph numbers, bulleted paragraphs, various types of indentation, and more. Although these styles can be very useful, you should read the section "Outlines" before using WordPerfect's default paragraph styles.

Selecting Styles from the Ribbon

With WordPerfect's Ribbon, which you can turn on or off from the View menu, you can make several of the most common formatting changes without going through menus or dialog boxes. One of the most useful Ribbon options lists your document's paragraph styles. To select a paragraph style by using the Ribbon, click the second drop-down arrow and select one of the listed styles. You may need to scroll to see all the available style names. The Ribbon lists only paragraph styles, not open or character styles. You must use a mouse to select styles from the Ribbon.

more ▶

Create a Paragraph Style

1. Choose **L**ayout, **S**tyles.

2. Choose **C**reate.

3. Enter a short name for the style.

4. Accept the default Style **T**ype of **P**aragraph Style.

5. If you want WordPerfect to copy the current formatting, choose **C**reate From Current Paragraph.

6. Choose OK.

   WordPerfect displays the Edit Style dialog box.

7. Choose **D**escription and then enter a longer description of the style.

8. Choose Style **C**ontents.

9. Insert any formatting codes you want, using the function keys or pull-down menus. You can also delete codes that you don't want included in the style.

10. Press F7 when you're done adding codes.

11. If desired, choose **E**nter Key Action, then choose one of the following:

    Turn Style O**ff**.

    Turn Style Off and Back **O**n.

    Turn Style Off and Link To: then select a second style from the list that appears.

    Choose OK.

12. Choose OK to return to the Style List dialog box.

13. Choose Close to return to the document window.

Troubleshooting

If you insert the wrong code into a style definition, simply delete the code just as you delete any code in Reveal Codes. If you don't discover the mistake until later, you can edit the style.

Shortcut Key	
Styles	Alt+F8

Apply a Paragraph Style

1. Choose **L**ayout, **S**tyles.

2. Highlight a paragraph style.

3. Choose **S**elect.

Troubleshooting

If you select the wrong paragraph style, simply select a different style. If you don't want a paragraph style after all, choose None. If a style doesn't format a paragraph in the manner you expected, edit the style to change its formatting, or create a new paragraph style with the desired formatting.

Shortcut Key

| Styles | Alt+F8 |

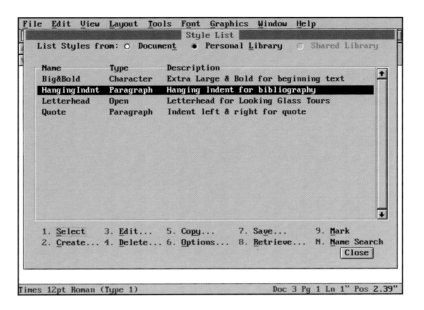

Even if you use a particular style only once a month or so, you can save at least a few keystrokes—and maybe a few minutes of formatting time—by using the style.

Because a style can contain font changes, special characters such as bullets, a particular indent format, and so on, changing the style can radically change the look of the paragraph.

STYLES

Save collections of styles you use frequently as style libraries. Then retrieve those styles into other documents.

When you create a style, the style definition becomes part of the current document, and you can use the style as many times as you like within the document. When you start a new document, however, it doesn't contain any styles you created for a different document. To use the style in the new document, you can re-create the style, but you don't have to. Instead, you can save styles in a *style library* and reuse your styles with other documents.

What Is a Style Library?

A style library is a WordPerfect document that usually contains nothing but style definitions. By convention, style libraries have a file name extension of STY, but you can give any file name or extension to a library file.

Building Custom Style Libraries

Creating a style library is no more difficult than saving a document. If you have created styles in a document, you can simply choose Save in the Style List dialog box. WordPerfect asks you for a file name, then copies all the style definitions you've created in the document into that file. Because this process creates a style library, you may want to give the new file an STY extension.

You can create as many style libraries as you like. You probably create several different types of documents—letters, reports, invoices, newsletters—and each type of document has different formatting needs. If you create a different library for each type of document, with names such as LTR.STY, INVOICE.STY, or NEWSLTR.STY, you can always use styles you have designed precisely for the current type of document.

When you create additional styles, you can add them to an existing style library. When you highlight a style name in the Style List dialog box, you can choose Copy to have WordPerfect copy the style to your personal or shared library.

Creating Default Style Libraries

Although style libraries are in fact normal WordPerfect documents, WordPerfect treats them like other system files. If you designate a specific directory for style libraries in the Setup Location of Files dialog box, WordPerfect automatically saves new libraries in that directory and looks in that directory whenever you use a style library. You can designate a directory for *personal* style files and the same directory or a different directory for *shared* style files. See "Customizing" for help in setting your program file locations.

When you specify directories for your library files, you can also designate a default personal library and a default shared library. You then can use the styles contained in either default style library with any other document without taking any special steps.

Using a Style Library

When you call up the Style List, the dialog box displays the style definitions contained in the document, as well as several of WordPerfect's own styles. You can also display the styles contained in a style library and use those styles in your document.

Using Default and Shared Libraries

To use styles defined in a style library, you need to assign the library to the current document. WordPerfect lets you assign two libraries at a time: a personal library and a shared library. If you designated a default personal or shared style library in Location of Files, these libraries are already assigned. If you didn't designate a default personal or shared style library, their radio buttons are grayed in the Style List, and you must assign a library before you can use library styles. You can assign a different library to a document at any time.

Shared vs. Personal Libraries

The difference between shared and personal libraries is somewhat arbitrary, and depends on your work environment. If you work in an office environment with a local area network, shared libraries may contain styles created for the use of anyone in the office, while personal libraries may contain your personal styles. If you work by yourself, the shared libraries may contain styles you use with many types of documents, while personal libraries may contain special-purpose styles.

Viewing and Applying the Library Styles

After you assign a library to a document, you can see the list of styles the library contains by choosing the Personal Library or Shared Library radio buttons at the top of the Style List dialog box. You can use any library style exactly as you use a style contained in the document, whether the style is a character, open, or paragraph style.

When you use a library style, WordPerfect automatically copies the style's definition to the current document. As a result, if you later change the style library assigned to the document, the library styles you have already used remain with the document.

more ▶

Create a Style Library

1. Choose **L**ayout, **S**tyles.

2. Choose Sa**v**e.

3. Enter a file name.

Copy a Style

1. Choose **L**ayout, **S**tyles.

2. Highlight a style name.

3. Choose Co**p**y.

4. Choose **P**ersonal Library or **S**hared Library.

Troubleshooting

If you make a typo while saving a style library, you can use the File Manager to rename the style library, just as you rename any other file. WordPerfect saves style libraries in the location specified in the Location of Files setup screen or in the current directory if no location has been specified for style files.

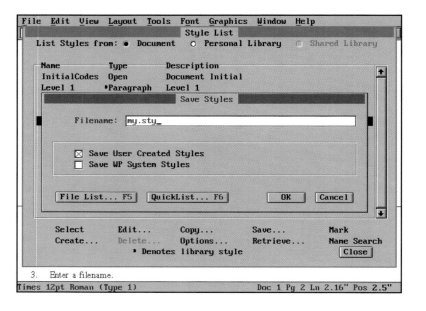

The STY extension isn't required. To keep your style libraries organized, however, you should use common naming conventions and/or save your libraries in a special directory.

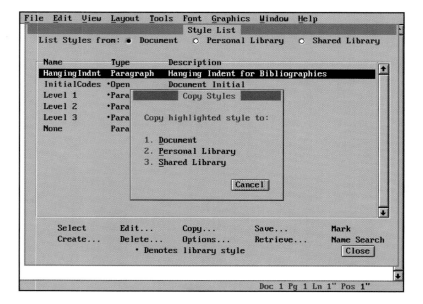

Copying existing styles can save a lot of time and effort. Why re-create styles that are already perfect?

162 **Styles**

Select a Style Library

1. Choose **L**ayout, **S**tyles.

2. Choose **O**ptions.

3. Choose **L**ibraries Assigned to Document.

4. Enter a file name for the Personal library, or select a file using the File List or QuickList.

5. Enter a file name for the Shared library, or select a file using the File List or QuickList.

6. Choose OK.

Troubleshooting

If you assign the wrong style library as the personal or shared style library, simply assign a different library.

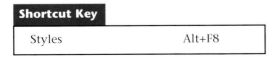

Shortcut Key	
Styles	Alt+F8

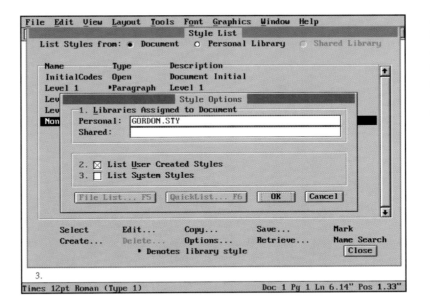

If the library you want is in a different directory, use the File List or the QuickList to find the right file. See the section "Files" for details.

Line styles let you save and reuse graphics lines just as paragraph styles let you save and reuse format codes.

Whenever WordPerfect draws lines in a document—graphics lines, graphics boxes, and paragraph, page, and column borders—the program uses *line styles* to control the appearance of the printed lines. Each line style defines the appearance of one or more lines: number of lines and the thickness, color, and pattern of each, as well as the space between each pair of lines.

When you create a line, box, or border, you can select one of WordPerfect's built-in line styles, edit a style, or create a new line style. Once you've created or edited a style, you can copy the new style to a style library, which can contain all types of styles; when you select a paragraph style, you don't see the line styles, and vice versa.

You can reuse line styles. Once you create a line style, selecting a complicated pattern of thick or thin lines takes no longer than selecting an individual thick or thin line. If you use a line style repeatedly throughout a document and then edit the line style, the appearance of the lines changes throughout the document where you used that style.

Line Style Contents

When you create or edit a style, you can control these elements:

◆ *Components*. Each line style can contain many individual lines. You can insert a new line before, between, or after any line components that are already part of the style.

◆ *Thickness*. You can specify an exact thickness for each line component of a style, to three decimal places.

◆ *Interline Spacing*. When a style contains more than one line, you control the spacing between each pair of lines.

◆ *Color*. You can choose from a list of predefined colors or define your own color for each line component. (You must have a color printer to print colored lines.)

◆ *Pattern*. Select from a wide range of line patterns: solid, dotted, dashed, and various combinations and lengths of dots and dashes.

Editing a Line Style

You can create and edit line styles through the **G**raphics menu.

When you create or edit a style, Word-Perfect displays the Edit Line Style dialog box. The individual line components that make up the line style appear at the left of the screen. WordPerfect draws a red border around one of the components so you can tell which line you're editing; scroll up or down to select a different line.

The Edit Line Style dialog box displays a box corner, using the style as it is currently defined. When you change the line style,WordPerfect updates the display to reflect your changes.

Edit a Line Style

1. Choose **G**raphics, Graphics **L**ines, St**y**les. WordPerfect displays the Line Styles dialog box.

2. Choose **C**reate to create a new line style; or highlight an existing line style and choose **E**dit.

3. If necessary, press the up arrow or down arrow to highlight a line component you want to edit.

4. To add a new line component, choose **C**reate. WordPerfect inserts the new line *above* the currently highlighted component.

5. To delete a line component, highlight the line and choose **D**elete.

6. To change a line component's thickness, choose **T**hickness and enter a different value.

7. To change the spacing between the selected line component and the component below, choose Interline **S**pacing and enter a different value.

8. To change a line's color, choose C**o**lor and select a shade from the list of colors that appears. To change a line's pattern, choose **P**attern and select a pattern from the list that appears.

9. When you're finished making changes, choose OK; then Close the Line Styles dialog box.

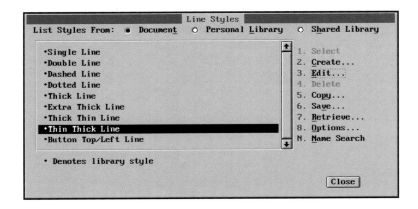

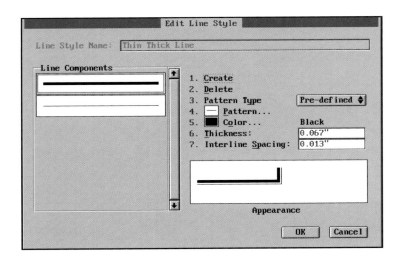

Troubleshooting

If you aren't happy with the appearance of a line style, you can edit the style to add or delete line components, or change any attributes of the existing components.

Newspapers, agendas, and scripts are all examples of documents that use columns. You can use WordPerfect's Columns feature to create these types of documents.

Before WordPerfect can format a document in text columns, you need to tell the program how you want the columns to appear. You need to define what type of columns you want—newspaper, balanced newspaper, parallel, or parallel with block protect—how many columns you want, and how much space you want between columns.

How Columns Work

When you define columns, WordPerfect inserts a column definition code at the beginning of the current paragraph and formats any following text according to the definition. You can define columns in the Text Columns dialog box or by selecting the number of columns you want by using the Ribbon's columns drop-down list.

Calculating Columns and Gutters

You can create up to 24 columns of any type. Of course, the more columns you create, the narrower each column will be. The width of each column depends on the number of columns you select, the space available between the left and right margins of the document, and the amount of space between the columns. By default, Word-Perfect makes all the columns the same width.

The empty space between two columns is called a *gutter*. Changing the Distance Between Columns setting changes the width of your document's gutters. If you make the gutters wider, WordPerfect makes your columns narrower, leaving less room for text on a page. Likewise, narrow gutters leave more room for text. WordPerfect's default gutter width is $1/2$ inch, which is usually too much space between columns. In most cases, you should specify a smaller measurement, such as $1/3$, $1/4$, or $1/5$ inch.

Turning Off Columns

You can turn off columns by choosing Off from the Text Columns dialog box or by selecting 1 Col from the Ribbon's Column button. If you want to turn columns back on at some later point in your document, you must actually insert a new column definition. WordPerfect retains your previous setting for Distance Between Columns, but you must reselect any other values. You can also copy the original column definition code and paste it in at a new location.

Define Text Columns

1. Place the cursor where you want columns to begin.

2. Choose **L**ayout, **C**olumns.

3. Choose Column **T**ype and specify the type you want from the following:
   Newspaper
   Balanced N**e**wspaper
   Parallel
   Parallel with **B**lock Protect

4. Choose **N**umber of Columns and enter a value.

5. Choose **D**istance Between Columns and enter a value; you can use decimals or fractions.

6. Choose OK.

   WordPerfect immediately formats into columns any text that follows the definition.

Troubleshooting

If you aren't happy about any aspect of your columns' appearance, move the cursor to the paragraph you defined columns in, choose **L**ayout, **C**olumns, then change any setting.

Shortcut Key

| Columns/Tables | Alt+F7 |

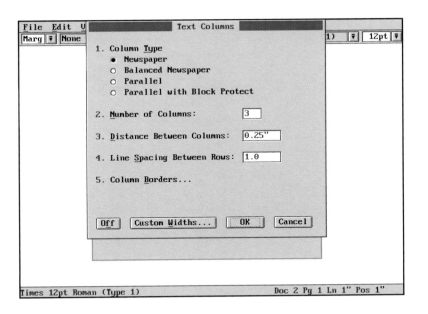

Because WordPerfect sets up the columns, you can just make guesses for the initial settings. If you don't like the result, simply adjust the settings.

File Edit View Layout Tools Font Graphics Window Help

In Congress July 4, 1776
The Unanimous Declaration of
The Thirteen United States of America

When in the course of human events, it becomes necessary for one people to dissolve the political bands which have connected them with another, and to assure among the Powers of the earth, the separate and equal station to which the Laws of Nature and of Nature's God entitle them, a decent respect to the opinions of mankind requires that they should declare the causes which impel them to the separation.

We hold these truths to be self-evident, that all men are created equal, that they are endowed by their Creator with certain

established should not be changed for light and transient causes; and accordingly all experience hath shown that mankind are more disposed to suffer, while evils are sufferable, than to right themselves by abolishing the forms to which they are accustomed. But when a long train of abuses and usurpations pursuing invariable the same Object evinces a design to reduce them under absolute Despotism, it is their right, it is their duty, to throw off such Government, and to provide new Guards for their future security. Such as been the patient

Doc 1 Pg 1 Ln 1.24" Pos 1"

A two-column structure like this is easy to read and looks attractive in print.

Changing the Column Layout

You can be as inventive as you like with your column layout. You can change the number of columns and create uneven column widths.

Occasionally, you may want to change the columns you specified for a document layout. Perhaps the lines look too ragged because the columns are too narrow. Maybe you want to change the type of columns you're using or change the number of columns.

Changing the Columns

Whenever you want to change a column definition after you've typed some text, make sure that you move the cursor back to the first line of columnar text before calling up the Text Columns dialog box. Otherwise, you create a second column definition at the row in which the cursor is currently located, and the format of the previous rows aren't changed.

When you return to the location of the original column definition, call up the Text Columns dialog box.

Make any changes to the settings:

◆ Select a new column type.

◆ Select a different number of columns.

◆ Change the distance between columns.

◆ Change the line spacing between rows.

◆ Add column borders. (See the article, "Adding Column Borders.")

WordPerfect replaces the first column definition code with a code containing your new settings.

Creating Custom Column Widths

WordPerfect automatically makes all column widths the same. For some documents, you'll want to make some of your columns wider than others if you have different amounts of information in different columns, or if you want to create a sidebar effect with one wide column and one narrow column. You can set specific widths for each column and gutter by choosing Custom **W**idths in the Text Columns dialog box.

You can change the width of any or all columns and gutters. If your combined custom column and gutter widths are less than the space between the margins, WordPerfect makes the columns slightly wider so that they fill the margin width. If your column and gutter widths are too wide to fit on the page, WordPerfect prompts you that text columns can't overlap, and you must re-adjust the width of one or more columns or gutters.

Create Custom Column Widths

1. Place the cursor in the first row of columnar text.

2. Choose **L**ayout, **C**olumns.

3. Choose Custom **W**idths.

4. Highlight a column whose width you want to change and then choose **E**dit.

5. Choose **W**idth and enter a different width. You can use decimals or fractions.

6. Choose OK.

7. Change any other column widths or choose OK.

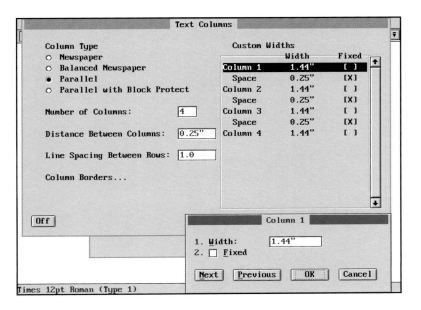

Try making the columns in a two-column setup two different widths. The larger column draws the eye; this "unbalanced" effect can add emphasis to the text.

Troubleshooting

If you don't move the cursor back to the paragraph in which you defined columns before you edit a column definition, WordPerfect creates a new definition in the current paragraph, and any previous columnar text remains unchanged. To fix this, choose Undo, then move the cursor back to the beginning of the columns and re-edit the definition.

Working in Newspaper columns is just like working in a very narrow document. Parallel columns are good for agendas, plays, and itineraries. If you have to create these types of documents or similar documents, investigate Parallel columns.

Once you have defined Newspaper columns, you can type in columns just as you would in a normal document. Text automatically wraps at the end of each line within the column and from the bottom of one column to the top of the next.

Moving Around in Columns

Cursor movement within a column is the same as in a normal document, with the addition of two commands to move between columns:

◆ Press Alt+right arrow to move the cursor one column to the right.

◆ Press Alt+left arrow to move the cursor one column to the left.

With a mouse, simply click in a different column to move the cursor.

Inserting Column Breaks

When you type in Newspaper columns, as your text fills a column, WordPerfect automatically wraps the following text to the next column. But you can also force a column break at any point by pressing Ctrl+Enter.

In normal text, this keystroke inserts a [HPg] code, but in columnar text it inserts a [HCol] code, instead. The latter action forces the following text to the top of the next column and leaves the remainder of the column below the page break code empty.

Changing the Font

Because columns are much narrower than the normal line width, you may need to select a smaller font size; otherwise, left-justified text may have a ragged-right margin, and some lines of full-justified text may look abnormally spread out or compressed.

TIP

The more columns you define, the smaller your point size should be; you should average 10 to 12 words per line. Proportionally spaced fonts adjust better than fixed-width fonts, and some fonts at the same point size are narrower than others.

See "Changing the Font Size" for more information.

Changing the Justification and Alignment

Justification and alignment codes work in columns exactly as they do in normal text. To center a heading, for example, you can center-align a single-line heading or center-justify a multiline heading. In either case, WordPerfect centers the text between the current margins, whether they're full-page margins or column margins. The other alignment and justification commands act in a similar manner (see "Setting Tabs" and "Changing Justification" for more information on aligning and justifying text).

TIP

You can improve the appearance of columnar text by manually hyphenating some long words that have wrapped to the following line, but you should avoid placing hyphens on several successive lines.

Working in Balanced Columns

With standard Newspaper columns, if you turn off Columns in the middle of a page, WordPerfect leaves the remainder of the column empty and forces any text that follows to the top of the next page. With Balanced Newspaper columns, WordPerfect continually adjusts the length of all columns so that they end at approximately the same line. If you turn off Balanced Newspaper columns, any text that follows the Column off code appears below, on the same page.

TIP

Because WordPerfect continually adjusts your column lengths, typing in Balanced Newspaper columns can be slow. As soon as you finish typing each line of text, WordPerfect adjusts the lines of text in each to keep the column lengths as even as possible. You may find it easier to type your text first and then add the balanced column definition.

Even though you select Balanced Newspaper columns, all your columns may not be *exactly* the same length; it's impossible to fit four lines of text evenly into three columns. Also, widows and orphans, paragraph spacing, and larger type sizes for headings can all cause your columns to have slightly uneven lengths. However, no column should be more than one line shorter or longer than the average number of lines in all columns.

Where Newspaper columns typically feature large amounts of text flowing continuously from column to column, Parallel columns contain shorter blocks of text that you read across the page from left to right like a table. These blocks of text can be any length, from individual words and short phrases to long paragraphs. As a result, you can use Parallel columns for a wide variety of documents, from itineraries to screenplays.

Defining Parallel Columns

The steps for defining Parallel columns are similar to those for creating Newspaper columns, but you must define Parallel columns using the Text Columns dialog box; you can't use the Ribbon. Also, whereas Newspaper columns are usually evenly spaced and need little, if any, adjustment after definition, Parallel columns can have greatly differing widths.

TIP

For the best appearance, you may need to edit the column definition after you've entered some text. Although you should plan in advance the number of columns you need and their approximate widths, don't spend a lot of time making complex calculations that you will probably change anyway. See "Changing the Column Layout" for help in creating custom column widths.

Spacing between Rows

When you create Parallel columns, WordPerfect puts one blank line between each row of text blocks. To increase or decrease that amount of space, choose Line Spacing Between Rows in the Text Columns dialog box and specify the desired amount of space. A value of 2.0 creates a double space between rows; a value of 1.5 creates a space and a half. If you enter a value of 0, WordPerfect doesn't add any space between rows.

more ▶

COLUMNS

Typing Text in Parallel Columns

When you type in Parallel columns, you must press Ctrl+Enter to insert a [HCol] code at the end of each block of text to tell WordPerfect where to break text between columns. Otherwise, WordPerfect treats everything that follows as part of the same column. Therefore, when you finish typing the block of text in the first column, press Ctrl+Enter, and WordPerfect moves the cursor to the second column. Do the same for any subsequent columns. After you finish the text block in the last column, again press Ctrl+Enter. WordPerfect moves the cursor to the beginning of the first column, below any text you've entered.

If you need to add a new row in the middle of your existing text, place the cursor at the beginning of a row and begin typing. When you finish the first column, press Ctrl+Enter as normal to move to the second column. WordPerfect pushes the existing blocks of text out of the way so that you can type the text for the next column. Continue in this manner, pressing Ctrl+Enter at the end of each column; at the last column, this action moves the existing text block to the beginning of the next row.

Block-Protected Columns

When you select the Parallel column type, WordPerfect allows a block of text to extend over a page break. This situation is acceptable for screenplays and other documents where a text block may be several paragraphs or pages long. In other cases, particularly when text blocks are short, you may want to prevent blocks of text from being split by a page break. To do so, use the Parallel with Block Protect column type when defining columns.

Block-protected Parallel columns look and act like standard Parallel columns. In Reveal Codes, the column definition code appears as [Col Def:Parallel with Protect], but WordPerfect provides no other indication that block protection is active. Each text block ends in a [HCol] code. If a text block extends past a page break, however, WordPerfect moves the entire row of text blocks to the next page.

Troubleshooting

◆ If you copy and paste text from more than one column at a time, WordPerfect copies and pastes the [HCol] code as well, which shifts every following block of text over by one column, and text that was in the last column is now in the first column. To restore your column structure, delete the extra [HCol] code. The text then reverts to its previous position.

◆ If you delete a [HCol] code by accident, you can press Ctrl+Enter to insert a new code.

◆ If you aren't happy with the appearance of your columnar text, you can change any aspect you don't like. See "Changing the Column Layout" for help in changing the number of columns or their widths. See "Formatting" for help in changing the font, justification, or alignment.

Remember not to mix too many fonts or font styles. Otherwise, your newsletter ends up looking like a ransom note.

Notice that a graphic line dropped between columns helps to guide the eye and prevent the reader from jumping across columns by accident.

Adding a graphic to your newsletter really enhances its appearance and makes the text attract the reader. The graphic may be tied to the text or completely unrelated.

Use horizontal lines to distinguish between parts of the newsletter.

For an itinerary like this, you can use a column setup or create a table. See the "Tables" section for details on creating a table.

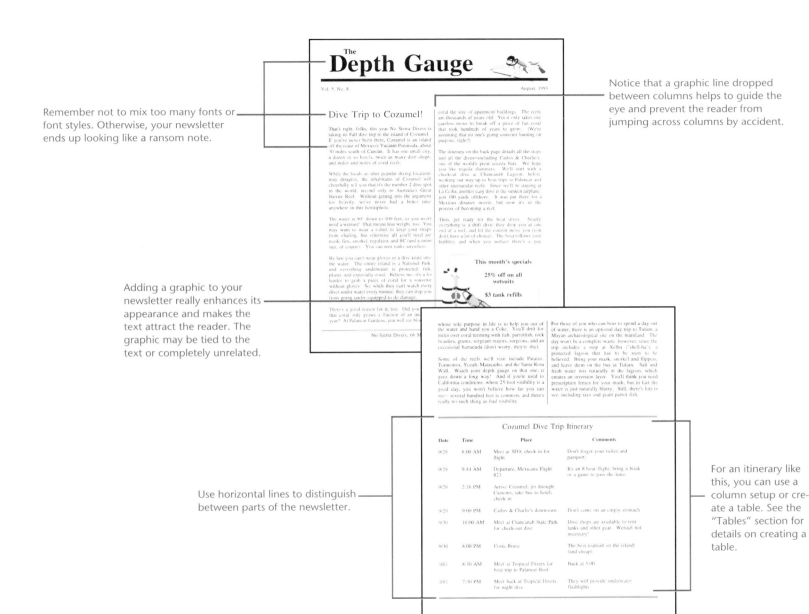

You can dress up the appearance of your columns by adding borders or shading.

Wordperfect can draw a single line in the gutter between each pair of columns, a rectangular border outside your columnar text—much like paragraph borders—or a border both outside and between columns. Column borders don't surround headers, footers, or page numbers.

Line and Fill Styles

If you simply turn on Column Borders without choosing any other border options, WordPerfect automatically draws a single line gutter between columns. You can select a different line appearance, however, from a list of line styles, including double, dotted, dashed, thick, thin, and more.

At the same time, you can also select a fill style. Most fill styles are uniform gray shades of different densities, although you can also select a "button fill," which uses light and dark shading on the edges to simulate a push button. In addition, you can create a custom column border with a drop shadow, rounded corners, a gradient fill, color (if your printer supports it), or other options.

 TIP For information on creating custom borders, see "Creating Lines."

Turning Borders On and Off

After you turn on Column Borders, WordPerfect puts a border around all following columnar text until you turn off borders. To turn off Page Borders, repeat steps 1 and 2 (from the steps on the next page) and then choose **O**ff. If you don't turn off Column Borders, WordPerfect draws a border around all columnar text that follows. Turning off Columns also turns off Column Borders.

Parallel Column Borders

If you use Column Borders with Parallel columns, WordPerfect draws a border around (or between) each row of columns but does not draw borders in the space between rows. Likewise, if you select a fill style, each row is shaded, but not the space between rows.

Turn On Column Borders

1. Select a block of text.

2. Choose **L**ayout, **C**olumns, Column **B**orders.

3. If you want to, choose **B**order Style and select a different style from the list box.

4. If you want to, choose **F**ill Style and select a style from the list box.

5. Choose **C**ustomize to create a drop shadow, rounded corners, gradient fill, or other options if you want.

6. Choose OK to close all open dialog boxes.

Troubleshooting

◆ If you choose Column **B**orders from the Text Columns dialog box by accident, press Esc or choose Cancel.

◆ If you select a line or fill style but don't like your selection, place the cursor in the first line of columnar text with a border. Then repeat the steps and select different styles, or choose **O**ff to remove the border completely.

◆ You also can turn on Reveal Codes and delete the [Col Border] code. WordPerfect places column border codes at the beginning of the current paragraph.

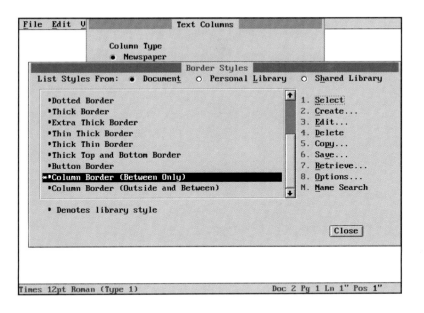

You can choose from a wide variety of border styles. Be careful, though, about combining thick borders and dark graphics. This combination can look oppressive.

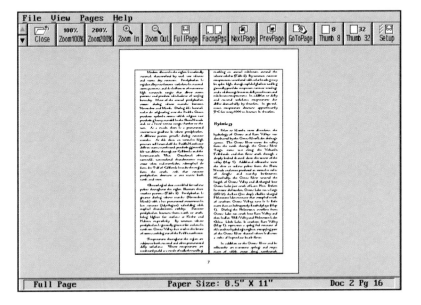

Notice that these balanced columns are visually appealing. The column borders make them easy to read, too.

Creating a table is simply a matter of telling WordPerfect how many rows and columns you need.

A WordPerfect table is a grid of cells arranged in columns and rows. The intersection of a column and row is called a *cell*. WordPerfect automatically draws lines around each cell.

After you've created a table, you can put just about anything in a cell—text, numbers, spreadsheet formulas, graphics—and WordPerfect automatically adjusts the table structure to hold the information.

Adjusting Columns

When you first create a table, WordPerfect leaves you in table edit mode so that you can make initial changes to the table's format.

◆ Press Ctrl+right arrow to make a column wider.

◆ Press Ctrl+left arrow to make a column narrower.

◆ Press F7 or choose Close to exit table edit mode.

When you work in a table, each cell is like a mini-document. WordPerfect formats the text in each cell separately, and you use special commands to move from cell to cell.

When you first create a table, each row is one line high. As you type information into a cell and reach the right edge of the cell, WordPerfect wraps the following text down to a second line and expands the height of the cell—and every other cell in the row— to fit. As long as you keep typing in the cell, WordPerfect keeps expanding its height.

If you want to create a second line within a cell but don't want text to wrap, you can press Enter, just as you do anywhere else in a document, and WordPerfect inserts a [HRt] code. Likewise, if you want to force a page break in a long table at a particular row, you can press Ctrl+Enter, and Word-Perfect inserts a [HRow-HPg] code.

When you fill in the last cell in the last row, simply press Tab if you want to keep adding information to the table. WordPerfect automatically adds another row to the bottom of the table.

You can click in any cell with your mouse to move the cursor to that cell. However, using cursor keys to move the cursor within a table is somewhat different from moving within a normal document. You can scroll from cell to cell, but if a cell contains text, WordPerfect scrolls through all the text in the cell before moving the cursor to the next cell.

Moving Around in a Table

Tab	Next Cell
Shift+Tab	Previous Cell
Alt+↓	One Cell Down
Alt+↑	One Cell Up
Ctrl+Home, Home, ↑	First Cell in Column
Ctrl+Home, Home, ↓	Last Cell in Column
Ctrl+Home, Home, ←	First Cell in Row
Ctrl+Home, Home, →	Last Cell in Row
Ctrl+Home, Home, Home, ↑	First Cell in Table

Create a Table

1. Choose **L**ayout, **T**ables, **C**reate.

2. Enter the number of columns you want.

3. Enter the number of rows you want.

4. Choose OK.

5. Make any initial changes you want in table edit mode.

6. To leave table edit mode, choose Close or press F7.

7. Type the table text.

Troubleshooting

◆ If you chose the wrong number of rows, don't worry about it now; you can easily add or delete rows later.

◆ If you chose the wrong number of columns, you should add or delete columns before adding any text; see "Inserting or Deleting Columns."

◆ If you want to delete the table, exit from table edit mode, block the entire table, and press Del.

Shortcut Key

Tables/Columns	Alt+F7

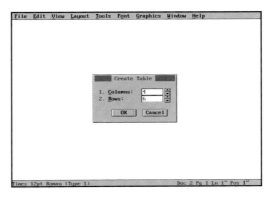

Select the number of rows and columns you want.

Adjust the column widths if necessary.

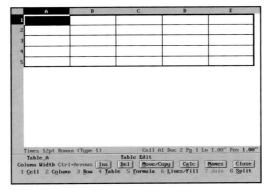

The finished table.

You can add or delete rows anywhere in a table at any time.

When you create a table, you may not know how many rows or columns you need. But don't worry. If your table is too short, you can easily add rows at the end as you type. You can also insert or delete rows in the middle of a table.

Adding Rows Automatically

WordPerfect automatically adds rows to the end of a table as you need them. When you fill in the last cell in the last row and press Tab, the program adds another row to the bottom of the table. With each additional row that you finish, again press Tab to add another row.

Inserting or Deleting One Row

You have to make most changes to a table structure in table edit mode, but you can insert or delete a single row in the normal document window.

To insert a row, move the cursor to any row in the table and then choose Insert Row. WordPerfect inserts a new row above the current row.

To delete a row, use the Delete Row command. The program makes you confirm the deletion, and then it deletes the row at the cursor position.

Inserting or Deleting Several Rows

If you want to insert or delete more than one row at a time, you must go into table edit mode. There you can choose the **I**ns or **D**el command and select rows. WordPerfect then lets you choose how many rows to insert or delete. If you're inserting, the program also lets you choose whether to insert the new rows above or below the current row.

Insert or Delete Table Rows

1. Choose **L**ayout, **T**ables.

2. Choose **E**dit.

3. Move the cursor to the desired location.

4. Do one of the following:

   To insert, choose **I**ns; then choose **B**efore Cursor Position or **A**fter Cursor Position.

   To delete, choose **D**el.

5. Choose **R**ows.

6. Choose **H**ow Many? and enter a value.

7. Choose OK.

Troubleshooting

◆ If you create an unwanted row by accidentally pressing Tab in the last cell of a table, use the Delete Row command to delete the row.

◆ If you delete one or more rows by accident or delete too many rows, immediately choose Undo. You can undo in table edit mode by pressing Ctrl+Z.

Shortcut Keys

Insert 1 Row	Ctrl+Insert
Delete 1 Row	Ctrl+Delete
Table Edit	Alt+F11

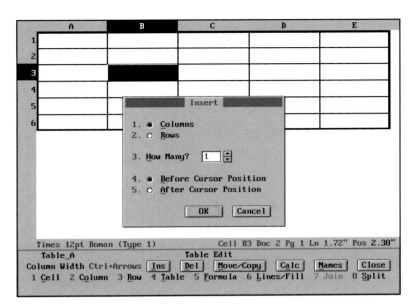

Inserting rows.

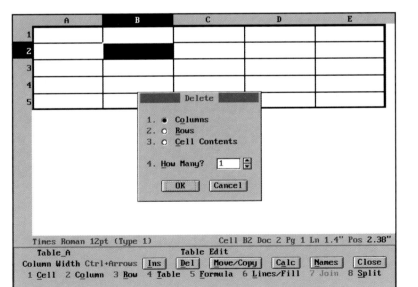

Deleting rows.

TABLES

If you don't have enough columns, add some. Or if you have too many, delete the ones you don't need.

A WordPerfect table can effectively be any length (the technical limitation is many thousands of lines) but must fit within the width of a page. As a result, when you insert a column, WordPerfect has to squeeze other columns to make room. When you delete a column, WordPerfect leaves the other column widths the same, which makes the table narrower and leaves a gap between the table edge and the right margin. In either case, you probably want to adjust column widths.

Inserting Columns

When you choose the **I**ns command in table edit mode, by default WordPerfect assumes you want to add or delete columns. You can choose how many columns you want to insert or delete. When inserting, you can add the new columns either to the left or right of the cursor position.

When you insert a column, WordPerfect actually makes the current column narrower so that your table now has two columns, which together take up the same width as the original column. If you insert several columns, the program again makes them fit within the width of the current column so that all the new columns become very narrow.

Deleting Columns

When you delete one or more columns, WordPerfect doesn't adjust the width of the remaining columns. If you want the table to be the full-page width, you must adjust the width of the remaining columns.

Insert or Delete Columns

1. Choose **L**ayout, **T**ables.

2. Choose **E**dit.

3. Do one of the following:

   To insert, choose **I**ns, **C**olumns; then
   choose **B**efore Cursor Position or **A**fter
   Cursor Position.

   To delete, choose **D**el, **C**olumns.

4. Choose **H**ow Many? and enter a value.

5. Choose OK.

Troubleshooting

If you insert or delete columns by mistake
or if you choose the wrong number of
columns to insert or delete, immediately
choose Undo.

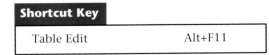

| Table Edit | Alt+F11 |

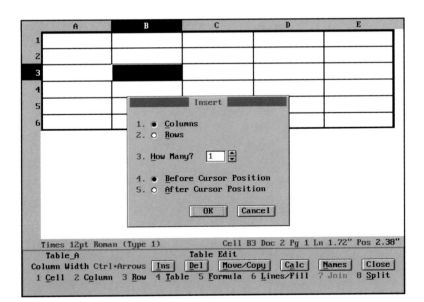

Inserting columns.

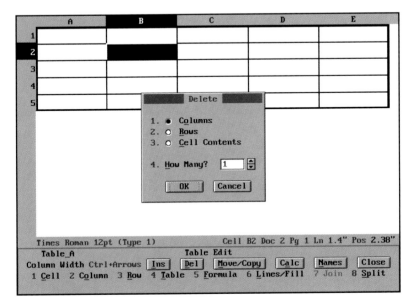

Deleting columns.

TABLES

You can control how the data in your table is formatted: you can select a format for the entire table, a specific column, or a specific cell.

In WordPerfect, you can set a variety of formatting options, including justification, decimal alignment position, font attributes, number type, and column margins. You can also join cells.

Formatting the Table, Column, or Cell

You can set options for the table as a whole, for a column, or for an individual cell or block of cells. Column formatting overrides table formatting, and cell formatting overrides column formatting. Your first decision is what part of the table to format.

◆ If the majority of a table shares the same format, set options for the table as a whole, then change format of any individual columns, and finally set the format for individual cells such as headers or totals. The majority of your columns many contain numbers, for example, but the first column usually contains text. You may want to format the table as decimally aligned and then format the first column as left or full justified.

◆ If each column contains different types of information, set options for each column individually. Then change any individual cells that you need to.

◆ If the cells in each column are different, you may want to format each cell individually.

Formatting Options

Here are the formatting options available to you:

◆ *Attributes.* You can apply any of WordPerfect's font attributes to a table, column, or cell. Any information in the affected cells is automatically formatted with the attribute(s). You can make a cell or column bold or italic, for example.

◆ *Justification.* By default, information in table cells is left justified. You can, however, select Center, Right, or Full justification, as well as Full, All Lines. Most useful in a table, however, is decimal align, which automatically lines up numbers in a table as if you had set a decimal tab.

◆ *Decimal Align Position (table and column format only).* If you select decimal alignment, WordPerfect automatically leaves room for two digits after a decimal point. If your numbers have four decimal places, however, they don't fit. You can either tell WordPerfect how many digits to leave room for or specify how far from the right cell margin the program should align the decimal point in the column.

◆ *Vertical Alignment (cell format only).* You can vertically align the information in specific cells so that a cell's contents are centered top to bottom or aligned at the top or bottom of the cell. In particular, header cells often look best when centered vertically. WordPerfect doesn't display vertical alignment on-screen but does print properly.

- *Number Type.* Using this option, you can specify whether the contents of a cell are text or a number with a specific format, such as currency, with commas, or a fixed number of decimal places. Number type is most useful when you want to use a table as a small spreadsheet.

- *Column Margins (table and column format only).* WordPerfect leaves a small amount of space between the left and right edge of each cell so that its contents don't run into any lines between cells or the contents of adjoining cells. You can change the settings for the table as a whole or for individual columns. When you use smaller margins, you may be able to squeeze an extra character or two in cells if you're tight on space.

- *Column Width.* You can specify a precise column width and even prevent that width from changing by choosing **F**ixed width. However, you may find it easier to adjust the width of individual columns by hand using the Ctrl+arrow keys.

Joining Cells

A table's heading usually has a format very different from the rest of the table. You can join cells to create a heading.

Table headings often don't fall into a neat arrangement of columns and rows. Instead, some headings span two or more columns and require additional subheadings for the individual columns. Other headings may need to be two or more rows high.

In WordPerfect, you can modify your table structure any way you like by joining cells. When you join cells, the program actually combines two or more cells into one big cell. WordPerfect adjusts the text in affected cells to wrap correctly within the new cell margins.

- You must be in table edit mode to join cells.

- You can join any block of cells, although you usually join cells in the same row or column.

more

Formatting Columns and Cells 183

Change a Column's Format

1. Choose **L**ayout, **T**ables.

2. Choose **E**dit.

3. Choose **C**olumn.

4. Choose **J**ustification and then choose a justification type.

5. If you choose decimal align, choose **D**ecimal Align Position and specify a number of digits or a distance from the right margin.

6. If you want to, choose **A** or **S**ize and then choose one or more font attributes.

7. If you want to, choose Number **T**ype and choose a number type.

8. If you want to, choose **C**olumn Margins and enter smaller values for left and right margins, such as **0.06** or **0.04**.

9. Choose OK.

Troubleshooting

If you select the wrong format options for a column or cell, repeat the steps and choose different settings.

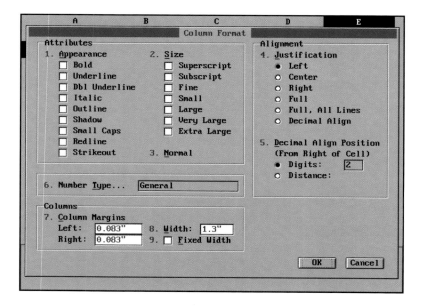

Changing the column format.

Join Cells

1. Choose **L**ayout, **T**ables.

2. Choose **E**dit.

3. Select a block of cells.

4. Choose **J**oin.

5. Choose **Y**es.

Troubleshooting

If you accidentally join too many cells, you can split the joined cell back into its original cells and then select a smaller block of cells to join. If you meant to join more cells, you can select another block that includes the joined cell and then choose **J**oin again.

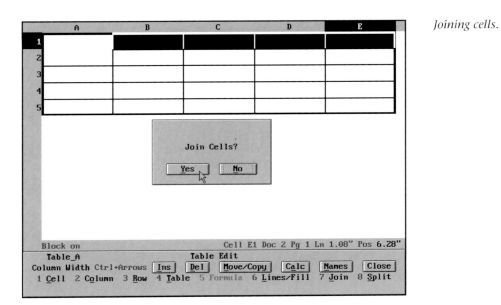

Joining cells.

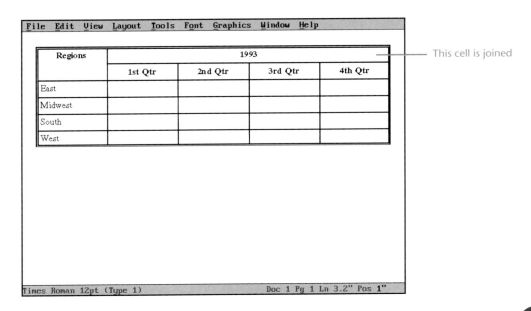

This cell is joined

Formatting Columns and Cells 185

Just as you can set table, column, and cell format options, you also can set several row options: the top and bottom row margins, the row height, the lines of text to allow in a row, and whether or not the row is a header.

When you create a WordPerfect table, the height of each row depends on the contents of the row. The program automatically leaves room for one line of text in the current font size. If you select a larger font, WordPerfect adjusts the height of each row to make room. WordPerfect also automatically wraps text within a cell. If a cell contains two or three lines of information, the program adjusts the height of the entire row.

But what if you're duplicating a form using a WordPerfect table? When you create forms, you usually want rows to be a precise, fixed height. In that case, you don't want WordPerfect to adjust the height of your table rows. Luckily, you get to choose.

Row Options

Here are the Row options available to you:

◆ *Auto Row Height* is the default; WordPerfect adjusts the height of the row based on the row's contents.

◆ *Fixed Row Height* lets you specify an exact measurement for a particular row's height. If you choose this option, WordPerfect doesn't let you type any more information into a cell than fits in the specified height.

◆ *Multiple Lines of Text* is the default. It allows text to wrap within a cell.

◆ *Single Lines of Text* prevents text wrap and allows only one line of text within any cell.

◆ *Row Margins* lets you specify the top and bottom margins of the row. Using smaller row margins, you can squeeze more lines onto a page. The default values add up to roughly one half space between rows.

◆ *Header Row* lets you identify a line as being part of the header. If your table is longer than a page, WordPerfect automatically prints any rows marked as header rows at the top of the next page and any subsequent pages that the table covers.

Change a Row's Format

1. Choose **L**ayout, **T**ables.

2. Choose **E**dit.

3. Highlight a cell in the row you want to change.

4. Choose **R**ow.

5. Do one of the following:

   To set a specific row height, choose **F**ixed and then enter a measurement.

   To let WordPerfect adjust the row's height, choose **A**uto.

6. Do one of the following:

   To limit cells to one line of text, choose **S**ingle.

   To allow multiple lines of text in a cell, choose **M**ultiple.

7. If you want to, adjust top or bottom row margins or choose **H**eader Row.

8. Choose OK.

Troubleshooting

If you select the wrong row options, repeat the steps and select different options. You can't undo changes made in table edit mode, and Reveal Codes doesn't show row option codes.

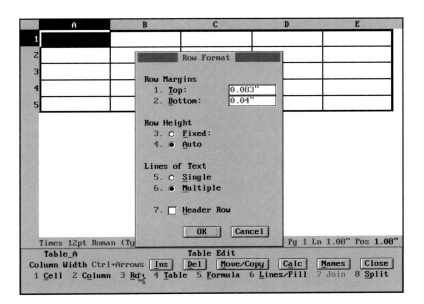

Changing a row's format.

Using WordPerfect's graphic lines can make your tables look truly professional.

Whenever you create a table, the program automatically draws a rectangular grid around the cells and surrounds the entire table with a double-line border. If you don't like Word-Perfect's table lines, though, you can change them. You can use any of Word-Perfect's line styles—single, double, dotted, dashed, thick, and more—or create your own styles. You can change the border or the lines in the table. You also can turn off all the lines or use lines only with selected cells.

Line Styles

You can change the default lines for the entire table, for the border around the table, or for the current cell or block of cells. Like paragraph, page, or column borders, table lines use WordPerfect's line styles. You can select any line style, edit existing styles, or create your own. See the section "Styles" for more information on line styles.

◆ You use the Default Line option to select the appearance of all the lines in the table. If you choose [None], the table prints without lines. If you choose Dashed Line or Dotted Line, all the lines in the table are dashed or dotted.

◆ You use the Border/Fill option to control the table's border separately from the rest of the table. If you choose [None] for the border, the outside edges of the table print with the default interior line style. Otherwise, the Border/Fill setting overrides the default line style for the outside edges.

◆ If you select any block of cells within the table, you can override the default line style for any part of that block: left, right, top, bottom, inside, or outside. If you select a row of cells, choosing a line style for the top or bottom of the block draws a line of that style across the entire table.

◆ You also can select a fill style to shade the background of the table, cell, or block of cells.

Change Table Lines

1. Choose **L**ayout, **T**ables.

2. Choose **E**dit.

3. Choose **L**ines/Fill.

4. To change all interior lines, choose **D**efault Line; then choose a line style or choose [None].

5. To change the exterior lines, choose Bord**e**r/Fill; then choose a border style or choose [None].

6. Choose Close.

7. To override the default lines for a block of cells, select a block and then choose **L**ines/Fill.

8. Choose one of the following: **L**eft, **R**ight, **T**op, **B**ottom, **I**nside, or **O**utside.

9. Choose a line style or choose None.

10. Choose Close.

Troubleshooting

If you choose the wrong line style for a block, reselect the block and choose a different line style.

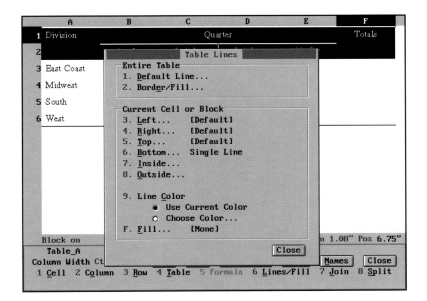

Changing table lines.

A table with different line styles.

Division	Quarter				Totals
	1st Qtr	2nd Qtr	3rd Qtr	4th Qtr	
East Coast					0
Midwest					0
South					0
West					0
Totals	0	0	0	0	0

You can put a formula in any cell in a table and tell WordPerfect to calculate it. The table then displays the result of each formula in the appropriate cell.

hen you create a table of numbers, you frequently want to add those numbers to reach one or more totals. In many ways, a WordPerfect table is a spreadsheet. You can create simple to complex formulas, just as you can do in a spreadsheet.

Subtotals, Totals, Grand Totals

To calculate a subtotal, total, or grand total, first select the cell. Then enter one of the following functions. You can't just type + or = into the cell. You must use the Formula command.

+	Subtotal	Adds any numbers in the column above
=	Total	Adds any subtotals in the column above
*	Grand Total	Adds any totals in the column above

Calculating Totals

Unlike a spreadsheet, WordPerfect can't automatically calculate the totals and other formulas in a table whenever you make a change. Therefore, for the program to display accurate totals, you must choose C**a**lculate All from the Tables submenu when you've finished adding information into a table or whenever you change a value in the table.

TIP

If you simply want to add a column of numbers, you should use a subtotal. You should use a total only if you have several subtotals in the column.

Ignoring Cells

If a column heading contains a date such as 1993 or a phrase such as 1st Quarter, WordPerfect adds the numbers in the heading. To prevent WordPerfect from adding the numbers in the headings, select any heading cells containing numbers, call up Cell Format, and choose **I**gnore when calculating.

If you want to add up a row, you must use a spreadsheet function (see "Table Functions and Formulas").

Add a Column of Numbers

1. Choose **L**ayout, **T**ables.

2. Choose **E**dit.

3. Highlight the cell that you want to contain the total.

4. Choose Formula.

5. Enter a plus (+).

6. Choose OK.

Troubleshooting

To erase a formula, highlight the cell in table edit mode and press Backspace. To change a formula, repeat the steps in this article, and at step 3, you can edit or replace the formula.

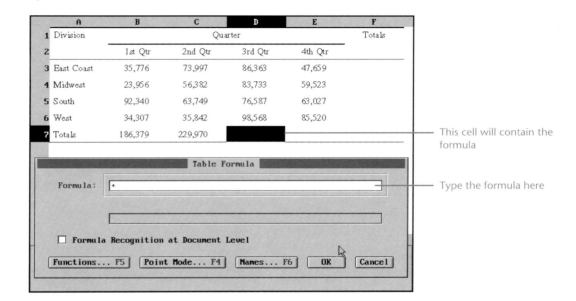

This cell will contain the formula

Type the formula here

You can create formulas that perform calculations on the data in your table.

WordPerfect's shortcut functions for adding subtotals, totals, and grand totals are useful when you want to add information in columns, but they're no use whatsoever when you want to add information in rows. To add a row, you need to create a true table formula.

What's a Formula?

If you've used a spreadsheet program, you already know how WordPerfect's table formulas work because the concepts are identical. A table formula is a short mathematical equation that usually refers to one or more cell addresses in the table and often uses a table function.

To refer to a cell in a formula, you use the cell's address. A cell address is simply a combination of the cell's column letter and row number. The first cell in a table is always A1, the cell to the right of A1 is B1, and the cell below A1 is A2.

You can create simple formulas using nothing but cell addresses and the standard mathematical operators +, –, *, and / for addition, subtraction, multiplication, and division. For example, A1+A2 adds the contents of cells A1 and A2, and B2*C3 multiplies the contents of cell B2 by the contents of cell C3.

What's a Function?

You can add the contents of cells B3 through E3 by adding the individual cells with the formula B3+C3+D3+E3. If a row has many columns or if you need to add the contents of many rows, however, adding all the individual cells becomes tedious. Instead, you can use a table function.

A table function is a command that performs a mathematical task. WordPerfect has nearly 100 table functions including trigonometric functions such as sine and cosine, and financial functions such as present value and future value. The available functions and their meanings are listed in an appendix of your WordPerfect manual.

The most common function is SUM, which simply adds a list of numbers or cell addresses. The list can be several individual cells, or it can be a range of cells. A *cell range* is a rectangular block of cells, identified by the first and last cells in the block. For example, A1:C1 refers to the first three cells in row 1. A1:C4 refers to the first three cells in each of the first four rows, a total of twelve cells.

Calculating the Formula

If a table formula refers to a cell or range of cells, you must choose Calculate All to recalculate the formula when you add to or change the information in any of those cells.

Use a Function

1. In table edit mode, highlight the cell to contain the formula.

2. Choose **F**ormula.

3. Choose Functions (F5).

4. Type **sum** and choose Insert.

5. To include a range, do one of the following:

   Type a range in the format A1:C1.

   Choose Point Mode (F4), highlight the cell that begins the block, and press Enter. Then type a colon, again choose Point Mode (F4), highlight the cell which ends the block, and press Enter.

6. Choose OK to insert the range into the formula.

7. Choose OK to insert the formula into the cell.

Troubleshooting

If you make a mistake in building a formula, you can either edit the formula or delete it and start over from scratch. To delete the formula, highlight the cell in table edit mode and press Backspace. To edit the formula, highlight the cell and choose **F**ormula. Then edit the formula as you do any word or phrase.

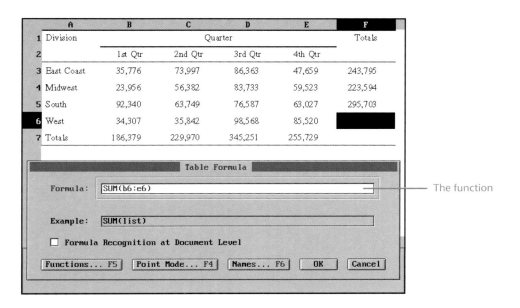

The function

	A	B	C	D	E	F
1	Division		Quarter			Totals
2		1st Qtr	2nd Qtr	3rd Qtr	4th Qtr	
3	East Coast	35,776	73,997	86,363	47,659	243,795
4	Midwest	23,956	56,382	83,733	59,523	223,594
5	South	92,340	63,749	76,587	63,027	295,703
6	West	34,307	35,842	98,568	85,520	
7	Totals	186,379	229,970	345,251	255,729	

Table Formula

Formula: `SUM(b6:e6)`

Example: `SUM(list)`

☐ **Formula Recognition at Document Level**

`Functions... F5` `Point Mode... F4` `Names... F6` `OK` `Cancel`

TABLES

A simple horizontal or vertical line can dramatically change the appearance of a page.

WordPerfect can draw horizontal or vertical lines of any length or thickness in a document. You may want to draw a thin hairline to separate a header or footer from the rest of the document, or a heavy line underneath a chapter title. Likewise, a vertical line can separate a sidebar from the main document visually or simply add an interesting graphics element to a page's layout.

Line Options

When you tell WordPerfect to create a graphics line, it calls up the Create Graphics Line dialog box. You can change any or all the values and then choose OK to insert the line. Here's what you can change:

◆ *Line Orientation.* A line can be horizontal or vertical. The default is horizontal.

◆ *Horizontal Position.* For a horizontal line, the default value of Full automatically draws a line from the left margin to the right. If you want a shorter line, choose **L**eft, **R**ight, or **C**enter to anchor a line on either margin or the center of the page, or choose **S**et to start the line a specific distance from the left edge of the page. Similarly, a vertical line can be Left, Right, Centered, Set, or Between Columns.

 You also can double-click the line to call up the Edit Graphics Line dialog box.

◆ *Vertical Position.* For a horizontal line, the default value of Baseline lets the line "float" with the surrounding text. You also can choose **S**et to anchor the line a specific distance from the top edge of the page. For a vertical line, the default value of Full automatically draws a line from the top margin to the bottom. You can also choose **T**op, **B**ottom, **C**enter, or **S**et a specific measurement from the top edge of the page.

◆ *Thickness.* The default value of Auto lets the Line Style control the line thickness. You also can set a specific value.

◆ *Length.* If a horizontal or vertical line is set to Full, you can't select a length. If you select a specific position, you can set the length to any measurement.

◆ *Color.* If you have a color printer, you can select a specific line color.

◆ *Spacing.* If you want to leave a certain amount of space blank above or below a horizontal line, you can enter values here. If you create a vertical line along the left or right edge of your document, this option controls how far outside the margin the line prints.

Viewing Graphics Lines

When you use Graphics mode or Page mode, WordPerfect displays your graphics lines on-screen while you work. When you use Text mode, you cannot see the lines on-screen while you edit. You can call up Print Preview to see how the lines will print.

Create a Horizontal Line

1. Choose **G**raphics, Graphics **L**ines, **C**reate.

2. Choose **H**orizontal Position.

3. Do one of the following:

   To start the line a specific measurement from the left edge of the page, choose **S**et and then enter a distance.

   To start the line at the left margin, choose **L**eft.

   To draw the line backward from the right margin, choose **R**ight.

   To center the line between the left and right margins, choose **C**entered.

   To draw the line between the margins, choose **F**ull.

4. If you select a position other than Full, choose **L**ength and enter a measurement.

5. If you want to change line style, choose Line St**y**le and select a different style.

6. Choose OK.

Troubleshooting

To delete a graphics line, click the line with your mouse and press the Delete key.

Or you can turn on Reveal Codes and delete the [Graph Line] code.

more ▶

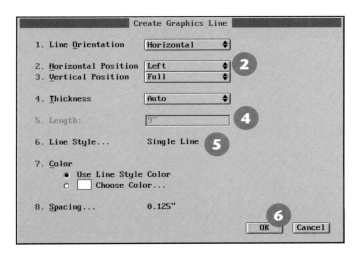

Creating a horizontal line.

An example of horizontal lines.

Create a Vertical Line

1. Choose **G**raphics, Graphics **L**ines, **C**reate.

2. Choose **O**rientation, **V**ertical.

3. Choose **H**orizontal Position. Set the horizontal position as described on previous page (step 3).

4. Choose **V**ertical Position.

5. Do one of the following:

   To draw the line a specific measurement from the top of the page, choose **S**et and then enter a distance.

   To start the line at the top margin, choose **T**op.

   To start the line at the bottom margin, choose **B**ottom.

   To center the line between the top and bottom margins, choose **C**entered.

   To draw the line between the top and bottom margins, choose **F**ull.

6. If you select a Vertical Position other than Full, choose **L**ength and enter a measurement.

7. If you want to change line style, choose Line St**y**le and select a different style.

8. Choose OK.

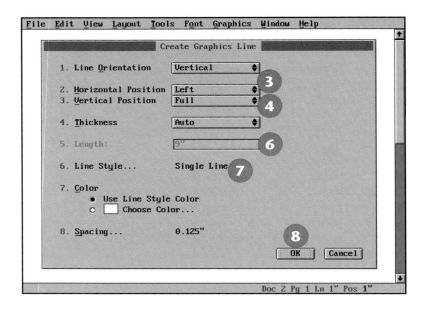

Creating a vertical line.

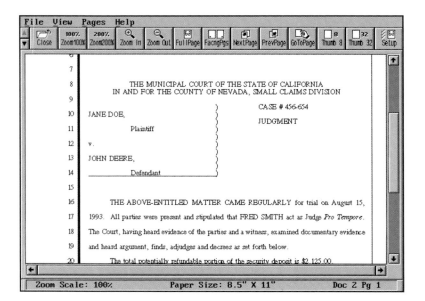

An example of a vertical line.

Edit Graphics Lines

1. Choose **G**raphics, Graphics **L**ines, **E**dit.

2. Change any of the values.

3. Choose OK.

Edit Lines with the Mouse

To move a line with the mouse, click on the line. Drag the line to a different position.

To resize a line with the mouse, click on it and then drag the handles. Make the line longer or shorter by dragging the end handles. Change the line's thickness by dragging the middle handles.

Troubleshooting

If you're not satisfied with any aspect of a line's appearance—its length, thickness, or position—you can edit the line at any time. You can double-click on the line to call up the Graphics Line dialog box and change one or more values; or you can click once on the line, then drag a handle to change the line's length or thickness, or drag the line itself to move it elsewhere on the page.

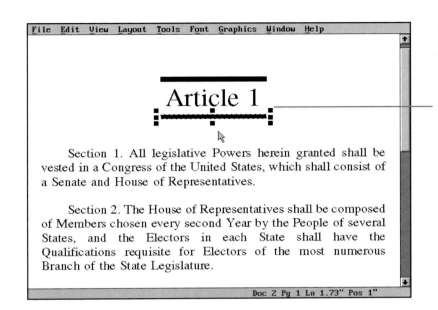

Drag to move the line. Drag the handle to resize the line.

Handle

You can easily retrieve most kinds of images into your documents. WordPerfect comes with many sample images.

When you retrieve an image, WordPerfect automatically creates a graphics box to hold the image, using default values for the box's size, position, and appearance. The box is half as wide as the document, and the program adjusts the box's height to keep the image in proportion, without distortion. WordPerfect ties the box to the current paragraph and aligns it along the right margin.

Using WordPerfect Graphics Files

WordPerfect comes with several graphics files you can insert in your document. When you perform a standard installation of WordPerfect, the Install program creates a GRAPHICS subdirectory under the WordPerfect program files and installs several dozen images in the WordPerfect Graphics (WPG) format.

TIP

If the file you want is in a different directory, you can use the File Manager to change directories and locate the file. You also can use the File Manager's Look command to preview the contents of a graphics file to make sure that it contains the image you want.

Changing the Graphics Box

You can adjust the size and position of the graphics box by using your mouse:

◆ To change the size, click on the box; WordPerfect displays handles at each of the box's corners and edges. Drag any of the edge handles to change the box's size in one direction or drag a corner handle to change the box's size in two directions at once. WordPerfect maintains the image's proportions within the box, and if necessary, adds extra white space within the box.

◆ To move the box, point at any location within the box and drag the box to a new location on the page.

If you don't have a mouse, or you want to set exact measurements for size or position, you can change all these options and more within the Edit Graphics Box dialog box. See the sections that follow on changing box attachment, position, and size.

Retrieve a Graphics Image

1. Choose **G**raphics, **R**etrieve Image.

2. Choose File List (F5).

3. Select a file from the list.

Troubleshooting

◆ If you retrieve the wrong graphics file, click on the graphics box to select it and then press Del.

◆ You also can turn on Reveal Codes and delete the [Para Box:1;Figure Box] code.

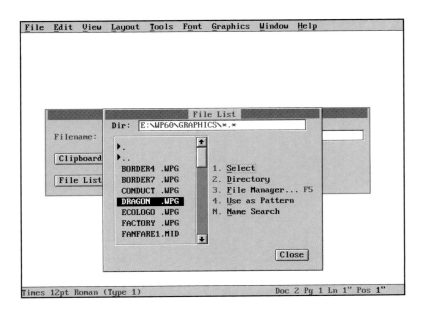

Choose the graphic you want to insert.

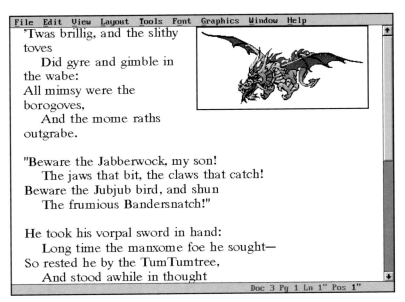

The graphic is inserted.

You can create a graphics box to hold an image, text, or equation. Or you can create a blank box— perhaps to use as a placeholder for something you plan to paste in later.

n some respects, the term *graphics box* is a misnomer because graphics boxes can contain text or equations as well as graphics images. You need to tell Word-Perfect what type of information you intend to put in the box and then either retrieve a file into the box or create the box contents yourself.

> **TIP**
> If you want to retrieve an image, you can use the shortcut discussed in "Retrieving an Image."

Graphics Box Contents

You can put four types of information in a graphics box: an image, text, a WordPerfect Equation, or nothing.

- *Image.* WordPerfect supports many graphics image formats, including its native WPG, paint-type images such as PC Paintbrush PCX files and Windows Bitmap (BMP); draw-type images such as CompuGraphics Metafile (CGM), Windows Metafile (WMF), and Migrografx (DRW); scanned images (TIFF); Encapsulated PostScript (EPS); and even standard Macintosh PICT paint-type images. You can retrieve all of these types of files directly into a graphics box. WordPerfect then displays and prints them all normally, except for EPS files. You must have a PostScript printer to print EPS graphics, and WordPerfect doesn't display them on-screen.

- *Text.* You can put up to a full page of text into a graphics box. You can retrieve a small file directly into a graphics box, type the text directly into the graphics box, or cut information from a document and paste it into the box. You also can create a *pull quote*—an important phrase or concept rendered in a large font size— to emphasize your points and add visual appeal to a page.

- *Equation.* Using WordPerfect's built-in Equation Editor, you can build complex mathematical equations. You can create sums, integrals, square roots, fractions, matrixes, and more. See the WordPerfect user's manual for help in using the Equation Editor.

- *Nothing.* If you want to, you can leave a graphics box completely empty. Depending on the border style you select, your box prints as an empty rectangle or as a blank space in a document. You may want to cut and paste something physically onto the printed document or just leave a fixed amount of space that will not be split up by a page break.

After you specify what you want the box to contain, you can retrieve an image or small document into the box, or you can create text or a WordPerfect equation in the box. Once you retrieve or create the contents of the box, you can edit the contents, change the box's border, or change the box's position and size. See the following articles for information.

Create a Graphics Box

1. Choose Graphics, Graphics Boxes, Create.

2. Choose Contents and then select one of the following: Image, Image on Disk, Text, Equation, or None.

3. Do one of the following:

   To retrieve a file, choose Filename and then follow the steps for retrieving an image.

   To create the contents of the box yourself, choose Create Text (or Create Equation). Press F7 to return to the Graphics Box dialog box.

4. Choose OK.

Troubleshooting

If you decide not to create a graphics box after all, choose Cancel or press Esc.

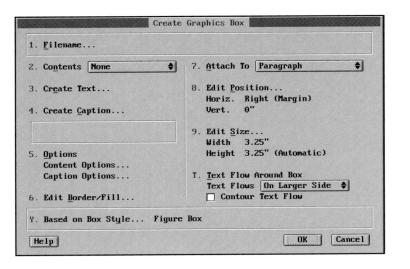

Creating a graphics box.

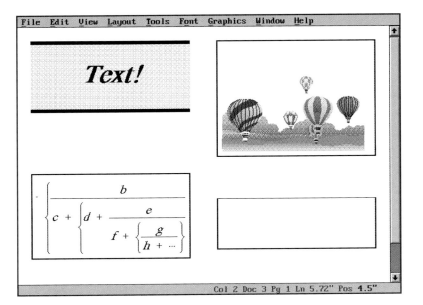

Examples of different graphics boxes.

After you retrieve an image into a graphics box, you may want to edit its appearance. WordPerfect can't actually edit an image in the way the program that created the image can, but WordPerfect can adjust an image in many ways.

Using the graphics box Image Editor, you can rotate an image, enlarge or reduce the image within the box, zoom in on a particular portion of the image, move the image horizontally or vertically within the box, flip it horizontally or vertically, and distort the image by expanding or compressing it.

Image Editor Options

These are the Image Editor options:

◆ *Rotation.* You can rotate any image through a full 360 degrees. You can choose Rotation and type in a value, or you can click the Rotate button and then drag the rotation handles that appear to a new orientation.

◆ *Flip.* You can obtain a mirror image by choosing Flip **H**orz, Flip **V**ert, or both.

◆ *Position.* You can move the image horizontally or vertically within the box by changing the X or Y value. An X value of 0.5 moves the image 50 percent to the right and cuts off the right half of the image; a value of 1.0 moves the image 100 percent to the right and, thereby, completely out of the box. As a result, useful X and Y values are between –1.0 and 1.0.

◆ *Black and White.* If you choose B/W, all dark shades become black, and all light shades become white.

> **TIP**
>
> The Image Editor has its own Button Bar. You can make many changes (such as rotating and zooming) most easily by clicking a button and then dragging within the image area.

◆ *Color.* You can adjust the brightness and contrast of an image just as you can adjust your computer monitor or a television screen. If you don't have a color printer, all colors print as shades of gray.

◆ *Enlarge.* You can enlarge or reduce the size of the image within the box by pressing PgUp and PgDn. You also can zoom in on a particular portion of the image by choosing Enlarge Area. You can click the button and drag a rectangle around the area you want to enlarge. If you don't have a mouse, you can choose **E**dit, **P**osition, Enlarge **A**rea and then indicate the area by using the cursor arrow keys, and using Enter to anchor the upper-left and lower-right corners of the area.

◆ *Scale.* When you enlarge or reduce an image, you change Scale Hei**g**ht and Scale **W**idth by equal amounts. If you change these values by different amounts, you can distort the image. A value of 0.5 makes the image half as wide or tall; a value of 2.0 doubles the height or width.

◆ *Invert.* You can invert the colors of an image, just like a photographic negative.

Edit an Image

1. Choose **G**raphics, Graphics **B**oxes, **E**dit.

2. Choose Image **E**ditor.

3. Make any desired changes to the image.

4. Choose OK to close the Image Editor.

5. Choose OK to close the Edit Graphics Box dialog box.

Troubleshooting

◆ If you want to reverse the changes you have made in the Image Editor, you can choose **E**dit, Reset All, or you can click the ResetAll button.

◆ You also can choose Cancel to exit the Image Editor and abandon any changes.

Shortcut Keys

Reset All	Ctrl+Home
Enlarge	PgUp
Reduce	PgDn
Brightness	, (less) . (more)
Contrast	< (less) > (more)

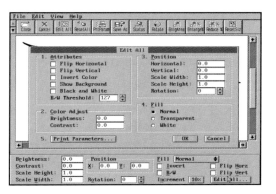

Make any changes you want.

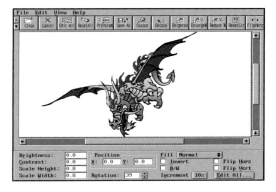

The image rotated and reduced.

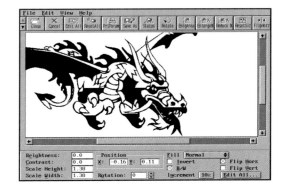

The image flipped horizontally and enlarged.

If you want to insert text in a graphics box, use the graphics box Text Editor. Use the text box to create pull quotes, for instance.

To create a text box, set the contents of a graphics box to text. Then choose Create Text (or later Edit Text) to call up the graphics box Text Editor.

The Text Editor

The graphics box Text Editor closely resembles the normal document window with the normal pull-down menus. Some pull-down menu items are grayed and cannot be selected. The width of the screen in which you can type depends on the width of the graphics box. The remainder of the screen is gray.

Using the graphics box Text Editor, you literally can create a document within a document. You can put almost anything in a graphics box that you can put in a normal document; the main exceptions are headers, footers, and footnotes.

You can do any of the following with text in a graphics box:

◆ *Formatting Codes.* You can use any formatting codes you normally use in a document, including font, font size, and justification.

◆ *Cut, Copy, and Paste.* You can type directly into the Text Editor. But you also can use any of the cut, copy, and paste commands to move information from the document to the graphics box or from the graphics box back to the document.

◆ *Tables and Columns.* You can create a WordPerfect table within a graphics box, or you can define columns.

◆ *Rotating Text.* WordPerfect can rotate the text within a graphics box in 90-degree increments. To rotate the text, press Alt+F9, choose Rotate Box Contents, and then select the degree of rotation. The text then appears normal in the Text Editor, but the box's proportions change. Unfortunately, not all printers can print rotated text.

◆ *Retrieving Files.* You can Retrieve—but not Open—document files directly into the Text Editor. WordPerfect adjusts the length of the box down to the bottom of the page, if necessary, to hold the retrieved information. Any excess text remains with the graphics box but isn't visible outside the Text Editor. To cut off the amount of text displayed in the box at a specific point, you can insert a hard page code.

◆ *Graphics Boxes.* You can create graphics boxes within graphics boxes with any of the normal contents.

Create a Text Graphics Box

1. Choose **G**raphics, Graphics **B**oxes, **E**dit.

2. Choose Co**n**tents, **T**ext.

3. Choose Cr**e**ate Text.

4. Insert any text or formatting you want.

5. Press F7 to exit the window.

6. Choose OK to close the Edit Graphics Box dialog box.

Troubleshooting

◆ You can edit the text in a graphics box just as you edit a normal document. To return to the text editor from the Graphics Box dialog box, choose **E**dit Text.

◆ If you want to abandon any changes you make in the text editor, press Esc and then choose **D**iscard changes and Exit.

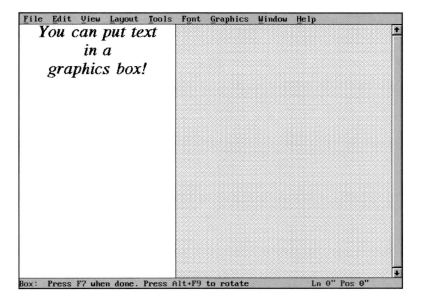

The Text Graphics Box window.

The text graphics box in the document.

Using WordPerfect, you can attach a graphics box to a specific page, to a paragraph, or even to an individual character.

When you create a graphics box, you usually have a good idea of where in the document it should go. You may want the box to go at the bottom of the current page, no matter what text is on the page. Or you may want the box to stay with a particular piece of text, no matter which page that text appears on. To specify the location, you attach the box to a page, paragraph, or character.

WordPerfect automatically attaches any new graphics box to the current paragraph, but you can change that option at any time. After you tell WordPerfect how to attach the box, you then can specify where the box should appear in relation to its attachment point—left or right margin, top or bottom, centered, or some set position.

Attachment Options

Here are the attachment options available to you:

◆ *Page.* If you attach a graphics box to a page, WordPerfect keeps that box in the same position on the page, whether or not you add or delete text to move the location of the code that controls the box. If the code gets moved to another page, WordPerfect moves the box to the new page, still in its original position.

◆ *Paragraph.* If you attach a graphics box to the current paragraph, WordPerfect keeps the graphics box with that paragraph. If you add or delete text that moves the paragraph higher or lower on the page, the box stays even with the paragraph. If the paragraph is close enough to the bottom of the page that the entire graphics box doesn't fit on the page, WordPerfect moves the box to the top of the following page.

◆ *Character.* If you attach a graphics box to the current character position, WordPerfect actually treats the box like a single, large character. If you add text to the beginning of the line that contains the box, WordPerfect moves the box over as far as the right margin. If the box doesn't fit within the right margin, the program wraps the box to the beginning of the next line, just like any other piece of text.

TIP

If you want to change the box's position and size, see the following articles for more information.

Attach the Box

1. Choose **G**raphics, Graphics **B**oxes, **E**dit.

2. Choose **A**ttach To.

3. Choose one of the following: **P**aragraph, P**a**ge, or **C**haracter Position.

4. Choose OK.

Troubleshooting

If you choose the wrong type of graphics box attachment, simply repeat the steps and select a different attachment type. Because changing attachment type also can change one or more position settings, you should also verify whether the position is still correct.

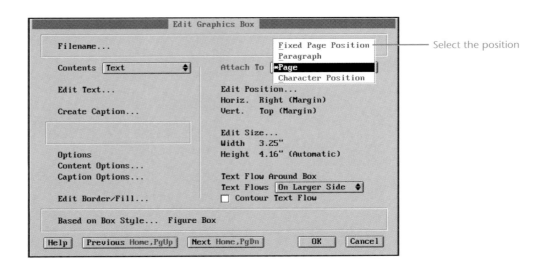

Select the position

You can position a graphics box anywhere on a page.

Whatever attachment type you select for a graphics box, you still need to decide exactly *where* you want the graphics box to appear. Do you want it along the left or right margin or along the full page width? Do you want it at the top or bottom of the page? If you have defined columns, do you want it within a column or between columns?

You can always drag a graphics box around with your mouse to find a position you like. When you drag a box, WordPerfect adjusts the position settings for that box. If you know exactly where you want your box to go, however, you often can specify its position more quickly and accurately by changing the position settings yourself.

Although some settings are similar, each anchor type has its own position settings.

Paragraph Position

Because a paragraph-type box "floats" with the paragraph, its position settings are relative to the top line of the current paragraph:

◆ Choose a **H**orizontal Position of **R**ight, **L**eft, or **C**entered to place the box along the right margin, left margin, or centered between the margins.

◆ To place the box a specific distance from the left edge of the page, choose a **H**orizontal Position of **S**et and then enter a measurement.

◆ Choose a Horizontal Position of **F**ull to have WordPerfect adjust the width of the box to fill the space between the margins and adjust the height in proportion.

◆ If you want to offset the box's position from the horizontal position, choose **O**ffset from Position, choose Left or Right, and enter a distance.

◆ If you don't want to align the box with the top of the paragraph, you can change the **D**istance from Top of Paragraph setting.

Page Position

Page-type graphics boxes have the same **H**orizontal Position settings available as paragraph-type boxes. In addition, you can change these options:

◆ With page-type graphics boxes, you can change what the horizontal position is relative to. The default Position **R**elative to setting is Margins, but you also can choose **C**olumns or **Co**lumn to set the box relative to one or more specific columns. You must have columns defined for this setting to have any effect.

◆ You also can set a **V**ertical Position for a page-type box. You can select **T**op, **B**ottom, **C**enter, **F**ull, or **S**et—similar to the horizontal position. You can also set an offset up or down from the vertical position.

Position a Graphics Box

1. Choose **G**raphics, Graphics **B**oxes, **E**dit.

2. Choose Edit **P**osition.

3. Choose **H**orizontal Position, then choose **L**eft, **R**ight, **C**enter, **F**ull, or **S**et.

4. If the graphics box is anchored to a Page, choose **V**ertical Position, then choose **T**op, **B**ottom, Centered, Full, or Set.

5. To position a Page graphics box between columns, choose Position **R**elative to, then choose **C**olumns or Co**l**umn, and specify which column(s).

6. Choose OK.

Troubleshooting

If you don't like a box's position, you can change it at any time. Either drag the box to a new position with your mouse or repeat the steps, making different selections.

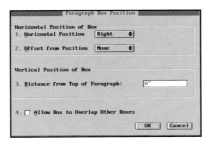

Paragraph Box Position options.

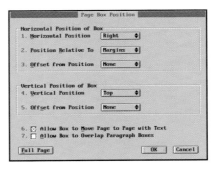

Page Box Position options.

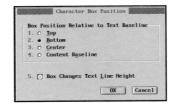

Character Position options.

Whether a box contains an image or text, you may want to change the box to a more appropriate size.

When you create an empty graphics box, WordPerfect automatically sets the box width to one-half the distance between the left and right margins—3 1/4 inches if you have standard 1-inch margins—and sets the box height to the same measurement. When you retrieve an image, WordPerfect adjusts the box height so that the image prints in the right proportions.

Using the Mouse

Just as you can change box position, you can also change a box's size by using your mouse. When you click the box, square handles appear at the box's corners and in the middle of each side. By dragging a side handle in or out, you can change the box's size in one direction. By dragging a corner handle, you can change the size in two directions at once. When you change a box's size disproportionately, WordPerfect doesn't distort the image. Instead, the program adds white space within the box.

Using the Edit Graphics Box Dialog Box

You also can change a box's size in the Edit Graphics Box dialog box. Changing size in this manner is more accurate than changing the size with your mouse.

◆ You can set specific measurements for the box's width, height, both, or neither. If your box contains an image, WordPerfect always adjusts the image size to keep it in proportion. If your box contains text, WordPerfect adjusts the line endings as if you have changed margins.

◆ If you set a specific width and a specific height, WordPerfect doesn't adjust the box size further, although it adjusts the contents of the box to fit.

◆ If you care about only one box dimension—either width or height—you can tell WordPerfect to calculate the other dimension automatically, based on the box's contents. If the box contains an image, WordPerfect again adjusts the other dimension to keep the image in proportion, without leaving extra space around the image. For text, you can set the box width and let WordPerfect calculate the height.

◆ If you want to display an image or some text (such as a WordPerfect table) at its original size, you can set both width and height to automatic. WordPerfect then calculates both dimensions for you.

Change Box Size

1. Choose **G**raphics, Graphics **B**oxes, **E**dit.

2. Choose Edit **S**ize.

3. Do one of the following:

   To set an exact width, choose Set **W**idth, and enter a value.

   To let WordPerfect calculate the width, choose **A**utomatic Width, Based on Box Content Width.

4. Do one of the following:

   To set an exact height, choose Set **H**eight and enter a value.

   To let WordPerfect calculate the width, choose A**u**tomatic Width, Based on Box Content Height.

5. Choose OK.

Troubleshooting

If you aren't happy with the size of the box, repeat the steps and select different values.

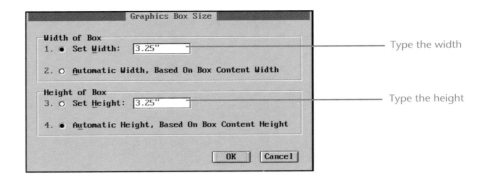

Type the width

Type the height

Two different box sizes.

When you put a picture on a wall, you usually frame the picture. When you put a graphics box in a WordPerfect document, you usually frame the box for similar reasons.

When you create a graphics box, WordPerfect puts a single line border around all four sides of the box to set its contents off from the surrounding document. You can change the line style for any or all of the sides, or you can remove the lines. You also can make the corners rounded, create a drop shadow, and fill the box with a shaded background. Finally, you can control the spacing between the edge of the box and the surrounding text, and between the edge of the box and its contents.

By default, a new graphics box has a single line border, square corners, no fill, and automatic spacing.

Border Options

Here are the Border options available to you:

◆ *Line Style*. You can select from any of WordPerfect's line styles—including single, double, dashed, dotted, thick, extra thick—or select [None]. You can select a line style for each edge individually or for all edges.

◆ *Shadow*. You can give the box a drop shadow. You can select which corner of the box is shadowed and how thick to make the shadow.

◆ *Corners*. The box can have square or rounded corners. If you select rounded, you also can set the corner radius.

◆ *Fill*. You can shade the background of the box by selecting a fill style.

◆ *Color*. If you have a color printer, you can select a color for the lines, shadow, or fill.

◆ *Spacing*. You can set both the outside spacing (the space between the border and the text) and the inside spacing (the space between the border and the contents). You can set outside or inside spacing for all four sides at once or for any side individually. You also can let WordPerfect choose the spacing for you automatically.

Change Box Border Options

1. Choose **G**raphics, Graphics **B**oxes, **E**dit.

2. Choose Edit **B**order/Fill.

3. Choose **L**ines, Select **A**ll.

4. Highlight a line style and choose **S**elect; then choose Close.

5. To create a drop shadow, Choose S**h**adow, Shadow **T**ype, then choose **U**pper Left, **L**ower Left, U**p**per Right, or Lo**w**er Right; then choose OK.

6. To round corners, choose **C**orners, **R**ounded; then choose OK.

7. To add a fill, choose **F**ill, Fill St**y**le. Highlight a fill style, and choose Select; then choose OK

8. Choose Close.

9. Choose OK to return to the document.

Troubleshooting

If you don't like any of the border options you select, repeat the steps, selecting different options.

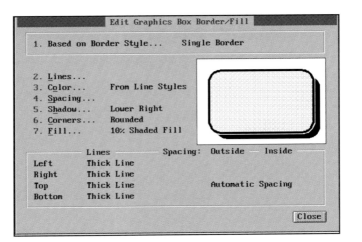

Changing the border and fill style.

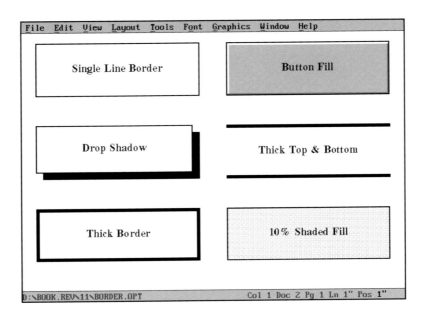

Examples of different lines and fill styles.

When you put a graphics box in a document, you usually want the text to make room for the box so that the two don't print on top of one another. WordPerfect can flow text around the box in several ways.

You can instruct the program to flow text around one specific side or around whichever side has more room for text. You also can have the text flow around both sides, neither side, or through the box. You can also have WordPerfect contour the text flow to the box *contents*, rather than the box itself.

Text Flow Options

Here are the Text Flow options available to you:

- *On Larger Side*, the default, lets the text flow around whichever side of the box has more room. If the box is on the right or left margin, text flows down the other side of the page. If the box is centered, text flows down the left side of the box.

- *On Left Side* or *On Right Side* specifies exactly which side of the box the text should flow. If, however, your box is on the right margin and you choose On Right Side, WordPerfect flows text on neither side, leaving the page to the left of the box empty.

- *On Both Sides* surrounds the box with text, and each line of text splits around the box.

- *On Neither Side* tells WordPerfect not to flow text around the box at all, leaving white space on both sides of the box.

- *Through Box* tells WordPerfect to ignore the box altogether and to simply flow text as if the graphics box weren't there. This option allows the box contents and document to print on top of one another. This option is most useful when you're putting graphics into posters and fliers.

- With any of the options, you can also choose **C**ontour Text Flow. WordPerfect ordinarily flows text around the rectangular outline of a graphics box. When you choose **C**ontour Text Flow, the program flows text around the outline of the box *contents*, usually an image. You can't adjust the contour shape that WordPerfect chooses, but you can adjust the space around the image by using the spacing option under Edit Border/Fill.

Note that a graphics box acts like a temporary margin change for the purposes of aligning and justifying text. If you center text next to a graphics box, the text is centered between the box and one margin, not between the normal document margins.

Select a Text Flow Option

1. Choose **G**raphics, Graphics **B**oxes, **E**dit.

2. Choose **T**ext Flow Around Box.

3. Choose Text **F**lows and then choose an option.

4. If you want to, choose **C**ontour Text Flow.

5. Choose OK.

Troubleshooting

If you don't like the way text flows around a graphics box, repeat the following steps and select a different option.

Contoured text flow.

Text doesn't flow on either side.

Text flows on left side.

Flowing Text around Boxes 215

A picture may be worth a thousand words, but sometimes a picture requires a few words of explanation. You can create a caption for any graphics box, with any description you like.

In a caption, you can include text that explains the contents. Or you can put a graphics box in the caption of a graphics box. You can also control on which side of the box the caption appears, whether the caption is inside or outside the border, and whether to rotate the caption.

> **TIP**
>
> If you have several graphics boxes, WordPerfect numbers them automatically. This feature is helpful for creating technical manuals or scientific manuscripts.

Creating a Caption

When you create a caption from the Edit Graphics Box dialog box, WordPerfect displays a screen that is virtually identical to the Text Editor. The screen already contains Figure 1 or a similar box number. If you don't want the caption to contain a box number, simply press Backspace. The number is actually a code, and backspacing deletes the code.

> **TIP**
>
> If you want to change the appearance of the box number, press Alt+F9, and then choose Caption Number Style, Edit.

You can type anything you like as a caption, with the same limitations on length as on text in a graphics box. When you add a caption, WordPerfect wraps text around the caption as well. The longer your caption, therefore, the larger the effective size of the graphics box for the purposes of text flow and adjusting its position on the page. Also, if your box is a full page, the size of the caption makes the contents of the box smaller.

Caption Options

To have complete control over the position of a caption, choose Caption options in the Edit Graphics Box dialog box:

◆ Select which **S**ide of the box the caption appears on: Top, Bottom, Left, or Right.

◆ Select where the caption appears in relation to the **B**order: Outside, Inside, or On the border.

◆ Choose **P**osition and then place the caption to the Left, Right, or Center.

◆ Choose **O**ffset and adjust the placement of the caption from that position to the left or right by a set measurement or percentage.

By default, the caption width is the same as the box width; however, you can change that width to a smaller set width or percentage. You can't make the caption wider than the box itself.

If your printer can rotate text, you can also rotate a graphics box caption in 90-degree increments.

Create a Caption

1. Choose **G**raphics, Graphics **B**oxes, **E**dit.

2. Choose Create **C**aption.

3. Type the caption.

4. Press F7.

5. Choose OK.

Troubleshooting

◆ If you delete the box number by mistake while creating or editing the caption, press Alt+F9 and then choose **C**aption Number Style, **I**nsert.

◆ If you make a mistake while creating the caption, repeat the steps and edit the caption like a normal document.

◆ If you don't like the position of the caption, choose **O**ptions, **C**aption Options and then select different options.

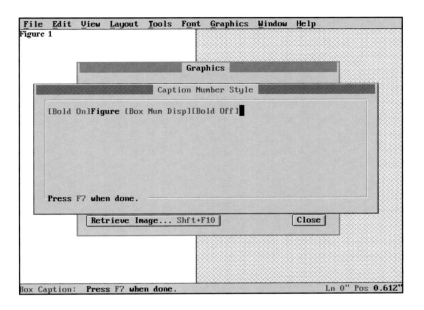

Type the caption.

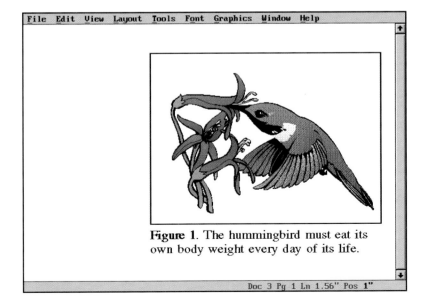

A graphics box with a caption.

Selecting a Graphics Box Style

If you have many boxes in your document and want them to look the same, use a graphics box style.

As you have seen, for each graphics box you can set dozens of options. Changing these options for one box is easy, but if your document requires many graphics boxes, changing many options for each box quickly becomes tedious.

Instead, you can set the options for any graphics box by selecting a single graphics box style, just as you can change the format of a paragraph by selecting a paragraph style. Each style controls all the options in the Edit Graphics Box dialog box: attachment type, position, size, text flow, border, and caption.

Using the Predefined Styles

WordPerfect provides a number of styles that you can use immediately:

◆ Figure Box has a single line on all four sides.

◆ Table Box has a thick line on the top and bottom but no side border.

◆ Text Box is similar to a table box but with a shaded background.

◆ Button Box has a shaded background and sculpted sides like a push button.

Each of the built-in styles has a specific numbering sequence attached to it as well. You can, for example, intermix Figure Boxes and Table Boxes in the same document, and WordPerfect numbers each type of box sequentially.

Creating Your Own Styles

If you don't like WordPerfect's built-in styles, you can edit them or create your own styles. You can create different styles for large figures and small figures, for example, and tie them to the same numbering sequence, or you can create versions of styles for different attachment types.

When you apply a style to a graphics box, WordPerfect changes all the options to match the style. You then, however, can change any option to a different setting if you don't care about exactly matching the style.

Select a Graphics Box Style

1. Choose **G**raphics, Graphics **B**oxes, **E**dit.

2. Choose Based on Box St**y**le.

3. To create a new style, choose **C**reate, then enter a new style name.

   WordPerfect displays the Create Graphics Box Style dialog box, which is nearly identical to the Edit Graphics Box dialog box.

4. Set any attachment, position, size, text wrap, border, or caption options you like.

5. Choose OK.

6. To use an existing style, highlight a style name and choose **S**elect.

7. Choose Close.

Troubleshooting

If you select the wrong graphics box style, repeat the steps and select a different style. You also can change various graphics box options individually.

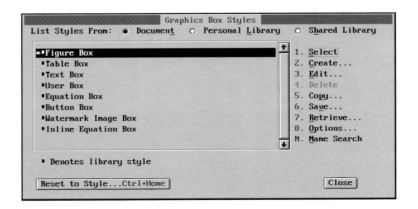

Select the style.

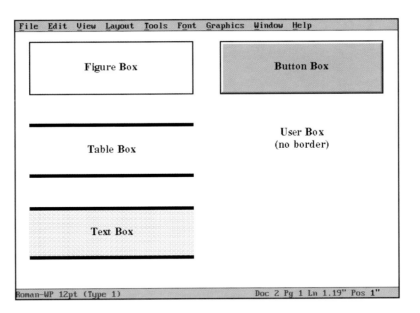

Existing box styles.

Part Four

Section 9—Outlines

When you want to organize a document, you create an outline. Your outline may be simple or quite complex, with multiple levels of topics and subtopics. It may consist of nothing but headings, or contain text beneath each heading. WordPerfect's powerful Outline feature lets you create outlines quickly and revise them easily.

Section 10—Special Printing

WordPerfect gives you unprecedented control over printing documents—before you print and while a document is printing. If you want to print on card stock or letterhead, you can tell the program what size and type of paper you want to print on, and where the paper is located in your printer. You can also print sideways on the page. You can print envelopes and mailing labels.

Section 11—Merge

You probably get mail every week that starts "You, Roy G. Biv, have just won 20 million dollars or a PCjr. All you have to do, Roy G. Biv, is …." Such "personalized" junk mail is an obvious use of a form letter. A form letter combines a letter with a list of names and addresses to create many individually addressed letters. You can use Merge to combine a form document with variable information.

Section 12—Document References

When you work on long documents, you often want to refer your readers to specific pages. Most books and magazines do this with a table of contents. WordPerfect can generate other document references in a similar way: lists of tables or figures; an index; a table of authorities for legal briefs; and cross-references.

When you want to organize a document, you create an outline. WordPerfect's powerful Outline feature lets you create outlines quickly and revise them easily.

You don't have to use the Outline feature to create an outline. You can type the outline numbers manually. But by using WordPerfect's Outline feature, you can quickly organize your thoughts, create a strong, logical outline for a document, and rearrange that outline as you develop your document.

Starting the Outline

The first thing you do when creating an outline is to select an outline style.

When you choose Begin New Outline, WordPerfect displays the Outline Style List dialog box, which looks identical to the list of paragraph, character, and open styles. Its contents, however, are all outline styles.

When you select an outline style, you tell WordPerfect exactly how you want your outline to appear. Just as paragraph styles can control the overall appearance of a paragraph, the overall appearance of an outline is controlled by its *outline style*. An outline style controls how an outline is numbered and how each outline level is formatted.

TIP
If none of the default outline styles meets your needs, you can edit a style or create your own.

Typing an Outline

When you select a style, WordPerfect inserts an [Outline] code in your document and automatically inserts the first paragraph number or bullet. You can immediately begin adding outline entries. See the following article for information on working in an outline.

The Outline Bar

To make it easier to manipulate an outline by using your mouse, you can display and use the *Outline Bar*, a screen tool similar to the Ribbon and Button Bar. With the Outline Bar, you simply point and click to change outline style, promote and demote items from one level to another, or hide or show families.

Create an Outline

1. Choose **T**ools, **O**utline.

2. Choose **B**egin New Outline.

3. Highlight the desired outline style and choose **S**elect. WordPerfect inserts the first paragraph number in your chosen style.

4. Type the first outline item, then press Enter. WordPerfect inserts the next paragraph number.

Troubleshooting

If you select the wrong outline style, from any place in the outline you can choose **T**ools, **O**utline, **O**utline Style and select a different style. WordPerfect changes the outline definition code at the beginning of the outline.

Shortcut Key

Outline	Ctrl+F5

more ▶

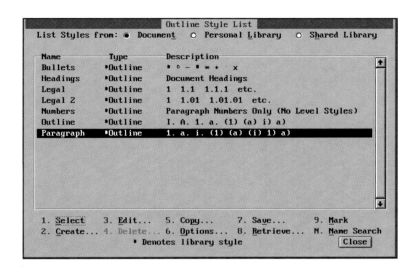

```
                    Outline Style List
List Styles from: ● Document   ○ Personal Library   ○ Shared Library

  Name          Type         Description
  Bullets      •Outline      • □ – ■ ✱ ◆   ✕
  Headings     •Outline      Document Headings
  Legal        •Outline      1  1.1  1.1.1  etc.
  Legal 2      •Outline      1  1.01  1.01.01  etc.
  Numbers      •Outline      Paragraph Numbers Only (No Level Styles)
  Outline      •Outline      I. A. 1. a. (1) (a) i) a)
  Paragraph    •Outline      1. a. i. (1) (a) (i) 1) a)



  1. Select    3. Edit...   5. Copy...    7. Save...     9. Mark
  2. Create... 4. Delete... 6. Options... 8. Retrieve... N. Name Search
                    • Denotes library style            Close
```

Outlining a document really helps you to organize your thoughts and make points in a logical order.

Outline Styles

WordPerfect's available outline styles fall into four general categories: indented and numbered, numbered without indentation, "legal" numbering, and headings without numbers or indentation. These are the styles from which you can choose:

◆ *Paragraph* is the default outline style. This style uses numbers for first-level items and indents each successive outline level to the next tab setting. You can create numbered lists quickly and easily with this style.

◆ *Outline* creates a more "traditional" outline, using Roman numerals for the first outline level. This style also indents each successive outline level to the next tab setting.

◆ *Bullets* creates a more informal outline. This style also indents each level, but uses a bullet to emphasize each entry instead of a number.

◆ *Numbers* uses the same numbering scheme as Paragraph, but doesn't indent levels in any way. You can use this style to number paragraphs that you don't want indented.

◆ *Legal 1* and *Legal 2* are special-purpose numbering schemes used mostly in legal applications. Instead of displaying the current level number for each item, these styles display the combination of outline levels, such as 1.3.2. Also, these styles use one indent for all levels, instead of successively indenting each level.

◆ *Headings* does not display numbers for any level. Instead, it formats first-level items as centered, bold, and very large, second-level items as bold and large, and so on. You can use this style in any document when you want to format your headings consistently but don't want the headings to be numbered.

Paragraph style.

```
 File   Edit   View   Layout   Tools   Font   Graphics   Window   Help
  1.     Word Processors
         a.     DOS
                i.      WordPerfect
                ii.     WordStar
                iii.    Microsoft Word
         b.     Windows
                i.      Word for Windows
                ii.     WordPerfect for Windows
                iii.    Ami Pro
         c.     Macintosh
                i.      Word
                ii.     WordPerfect
  2.     Spreadsheets
         a.     DOS
                i.      Lotus 1-2-3
                ii.     Quattro Pro
                iii.    PlanPerfect
         b.     Windows
                i.      Microsoft Excel
                ii.     Quattro Pro for Windows
                iii.    Lotus 1-2-3 for Windows
         c.     Macintosh
 D:\BOOK.REV\12\12ASCRN.TXT              Doc 1 Pg 1 Ln 1" Pos 1.5"
```

Outline style.

```
 File   Edit   View   Layout   Tools   Font   Graphics   Window   Help
  I.     Word Processors
         A.     DOS
                1.      WordPerfect
                2.      WordStar
                3.      Microsoft Word
         B.     Windows
                1.      Word for Windows
                2.      WordPerfect for Windows
                3.      Ami Pro
         C.     Macintosh
                1.      Word
                2.      WordPerfect
  II.    Spreadsheets
         A.     DOS
                1.      Lotus 1-2-3
                2.      Quattro Pro
                3.      PlanPerfect
         B.     Windows
                1.      Microsoft Excel
                2.      Quattro Pro for Windows
                3.      Lotus 1-2-3 for Windows
         C.     Macintosh
 D:\BOOK.REV\12\12ASCRN.TXT              Doc 1 Pg 1 Ln 1" Pos 1.5"
```

Bullets style.

```
File   Edit   View   Layout   Tools   Font   Graphics   Window   Help
   •      Word Processors
      o      DOS
                -      WordPerfect
                -      WordStar
                -      Microsoft Word
      o      Windows
                -      Word for Windows
                -      WordPerfect for Windows
                -      Ami Pro
      o      Macintosh
                -      Word
                -      WordPerfect
   •      Spreadsheets
      o      DOS
                -      Lotus 1-2-3
                -      Quattro Pro
                -      PlanPerfect
      o      Windows
                -      Microsoft Excel
                -      Quattro Pro for Windows
                -      Lotus 1-2-3 for Windows
D:\BOOK.REV\12\12ASCRN.TXT                    Doc 1 Pg 1 Ln 1" Pos 1.5"
```

Notice that changing the outline style dramatically changes the look and appropriateness of the document. Be sure to use the right style for the audience your document will reach.

Legal 1 style.

```
File   Edit   View   Layout   Tools   Font   Graphics   Window   Help
   1      Word Processors
   1.1    DOS
   1.1.1  WordPerfect
   1.1.2  WordStar
   1.1.3  Microsoft Word
   1.2    Windows
   1.2.1  Word for Windows
   1.2.2  WordPerfect for Windows
   1.2.3  Ami Pro
   1.3    Macintosh
   1.3.1  Word
   1.3.2  WordPerfect
   2      Spreadsheets
   2.1    DOS
   2.1.1  Lotus 1-2-3
   2.1.2  Quattro Pro
   2.1.3  PlanPerfect
   2.2    Windows
   2.2.1  Microsoft Excel
   2.2.2  Quattro Pro for Windows
   2.2.3  Lotus 1-2-3 for Windows
   2.3    Macintosh
D:\BOOK.REV\12\12ASCRN.TXT                    Doc 1 Pg 1 Ln 1" Pos 1.5"
```

After you select an outline style, adding text to your outline involves only typing outline entries, pressing Enter, and pressing Tab.

In your outline, each first-level entry may have several subentries, which in turn may have subentries of their own. WordPerfect lets you use up to eight outline levels, probably far more than you will ever need.

Switching between Outline and Text

A traditional outline is the skeleton of a longer document; each outline entry may correspond to some general point you want to make, or may be a specific document heading or subheading. In a WordPerfect outline, there is no real difference between the two. You can add any amount of normal text between outline entries, without affecting the overall structure of the outline itself.

You can either create your outline first and then add explanatory text between outline entries, or you can add an outline entry, write its explanatory text, and then add the next outline entry. Whether or not you have text between outline entries, Word-Perfect still treats the entries as an outline.

When you press Enter at the end of an outline entry, WordPerfect automatically adds a new entry at the current level. If you want to type normal text instead of a new outline entry, press Ctrl+T. WordPerfect removes the paragraph level style and moves the cursor to the left margin. You can now type a sentence, a paragraph, or many pages of normal text, which you can format in any way, including using other paragraph styles.

When you're ready to resume your outline, press Enter to end your text paragraph, then press Ctrl+T again. WordPerfect inserts a new paragraph number at the same level as the preceding outline entry. Ctrl+T is a toggle that changes any text into an outline entry, and any outline entry into normal text.

Note: If you're at the end of a paragraph, before the [HRt] code, when you press Ctrl+T, WordPerfect will change a paragraph from an outline item to text, or vice versa. If you meant to change the next paragraph instead, press Ctrl+T again to change the paragraph back, then press Enter to end the paragraph and press Ctrl+T once more.

TIP

If you want to create an outline out of several paragraphs of text, block the paragraphs, then press Ctrl+T. Word-Perfect inserts outline level styles at the beginning of each paragraph. You can then promote or demote any entry's level (see the following article).

Ending an Outline

When you're finished typing an outline, turn off the Outline feature. This is especially important if you include more than one outline in a document; turning off the first outline ensures that the second outline will be numbered correctly.

Edit Outline Levels

1. To add an entry, press Enter.

2. To promote or demote an entry, make sure that the cursor is immediately after the paragraph number code, then do one of the following:

To demote an entry to the next level, press Tab.

To promote an entry to the previous level, press Shift+Tab.

End an Outline

1. Choose **T**ools, **O**utline.

2. Choose **E**nd Outline.

Troubleshooting

If your cursor isn't immediately after a paragraph number when you press Tab or Shift+Tab, WordPerfect inserts a [Tab] or [Back Tab] code at the cursor position instead of demoting or promoting the level. Either Undo or delete the code, then move the cursor to the beginning of the entry before repeating your original keystroke.

Shortcut Keys

Next Level	Tab
Previous Level	Shift+Tab
Change Text/Outline	Ctrl+T

File Edit View Layout Tools Font Graphics Window Help

1.   First outline entry.

2.   Press Enter to create an entry at the same level.

    a.   Press Enter, then Tab to demote the next entry.

       i.   Press Enter, then Tab to demote the next entry.

    b.   Press Enter, then Shift+Tab to promote the next entry.

Press Enter, then Ctrl+T to change from an outline entry to a text paragraph. You can type as much text as you like before adding another outline entry.

    c.   Press Enter, then Ctrl+T to change from another text paragraph to an outline entry at the previous level.

3.   Press Enter, then Shift+Tab to promote the next entry.

Roman-WP 14pt (Type 1)   Doc 1 Pg 1 Ln 3.99" Pos 5.86"

You can combine an outline with regular text. Just end the outline when you're ready to add the regular text.

Changing Outline Levels

Here are the ways to change outline levels:

◆ When you finish typing an entry, if you want to demote the next entry rather than make it the same level, press Enter and then Tab. WordPerfect automatically selects the next outline level.

◆ Press Tab twice to make the next entry two outline levels lower.

◆ To select a higher outline level instead (promote the entry), press Back Tab (Shift+Tab).

◆ If you want to change the outline level of an entry you've already typed, move the cursor to the beginning of the entry, following the paragraph number or symbol, and press Tab or Back Tab to demote or promote the entry.

◆ With the cursor anywhere in an entry, you also can choose **T**ools, **O**utline, then **N**ext Level or **P**revious Level.

◆ Because outline levels are defined by paragraph styles, you can select a specific outline level by selecting its style from the Style List or Ribbon.

When you plan a document with an outline, it's best when you can rearrange the sections. WordPerfect makes it easy to move sections and the related information.

When you're creating an outline, you may discover that you want to change the order of several entries, or duplicate other entries. You can block and move individual entries and text, but ensuring that you move all the right codes and insert them in the proper location can be tricky. Instead, you can tell WordPerfect to move entire outline families for you.

What's an Outline Family?

If any outline entry has below it one or more subentries at higher level numbers, those subentries are considered part of the first entry's *family*. Any text in the entry or subentries is also part of the family. An *outline family*, therefore, is one outline entry at a given level and everything up to the next entry at the same level.

Any family may be part of a larger family, with the exception of families based on first-level entries.

Cutting, Copying, Pasting, and Moving Families

You don't need to select a block when you cut or copy an outline family. As long as the cursor is anywhere in an outline entry when you tell WordPerfect to cut, copy, or move that entry, the program takes everything from the paragraph style at the beginning of the entry to the next style at the same outline level.

When you paste cut or copied outline information in a new location, you only need to place the cursor somewhere within an entry; WordPerfect inserts the information in front of that entry's paragraph style.

Moving a family combines cutting and pasting into one command. When you choose **M**ove Family, WordPerfect cuts the current family, then waits for you to move the cursor and press Enter before pasting the family in at the new location.

TIP
If you intend to make many changes to an outline's organization, save the document first so that you can abandon any unwanted changes and retrieve the original version, if necessary.

Cut, Copy, or Move an Outline Family

1. Move the cursor to the first entry in a family.

2. Choose **T**ools, **O**utline.

3. Do one of the following:

   Choose Cut Family.

   Choose Copy Family.

   Choose **M**ove Family.

4. Move the cursor to a new location.

5. Press Enter.

Troubleshooting

If you make a mistake while rearranging an outline, immediately choose Undo to restore the outline to its previous condition.

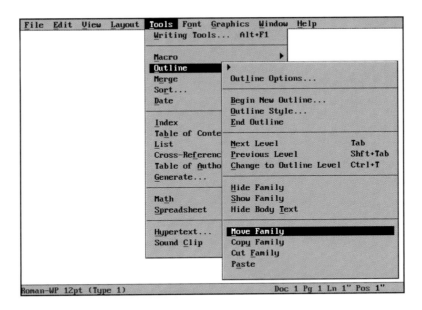

If you're not sure about the order of points in your outline, this feature makes it easy to switch them around.

When you want to concentrate on one particular aspect of an outline only, you can hide parts of the outline.

You can choose to hide all text in the document so that you can only see the outline, which can be useful for reorganizing an outline, or for printing just the outline. You also can hide the outline to see only the text; in this way, you can use an outline to organize your thoughts, but not show the outline entries when you print the document.

You also can choose to hide all outline levels and text below a specific outline level. Finally, you can choose to hide specific outline families, which lets you hide information that is confidential or irrelevant to the task at hand.

Hiding the Text or the Outline

If you want to concentrate on just the outline itself and not be distracted by any intervening body text, you can choose Hide **B**ody Text. On the other hand, you instead can hide your outline, by choosing Hide **O**utline. This capability lets you organize a document with an outline but print the final copy without the outline showing. If you choose both Hide **B**ody Text and Hide **O**utline, WordPerfect displays a blank screen.

Hiding a Family

WordPerfect defines an outline family as everything between an outline level code and the next code of the same level. A first-level entry may have three subentries at Level 2, each of which has two entries at Level 3.

If you place the cursor in the Level 1 entry and choose Hide Family, the entry itself remains visible but the Level 2 and Level 3 entries beneath it are hidden. If the next first-level entry also contains subentries, they aren't affected by hiding the previous family.

In this example, each of the three Level 2 entries also has a family, consisting of the Level 3 entries. Instead of hiding the entire Level 1 family, you can place the cursor in a Level 2 entry and hide its family instead.

When you hide a family, the hidden information is still there. When you want to see it again, place the cursor in the original entry and choose Show Family.

Choosing Levels To Hide or Display

The Hide Family command only hides the current family, although you can repeat the command to hide additional families. If you want to hide all information below a given outline level, you can use the Show Levels command. This action presents you with a small dialog box from which you can select an outline level or All levels.

If you select Level 2, for example, WordPerfect displays all Level 1 and Level 2 entries but hides all entries at Levels 3, 4, and so on. The program treats any text associated with an outline level in the same way. That is, any text under a Level 1 or 2 entry are displayed, but lower levels of text are hidden. When you want to see your entire document again, repeat the Show Levels command and select All.

Hide or Show Outline Levels

1. Choose **T**ools, **O**utline, Out**l**ine Options.

2. Choose **H**ide/Show.

3. Do one of the following:

To hide the current family, choose – Hide Family.

To show a hidden family, choose + Show Family.

To show only selected outline levels, choose **S**how Levels, then select the lowest level you want displayed.

To hide the outline, choose Hide **O**utline.

To hide everything but the outline, choose Hide **B**ody Text.

Troubleshooting

◆ If you're not sure what you have hidden, you can always see your entire document by choosing **S**how Levels and All.

◆ If you print a document with hidden families or outline levels, the hidden information doesn't print. To view or print the entire document, you merely need to show all outline levels again.

Shortcut Key

| Outline | Ctrl+F5 |

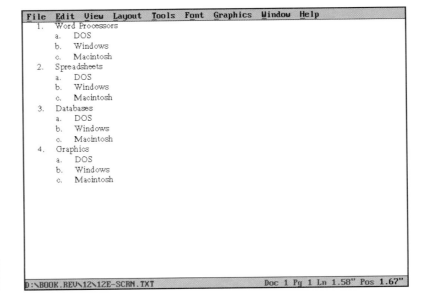

The entire outline.

Outline with only top two levels shown.

OUTLINES

When you create an outline, you might find it easy to use the Outline Bar and the mouse to do most of the common outline editing tasks.

Although editing an outline isn't terribly complicated, the commands are either in a submenu or a dialog box accessed through the submenu. If you need to make a lot of changes to the structure of an outline, using these commands repeatedly can get tedious. To make the task of editing an outline easier, WordPerfect provides the *Outline Bar*. The Outline Bar is a screen tool similar to the Ribbon and Button Bar.

Outline Bar Options

Each of the Outline Bar buttons is the equivalent of a command from the Tools Outline menu or Outline dialog box, although the Outline Bar doesn't contain a button for every possible outline command. To access the remainder of the commands, however, you can click the Options button described in the table on the next page.

Outline Edit Mode

When you display the Outline Bar, the status line prompt changes to `Press Ctrl+O for outline edit`. With the Outline Bar displayed, you can make changes to the outline structure by clicking various buttons, but you can still edit the outline contents.

When you press Ctrl+O, WordPerfect automatically switches into Outline Edit mode and displays the Outline Bar, if it isn't already on-screen.

When you choose Outline Edit mode, you can't make changes to the outline contents or use the pull-down menus. Instead, only the Outline Bar is active, and you can select all of its buttons (except the pair which promote or demote families) by using the keyboard. To choose **S**how, for example, you merely press S; if you try to press Alt+S, you get an error message.

To exit Outline Edit mode, press F7.

Changing Styles with the Outline Bar

The drop-down style list in the Outline Bar lets you select an *outline* style, whereas the drop-down style list in the Ribbon lets you select a *paragraph* style. By selecting a different outline style, you change the overall appearance of the outline. By selecting a different paragraph style, you can change the level and, therefore, the appearance of a single outline entry. If you change outline style, however, the list of paragraph styles available in the Ribbon may change because several outline styles contain paragraph styles with different names.

Turn On the Outline Bar

1. Choose **V**iew, **O**utline Bar to display the Outline Bar.

2. Click the desired button to edit the outline.

Troubleshooting

◆ If you display the Outline Bar by mistake, just turn it off again by choosing **V**iew, **O**utline Bar.

◆ If you select Outline Edit mode by mistake, press F7 to exit the mode.

◆ Because the Outline Bar buttons are merely shortcuts to the outline commands, you can reverse any change by using the normal commands.

Shortcut Key	
Outline Edit	Ctrl+O

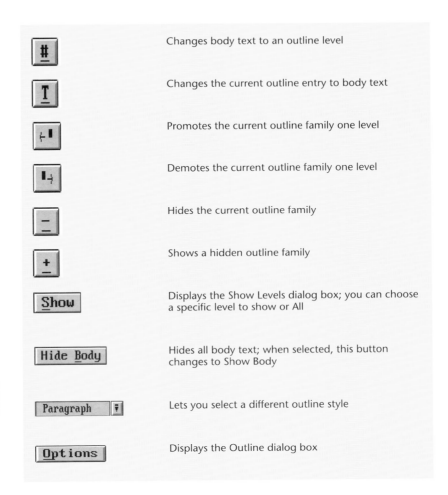

Changes body text to an outline level

Changes the current outline entry to body text

Promotes the current outline family one level

Demotes the current outline family one level

Hides the current outline family

Shows a hidden outline family

Displays the Show Levels dialog box; you can choose a specific level to show or All

Hides all body text; when selected, this button changes to Show Body

Lets you select a different outline style

Displays the Outline dialog box

If you have to print a wide table, WordPerfect lets you print sideways on the page.

You normally print documents on paper oriented in an upright manner—taller than it is wide. Occasionally, you may want to print a wide table or document sideways on the page. Technically, paper that is "upright" is in *portrait* orientation and paper that is "sideways" is in *landscape* orientation.

To print in landscape format on some printers, particularly dot-matrix printers, you feed the paper sideways. Other printers, like inkjet and laser printers, always feed paper the same way and print in landscape by printing the text and graphics sideways. Some printers cannot print in landscape at all.

When you print in landscape, the printable page area is wider than it is tall, and WordPerfect adjusts the document's line and page lengths accordingly. In a portrait document with 1-inch margins, each line is 6 $1/_2$ inches long, and each page has 9 inches of text from top to bottom. In a landscape document with 1-inch margins, the line lengths are 9 inches, and each page has 6 $1/_2$ inches of text from top to bottom.

TIP
To print *part* of a page in landscape and the rest of the page in portrait, create a graphics box and rotate the box contents 90 degrees. Not all printers can print portrait and landscape on the same page, however.

Paper Definitions

To print sideways on a page, you tell WordPerfect to print on a different *type* of paper. When you install WordPerfect and select a printer, the program installs a number of *paper definitions*. Each paper definition contains *paper size*—the paper's measurements and often a descriptive name, such as letter or legal—and *paper type*, such as standard, bond, or letterhead. Orientation is also included in the paper definition.

The default paper definition is letter-size 8 $1/_2$-by-11-inch paper.

Changing the Printing Codes

To use Landscape mode, you select the landscape paper definition from the Page Format dialog box; WordPerfect inserts a [Paper Sz/Typ] code. Change the paper definition at the beginning of the document or immediately following a hard page code. Otherwise, because [Paper Sz/Typ] tells WordPerfect that the following text prints on a different kind of paper, the program inserts a temporary hard page code.

A paper size/type code affects all text until the next comparable code. To print a landscape table in the middle of a portrait document, for example, insert a landscape code at the beginning of the page containing the table, then insert a portrait code at the beginning of the next page. You can change orientation as often as you like.

Print in Landscape

1. Move the cursor to the top of a document or page.

2. Choose **L**ayout, **P**age to open the Page Format dialog box.

3. Choose Paper **S**ize/Type to open the Paper Size/Type dialog box.

4. Select the appropriate landscape paper definition—in most cases, select Letter (Landscape).

5. Choose OK or Close to close all open dialog boxes.

Troubleshooting

◆ If a landscape paper definition isn't available for your printer, you must create one. See "Creating a Paper Definition" for more information. Also, some printers simply cannot print in Landscape mode. If you're unsure, check your printer manual.

◆ If you insert the wrong paper size/type code, repeat the steps to insert a different code or turn on Reveal Codes and delete the [Paper Sz/Typ] code.

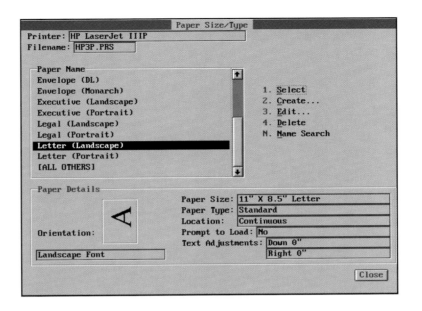

Notice that the example document shows the orientation of the printed text on the paper.

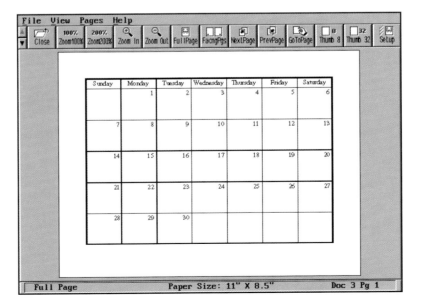

Landscape mode is ideal for creating full-page calendars using WordPerfect Tables.

Creating a Paper Definition

If you routinely print on letterhead, card stock, or other sizes or types of paper, you can save time by creating a new paper definition for each paper type and size.

Paper definitions tell WordPerfect how to format documents and how to handle the paper when printing. WordPerfect automatically installs paper definitions for many common paper sizes and types, including portrait and landscape versions of letter, legal, and A4 (the standard metric paper size used in England and Europe), as well as several sizes of envelopes.

If you use preprinted forms, you may want to create a paper definition for each form so that you can precisely line up where WordPerfect prints. You may also want to edit existing paper definitions to tell WordPerfect in which of your printer's paper bins or trays a particular type of paper is located.

Paper Definition Options

Each paper definition contains options you can set or change.

◆ *Paper Name.* This option is a descriptive label. WordPerfect displays a list of available paper names when you select a paper size/type and also displays the name if you highlight the [Paper Sz/Typ] code in Reveal Codes.

◆ *Paper Type.* Choose Standard, Bond, Letterhead, Envelope, Transparency, Cardstock, Glossy Film, Special, or Other. If you choose Other, enter any other name you like.

◆ *Paper Size.* This option contains the exact measurement of the paper and the paper size's common name, such as letter or legal. Choose from a long list of standard sizes, or choose Other and specify other dimensions.

◆ *Paper Location.* If your printer doesn't have a sheet feeder, choose Continuous or Manual. (For laser printers, the standard setting to print from the built-in paper tray is Continuous.) If you normally feed letterhead one page at a time by hand, choose Manual.

If you have a sheet feeder, specify in which bin number or paper tray WordPerfect should expect to find the paper.

◆ *Prompt to Load.* If you want WordPerfect to prompt you to change paper before printing, check this box.

◆ *Orientation.* This option tells WordPerfect the orientation of the paper as it moves through the printer, and the orientation of the text on the page. The example below the option shows the current orientation of page and text.

◆ *Adjust Text.* If the printed text doesn't come out exactly where you expect it, adjust the position of the printed information. You can adjust up, down, left, or right by any measurement, usually a fraction of an inch. This option is useful for lining up information on preprinted forms.

Create a Paper Definition

1. Choose **L**ayout, **P**age to open the Page Format dialog box.

2. Choose Paper **S**ize/Type to open the Paper Size/Type dialog box.

3. Choose **C**reate to open the Create Paper Size/Type dialog box.

4. In the Paper Name text box, type a name for the paper format. For example, type **letterhead**.

5. Choose Paper **T**ype and specify the desired paper type in the drop-down list. For example, select Letterhead.

6. Specify a Paper Size in the Paper **S**ize text box. The default size is 8 $1/_2$-by-11 inches.

7. If necessary, choose Paper **L**ocation and specify where the paper is in the printer. For example, select Manual to feed individual sheets by hand into the printer.

8. Choose OK.

9. To use the paper definition immediately, select the new paper name in the Paper Size/Type dialog box.

10. Choose OK to close the Page Format dialog box.

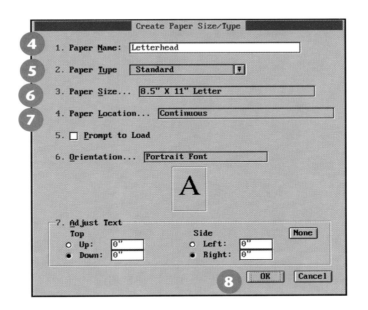

Troubleshooting

◆ If WordPerfect doesn't print as you expect when using a particular paper definition, return to the Paper Size/Type dialog box and edit the definition. WordPerfect uses the updated definition the next time you select that paper. You can also delete a paper definition in the same dialog box.

◆ WordPerfect stores paper definitions in printer drivers. If you use the same type of paper on several printers, you need to create a paper definition for each printer.

WordPerfect can do nearly all the work of printing an envelope for you.

Printing an envelope is one of the most common printing tasks and—until WordPerfect 6—among the most difficult. Envelopes are a different size and shape than standard paper and must have specific information printed in specific locations. WordPerfect can scan a letter for a mailing address, automatically generate a postal bar code, add a saved return address, format everything for any envelope size, and print the envelope.

Scanning for Addresses

When you indicate that you want to create an envelope, WordPerfect automatically scans the current document to find a mailing address. This scan will be unsuccessful if your document doesn't contain a mailing address or the address has a very unusual format, but you can always type the mailing address yourself. Even if WordPerfect finds an address in the document, you can modify the address to be printed on the envelope; for example, you can add an "attention" line.

TIP

If the printed envelope contains typos, the document's mailing address may have the same typos. Double-check the document and then re-create or correct the envelope.

Specifying the Return Address

WordPerfect can also print your return address. To prevent you from having to type your address every time, you can tell the program to save the current return address and to use it with all future envelopes. However, if you use envelopes with a preprinted return address, you don't want WordPerfect to print the address. You can tell the program to omit the return address on any particular envelope. You can also save an empty address as the default to permanently remove the return address.

Printing the Envelope

When you're satisfied with the envelope's appearance, you can print the envelope, add it to the document, or both. If you insert the envelope, WordPerfect inserts a hard page code at the end of the document and adds appropriate text and formatting codes. When you print the entire document, the envelope prints as the last page.

Print an Envelope

1. Choose **L**ayout, **P**age to open the Page Format dialog box.

2. Choose **E**nvelope to open the Envelope dialog box.

3. By default, WordPerfect formats for a standard COM 10 business envelope. If you prefer a different size, choose **E**nvelope Size and choose a different size from the drop-down list.

4. If necessary, choose **M**ailing Address to modify or create the address; press F7 when done.

5. If desired, choose **R**eturn Address to add your return address; press F7 when done.

6. If you want to include a postal bar code, choose POSTNET **B**ar Code and type the ZIP code. WordPerfect then generates a bar code that can be read by scanners at post office sorting centers.

7. To print the envelope, choose **P**rint.

8. To insert the envelope at the end of the document, choose **I**nsert. WordPerfect returns to the document and adds the formatted envelope.

Troubleshooting

If you insert an envelope at the end of a document by mistake, you can choose Undo or simply delete the inserted text and codes.

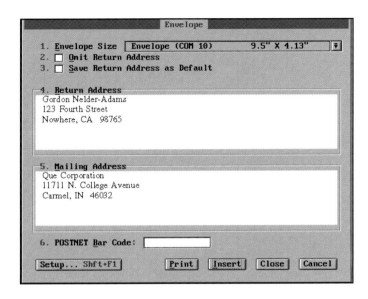

It's easy to print an envelope—just specify the options in this dialog box. Word-Perfect does the rest!

Envelope Options

If you don't like the way WordPerfect formats your envelopes, you can customize the envelope by changing the Envelope Setup options. From the Envelope dialog box choose Setup (Shift+F1), then change any of the following options:

◆ If your envelope size isn't listed, choose **E**nvelope Size, **C**reate to make a new paper definition (see previous article for help on setting paper definition options).

◆ If you don't like the positions WordPerfect uses for the mailing address or return address, choose Setup or press Shift+F1,

highlight the envelope size, and choose **A**ddress Positions. You can change the horizontal and vertical positions at which each address prints.

◆ To change the envelope setup so that WordPerfect automatically creates a bar code, enables you to create one manually, or disables bar codes altogether, choose **B**ar Code Creation, and choose **A**utomatically Create Bar Code, **M**anually Enter Bar Code, or **R**emove Bar Code Option.

If you need to send out dozens or hundreds of letters, you can print address labels instead of many individual envelopes.

Printing labels presents a special set of problems. There are dozens of label types, in long strips designed for a dot-matrix printer's tractor feeder, and in whole page sheets designed for inkjet and laser printers. For each label size, different numbers of labels fit on a single sheet and, of course, the individual labels are in different locations.

WordPerfect lets you specify what type of labels you want to use and then automatically formats a document, such as a mailing list, to print precisely on each label.

Label Definitions

WordPerfect comes with over 100 label definitions for Avery and 3M labels of all sizes, shapes, and descriptions. You can select from a list of label definitions, edit a definition, or add new definitions. WordPerfect has definitions for a variety of label types, including labels for file folders, floppy disks, audio and video tapes, name badges, Rolodex cards, and more. Each label definition name identifies the product by number and type, such as Avery 5260 Address. If your labels are a brand other than Avery or 3M, they may be comparably sized and formatted so that you can use one of the existing definitions.

The definitions specify the size of the label page, the size of the individual labels, the number of labels per column and row on the page, the top left starting position of the first label on the sheet, the distance between labels, and the margins to be used

with the labels. You can also specify printer locations, and you can adjust the printing area to properly align WordPerfect's printing on the labels.

Logical Pages

When you select a label definition, WordPerfect divides each physical piece of paper into a number of *logical pages*. Each logical page corresponds to one label. The label definition tells WordPerfect the location of each logical page on the physical page, but all you need to do is treat each label as a whole page, even though it's a very small one.

The size of each logical page depends on the label size. Because many labels are no more than an inch tall, WordPerfect's default margins of 1 inch on all sides are far too large. As a result, the margins in a label definition—often no more than 0.1 inch or 0.2 inch—override the normal margins.

Page Breaks

When you select a label definition, the page width that WordPerfect displays on-screen is the width of a single label. As you type, depending on the size of the label and the current font size, you may only get three or four lines on the page before WordPerfect inserts a soft page break, and the status line changes from Pg 1 to Pg 2. Anything you type after the page break will appear on the second label.

Create Mailing Labels

1. Start with a new document.

2. Choose **L**ayout, **P**age to open the Page Format dialog box.

3. Choose **L**abels to open the Labels dialog box.

4. Highlight a label type in the Labels list and choose **S**elect. The first time you select a label type, WordPerfect displays the Label Printer Info dialog box. This dialog box lets you set several paper size/type options, including the labels' location at your printer.

5. Choose OK to close the Page Format dialog box.

6. Type the mailing addresses, placing a hard return code after each address.

Troubleshooting

If you cannot fit as much information as you want on each label, use larger labels or a smaller font size. To change the label type, move the cursor to the beginning of the document and select a different label type. You can also turn on Reveal Codes and delete the [Paper Sz/Typ] code and the [Labels Form] code.

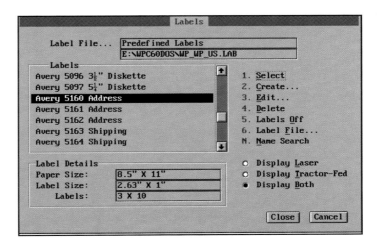

The Labels list includes more than 100 popular label types and sizes.

Printing the Labels

When you are ready to print, load the labels in your printer, then print as you normally would. When printing labels, if you tell WordPerfect to print the current page, the program prints an entire sheet of labels.

The first time you print on any type of labels, print a test page on plain paper. Then place the printed paper against the label form and hold them up together to a light to make sure that the labels print with the proper alignment. If not, you can edit the label definition's printer information to adjust where on the page WordPerfect prints. You can also edit the label's margins.

WordPerfect lets you control the quality of both printed text and graphics. You can also print multiple copies of a document and choose whether WordPerfect or the printer generates the extra copies.

When you print the final copy of a document, you usually want the highest quality output. For a draft copy, however, you may care more about getting the printout in a hurry. In general, the higher the quality, the slower the printing speed.

How Printers Create an Image

Modern printers (except daisy-wheel printers) create text and graphics by printing small dots. The size of the dots, the number of dots used to create an image, and how close together the dots are printed determine the quality of the printed image. To achieve the highest quality, many printers print each line several times. Printing high-quality text and graphics can take much longer than printing a draft copy.

On most laser printers, the quality of the text is always high quality, and neither printing speed nor quality change if you print a draft copy. With a graphic image, however, the difference between low, medium, and high resolution (75, 150, and 300 dots per inch) can dramatically affect printing speed and quality.

Changing the Print Quality

For text and graphics, you can select printing quality of High, Medium, Draft, and Do Not Print. If you tell WordPerfect not to print graphics, the program leaves the correct space where any graphic images belong and only prints the text around them. This setting also prevents graphics lines, borders, table lines, and background fills from printing.

When you change the print settings, WordPerfect saves the current setting with the document, so it continues to print at the same quality until you change the setting again.

Note: Changing the setting for one document doesn't affect other documents. If you want to change the default settings, from the Print/Fax dialog box select Setup (Shift+F1) and change the settings in the Print Setup dialog box.

Printing Multiple Copies

You can tell WordPerfect to print multiple copies of a document. Unlike print quality, changing this setting affects only the current printing and not future printings of this document.

If your printer has enough memory to store an entire page of information, WordPerfect can tell the printer to keep the page in memory and to print the extra copies. Otherwise, WordPerfect has to send the same information to the printer for each copy. Obviously, the less information WordPerfect has to send to your printer, the faster the job prints.

Change Print Options

1. Choose **F**ile, **P**rint/Fax to open the Print/Fax dialog box.

2. Make the desired changes as follows:

   To change the quality of text printing, choose **T**ext Quality and select an option.

   To change the quality of graphics printing, choose **G**raphics Quality and select an option.

   To change the number of copies printed, choose **N**umber of Copies and enter a quantity.

   To change whether your printer or WordPerfect generates extra copies, choose G**e**nerated by and select WordPerfect or Printer.

3. Choose P**r**int.

Troubleshooting

If you don't like the quality of a draft print job, or if a high-quality print job is taking too long, repeat the printing procedure and select a different quality for text and/or graphics.

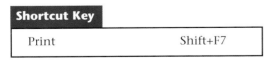

Shortcut Key	
Print	Shift+F7

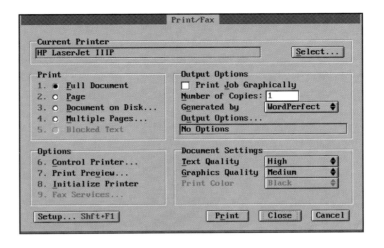

You change the print options with the settings in the right half of this dialog box.

SPECIAL PRINTING

If you need to stop one print job or rush another, WordPerfect lets you take control of the printer.

When you print a long document or print several documents at the same time, you may want to check on the progress of a print job, cancel a print job, or change the order of documents waiting to print. WordPerfect lets you perform all these tasks through the Control Printer dialog box.

Print Job Status

Every time you tell WordPerfect to print, the program creates a *print job*. A print job may be a single page or a huge document. The Control Printer dialog box displays a great deal of information about the current print job, including what page is printing, how many copies are printing, paper size and type, paper location, and the percentage of the document that WordPerfect has processed. It also indicates whether WordPerfect is actively printing, sending fonts to the printer, or creating temporary fonts. Finally, it can display error messages and suggest actions for you to take to fix the problem.

Changing the Print Queue

If you print additional documents before the first document finishes printing, WordPerfect creates a *print queue*, a list of print jobs waiting their turn at the printer. The Control Printer dialog box displays the current print queue. You can scroll through the list of print jobs, highlight a particular print job, and then cancel the job or rush it. You can also mark several print jobs with an asterisk (*) and change them simultaneously. Here's what the options do:

◆ *Cancel*. If you cancel a print job, WordPerfect prompts you to confirm before deleting the job from the queue. If you cancel the current job, WordPerfect tries to cancel the job and reset the printer. Depending on your printer's memory and capabilities, this may take some time. The program gives you the option of cancelling immediately; if you select this option, you may have to reset your printer manually.

◆ *Rush*. If you tell WordPerfect to rush a print job, the program gives you the option of interrupting the current print job. If you choose No, the rush job becomes the second item in the print queue and prints as soon as the current job finishes. If you choose Yes, WordPerfect suspends the current print job and begins printing the rush job instead. When the rush job finishes printing, WordPerfect starts the previous job from the beginning, *not* from where it left off.

◆ *Stop and Go*. If you need to stop a print job in the middle—to add more paper to your printer, for example—you can choose **S**top. When you're ready to resume printing, choose **G**o. If you stop and resume a print job, WordPerfect restarts the print job from the beginning.

Cancel, Rush, or Continue a Print Job

1. Choose **F**ile, **P**rint/Fax to open the Print/Fax dialog box.

2. Choose **C**ontrol Printer to open the Control Printer dialog box.

3. Highlight a print job. To change several print jobs at once, highlight each file and mark it with an asterisk (*), or press Home, * to mark all files.

4. To cancel a print job, choose **C**ancel Job; choose **Y**es to confirm the cancellation.

5. To rush a print job, choose **R**ush Job; choose **Y**es to interrupt the current job or **N**o to print the rush job next.

6. To stop a print job, choose **S**top. To restart the print job, choose **G**o.

7. Choose Close.

Troubleshooting

If you cancel a print job by mistake, simply reissue the print command.

Current job number

Error messages

Print queue

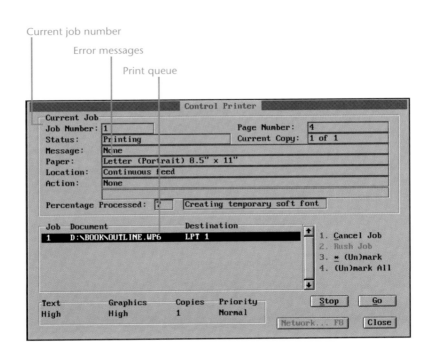

SPECIAL PRINTING

Performing a merge requires two files: a data file and a form file. The data file contains all the information needed to personalize the merged letter or other document.

A WordPerfect data file is really just a simple database file, organized in fields and records. A *field* is a single item of information, such as a name, phone number, or ZIP code. A *record* is a related group of fields, such as the name, address, and phone number of one person.

You can create a data file to keep track of employees, clients or customers, or any other type of information you like—recipes, catalogs of books or CDs, inventories of software and hardware, and so on.

Defining the Fields

The first step in creating the data file is to create the fields. A text data file can have up to 255 named fields in each record. You can make the fields specific or general. You can have a single Address field, for example, or individual fields for Street Address, City, State, and ZIP.

Naming the Fields

Field names indicate what information belongs in the field when you add records to the data file. When you create the form file to match the data file, you use the same field names.

Field names are not case sensitive, so you can use upper- or lowercase letters in any combination, and you can include spaces. For example, you can have a field called Last Name.

TIP Another way to create the data file is to create a table. See "Creating a Table."

You name the fields in the Field Names dialog box. Type the name of each field in order, pressing Enter after each name. When you're done, choose OK. WordPerfect inserts a FIELDNAMES merge code at the beginning of the file. This code lists all the field names you just entered. WordPerfect automatically inserts a hard page break after the code.

Entering the Records

After you define the fields, you enter the records for the data file. The records contain the specific information that you want to insert into a form letter or other form file. To add information, you type a field, insert a special code to indicate the end of the field, then type the next field. At the end of each record, you insert a different code to indicate the end of that record, then type the first field in the next record. When you add information to the file, WordPerfect displays the current field name on the status line, to help remind you what kind of data belongs in that field.

To tell WordPerfect where one field ends and the next begins, and where one record ends and one begins, you insert merge codes.

◆ To mark the end of each field, you insert an ENDFIELD code. WordPerfect automatically adds a hard return code ([HRt]) after each ENDFIELD code so that the following field starts at the beginning of the next line.

◆ To mark the end of each record, you insert an ENDRECORD code. WordPerfect automatically adds a hard page code ([HPg]) after each ENDRECORD code so that the following record starts on a new page.

You can put any information you like into any field. For example, you can enter **Smith**, **Fortescue-Smythe**, or nothing at all in the Last Name field. As far as WordPerfect is concerned, a field is anything before an ENDFIELD code—whether the field contains a few words, an entire paragraph or page, or is completely empty.

TIP

Make a list of the fields you need, their names, and the order of the fields. Then you can quickly enter the list into WordPerfect. You can use this list later to create matching field names in the form file.

Data Entry Rules

Keep these rules in mind when entering data:

◆ All records *must* contain the same number of fields. Even if a field is blank, you still must insert an ENDFIELD code as a placeholder.

◆ You must follow the same field order in each record. You can't type First Name first in one record and then Last Name first in the next record.

◆ Each field must end in an ENDFIELD code—even the last field in a record before the ENDRECORD code.

Changing the Data File

You can add records to a data file at any time. You can also edit records to update information, or delete records that are no longer needed. If you edit or delete the information in a field, make sure that you don't delete the ENDFIELD code at the end of the field. If you delete a record, make sure that you delete everything after the [HPg] code at the beginning of the record— through the [HPg] code at the end of the record.

more ▶

MERGE

Create a Text Data File

1. Choose **T**ools, M**e**rge, **D**efine.

2. Choose **D**ata [Text].

3. Choose Field **N**ames to open the Field Names dialog box.

4. Type the name of the first field, such as **Last Name**, and press Enter. Repeat this step for each additional field name.

5. After you type the last field name, press Enter one more time and choose OK.

   WordPerfect inserts a FIELDNAMES code, listing all your field names.

6. Type the information for the first field and press F9 to insert an ENDFIELD code. Repeat for each field in the first record.

7. After you insert the ENDFIELD code for the last field in the record, press Shift+F9 and choose **E**nd Record to insert an ENDRECORD code.

8. Repeat steps 6 and 7 for each record in the data file.

9. When the data file is complete, save and close the file.

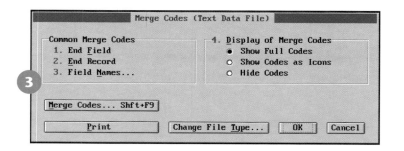

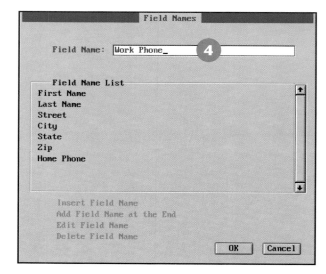

If you want to use data from an existing table, see the next article for details.

Notice that the field names are in common English. You don't have to type strange codes or character combinations.

Troubleshooting

If you forget to put an ENDFIELD code at the end of a field, when merging, WordPerfect treats that field and the following field as one large field. The merged document then contains the wrong information for the remaining fields in the record. If you forget an ENDRECORD code, WordPerfect combines two records, and the second half of the combined record isn't merged. You can edit the data file and insert additional ENDFIELD or ENDRECORD codes as needed.

Shortcut Keys

Merge Codes (Define)	Shift+F9
End Field	F9

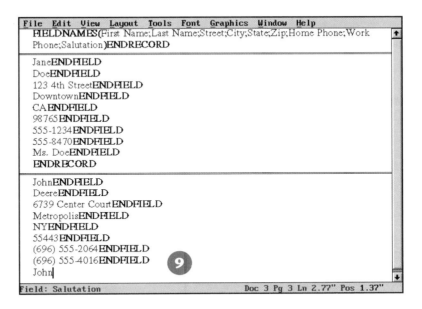

The data file may seem hard to read, but the Merge function needs these codes.

MERGE

A quick way to create a data file is to create a data table. When you use this approach, you don't have to worry about inserting **ENDFIELD** and **ENDRECORD** codes.

When you define a table data file, WordPerfect creates a table structure to hold the information. Each *cell* contains one field, and each *row* is a record. The first row in a table data file contains the field names.

Data File Format: Text versus Table

Here are advantages and disadvantages to using each type of data file:

◆ A text data file can have up to 255 fields per record. A table data file can have only 25 fields per record.

◆ In a text data file, you're responsible for inserting each ENDFIELD and ENDRECORD code. In a table data file, the table structure automatically separates fields and records.

◆ Fields in a text data file can be huge. Fields in a table data file aren't technically limited in size, but you probably shouldn't put a page of information into a single table cell.

◆ In a table data file, the cell and row boundaries make the divisions between individual fields and records obvious. In a text data file, the ENDFIELD codes appear at the end of a line, so as your eye scans down the beginning of each line, the field divisions aren't as immediately obvious.

◆ Large table structures can slow down WordPerfect dramatically. Therefore, if you need to maintain a data file with hundreds or even thousands of records, working in a text data file is faster.

Defining a Table Data File

Although both types of data files contain fields and records, defining a table data file is a slightly different process from defining a text data file. When you select a table data file, you must create a table with field names before you can enter any data.

After you create the table, entering your merge information is exactly like entering information in any other WordPerfect table. If you type more information in a cell than fits on one row, WordPerfect adjusts the height of the row as necessary to hold the information. You can press Tab and Shift+Tab to move forward and backward through the cells.

Create a Table Data File

1. Choose **T**ools, **M**erge, **D**efine.

2. Choose Data [**T**able].

3. Choose Create a Table with Field **N**ames.

   The Field Names dialog box appears.

4. Type the name of the first field, such as **Last Name**, and press Enter. Repeat this step for each additional field name.

5. After you type the last field name, press Enter one more time and choose OK.

6. Type the information for the first field into the first cell and press Tab to move the cursor to the next cell. Repeat for each field in the first record.

7. After you finish the last cell in the row, press Tab to insert a new row in the table.

8. Repeat steps 6 and 7 for each record in the data file.

9. When the data file is complete, save and close the file.

Troubleshooting

If you forgot a field when you defined the data table, return to the Merge Codes dialog box and add a column to the right or left of any existing column; then type a new field name in the cell in the first row. You can delete columns and add or delete rows anywhere in the table.

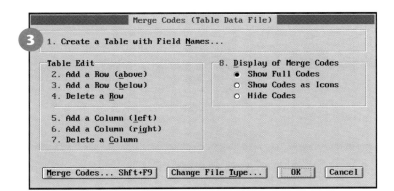

During setup, if you put a column or row in the wrong place, just delete it and start over.

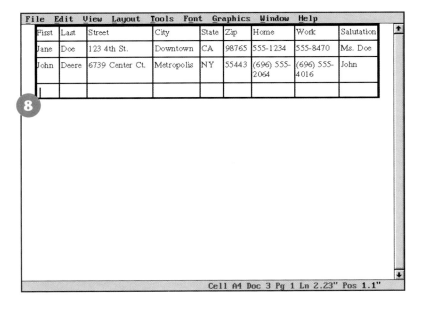

Remember to make the columns wide enough so you can read all the data.

MERGE

Shortcut Key	
Merge Codes (Define)	Shift+F9

The form file is the basis for a finished merge document. WordPerfect's fill-in-the-blanks approach lets you merge a form file with data from a data file to create form letters, mailing lists—even routing slips.

A *form file* is a WordPerfect document containing one or more merge codes. To send individually addressed letters to the people in a data file, for example, you create a letter with merge codes in place of a specific address or salutation. To create envelopes or mailing labels for that letter, you create another form file, formatted as an envelope or a page of labels.

You can create as many form files as you like to merge with a particular data file. You can also use a form file with more than one data file, as long as each data file contains field names that match the form file.

Defining a Form File

When you define a form file, you tell WordPerfect which fields from the data file will be inserted into the form, and where, by inserting merge FIELD codes. A FIELD code contains the name of a field in the data file, such as FIELD(*First Name*). When you perform the merge, WordPerfect replaces the code with the matching information from the data file.

> **TIP**
>
> Many merge codes and commands are available. For complex merges, consider a more detailed book on WordPerfect, such as Que's *Using WordPerfect 6*, Special Edition.

Merge Code Rules

Keep these rules in mind when creating a form file:

◆ The field name in a FIELD code must match *exactly* the field name in the data file, although field names are not case sensitive. If you merge the form file with a text data file, tell WordPerfect the name of the data file. Then, instead of typing field names from memory, you can select them from a list on-screen.

◆ You can use the same FIELD code more than once. For example, you can insert a FIELD(*First Name*) code as part of the address and again as part of the salutation.

◆ You don't have to use every field from your data file. You may need only a handful of the fields for your form file.

◆ You can insert FIELD codes in any order, regardless of the order in which the fields appear in the data file.

◆ You can insert a FIELD code anywhere in a form file, including headers and graphics boxes. You can't, however, insert a FIELD code in a Style definition.

Create a Form File

1. Choose **T**ools, **M**erge, **D**efine.

2. Choose **F**orm.

3. To insert the current date, choose **M**erge Codes (Shift+F9), select DATE, and press Enter.

4. To insert a field name from a data file, press Shift+F9 and then choose **F**ield. Choose List Field Names (F5) and enter the name of a data file. Then select a field name from the list. WordPerfect inserts a FIELD code containing that field name.

5. To insert another FIELD code, press Shift+F9. Then choose **F**ield, **L**ist Field Names (F5) and select a field name from the list.

6. Type the body of the document, inserting additional fields where appropriate.

7. When the document is complete, save and close the file.

Troubleshooting

If you make a typo when entering a field name for a FIELD code, you can edit the name between the parentheses. You also can delete a FIELD code, just as you can delete any other character.

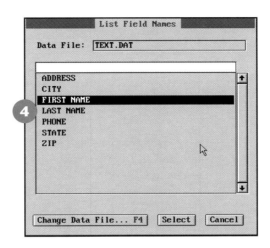

The data file uses a DAT extension.

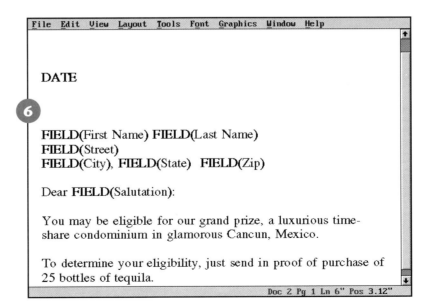

You can repeat fields as often as you like, wherever you want them.

Shortcut Key

Merge Codes (Define)	Shift+F9

MERGE

Are your form files and data files finished? You're ready to merge them to create a final document!

The merge process combines the form file and the data file to create a third document, which is usually displayed on-screen. You also can send the document directly to your printer or save it as a file on disk.

How the Merge Works

To begin the merge, you tell WordPerfect the names of the two files you want to merge. If the files are in different directories, you need to tell WordPerfect the path to the file(s) located elsewhere.

Note: If you type the wrong file name, or the file is in a different directory, WordPerfect displays File not found. *Correct the spelling of the file name or add the path if necessary.*

WordPerfect retrieves the form file into an unused document window. When the program encounters a merge FIELD code, it inserts the matching field from the first record in the data file. When WordPerfect reaches the end of the form file, the program inserts a hard page code and retrieves a second copy of the form file, this time inserting fields from the second record in the data file. WordPerfect repeats this process until all the records in the data file have been combined with a copy of the form file.

Depending on the number of records in the data file and the size of the form file, the merge operation may take anywhere from a few seconds to several hours.

> **TIP**
>
> If you find an error in the body of the final, merged document, *don't* correct the error on-screen because that error also is replicated in every other copy of the form file. Instead, close the merged document without saving, correct the mistake in the original form file, and repeat the merge operation.

After WordPerfect completes the merge operation, the result of the merge is a new, unnamed document on-screen. If the form file is one page long, the resulting document has one page for every record in the data file. If the form file is three pages long, the end document has three pages for every record in the data file.

> **TIP**
>
> Always scan a merged document on-screen before you print it. If the merge didn't work correctly, close the merged file (don't save it), correct the form file, and repeat the merge.

How Many Records Can You Merge?

WordPerfect has no built-in limit to the number of data file records you can merge with a form file. However, the amount of free space on your hard disk imposes a practical limit because WordPerfect needs to create a temporary file large enough to contain one full copy of the form file for every record in the data file. For really huge merge projects, you can get around the disk space limitation by sending the merge output directly to the printer instead of creating a document on-screen or on disk.

Merge a Data File and a Form File

1. Choose **T**ools, **M**erge, **R**un.

2. Choose **F**orm File and specify the form file you want to merge.

3. Choose **D**ata File and enter the name of the matching data file.

4. If desired, specify the output location: **C**urrent Document, **U**nused Document, **P**rinter, or **F**ile. If you merge to a file, specify the file name.

5. Choose Merge.

   WordPerfect merges the two files to create a finished document.

Troubleshooting

◆ To stop a merge operation, press Esc.

◆ You can correct a mistake in a single record of the merged document on-screen. Note the problem, however, and later correct that record in the data file.

◆ If the wrong information, or no information, is inserted for one or more FIELD codes in the merged version, either the wrong field name was specified, or the field name in the form file doesn't match the field name in the data file. Edit the form file and repeat the merge.

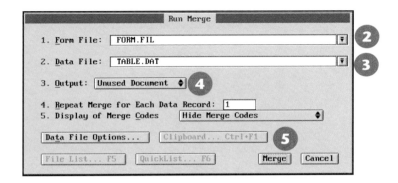

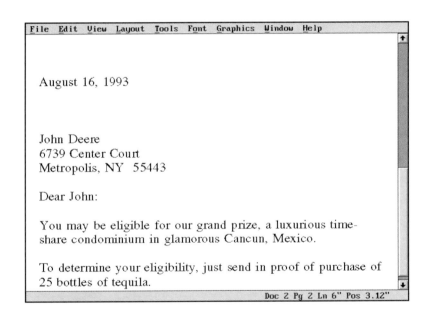

The finished merge document.

Shortcut Key

| Run Merge | Ctrl+F9 |

WordPerfect can create a table of contents automatically for any document—all you need to do is indicate what you want to include.

Specifying the entries you want to include is the first step in creating an automatic table of contents. WordPerfect doesn't know which titles, headings, or other items you want; you need to mark each entry. You can use two different methods to mark entries: mark them manually or mark them with styles.

Marking Text

To mark text to be included in a table of contents or other document reference, you begin by selecting a block of text—usually a heading. When you tell WordPerfect to mark the text for a table of contents, the program needs to know which table of contents *level* to use. Depending on the document, table of contents level 1 may be chapter titles or the names of major headings. Table of contents level 2 corresponds to the next lower headings or subheadings. You can mark up to 5 levels of headings.

When you mark a block of text to be included in a table of contents, the program puts a pair of [Mrk Txt ToC Begin] and [Mrk Txt ToC End] codes on either side of the block. If you highlight one of these codes in Reveal Codes, WordPerfect expands the code to show you the level number as well. *Everything* between these codes, including text and other format codes, is included when WordPerfect generates the table of contents.

Marking Headings with Styles

Marking every heading in a long document to be included in a table of contents can be tedious and time consuming. If you use styles to format your headings, however, you can mark all the headings automatically by including the table of contents mark codes in your styles.

WordPerfect provides some sample paragraph styles named Heading 1, Heading 2, and so on, which include table of contents marks. To use these styles, first select WordPerfect's Headings outline style. You can then select the individual paragraph styles from the main Style List or the Ribbon.

When you apply one of these paragraph styles to a heading, you automatically format the heading's appearance and mark it to be included in a table of contents. If you don't like the default appearance of WordPerfect's Heading styles, you can edit the styles or create your own. If you want to use a style to mark a heading *within* a paragraph, such as a heading that forms the first few words of a paragraph, you need to use a Character style.

See "Styles" and "Outlines" for more information on Paragraph styles, Character styles, and Outline styles.

Mark a Heading for a Table of Contents

1. Select a block of text.

2. Choose **T**ools, Ta**b**le of Contents, **M**ark.

3. If desired, type a new level number.

4. Choose OK or press Enter.

Mark Headings Using Styles

1. Before the first heading you want to mark, choose **T**ools, **O**utline, **B**egin New Outline. WordPerfect displays the Outline Style List.

2. Select the Headings outline style.

3. To mark a heading, place the cursor within the heading.

4. Choose **L**ayout, **S**tyles.

5. To mark a title, select the Heading 1 style. To mark a main heading, select the Heading 2 style. To mark a subheading, select the Heading 3 style.

Troubleshooting

If you select the wrong table of contents level while marking a heading, repeat the steps and select the appropriate level. If you want to unmark a heading, turn on Reveal Codes and delete one of the pair of table of contents marks.

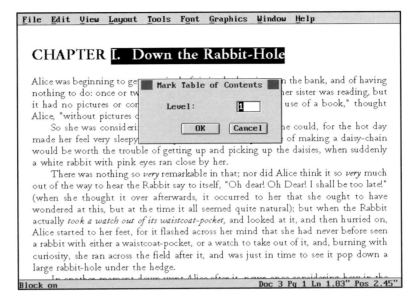

In this example, the chapter number and title are marked for a Level 1 table of contents entry.

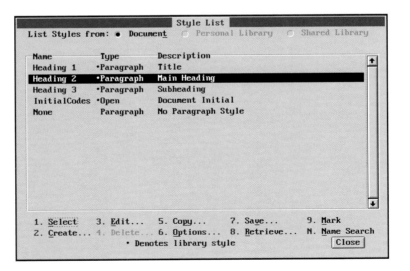

Use the Style List dialog box to specify the heading style for each heading. The heading styles include table of contents marks.

Generally a table of contents appears at the beginning of a document, but you may prefer it elsewhere—for example, in the bottom left corner for a newsletter. You can tell WordPerfect where to create the table and how you want it formatted.

After you mark what you want included, the next step in generating an automatic table of contents is to create a table of contents definition. WordPerfect inserts a table of contents definition code at the cursor position and builds the table of contents at that location.

Formatting the Table of Contents

The appearance of the table of contents is as important as the location. In the Define Table of Contents dialog box, you can choose how many levels to display, how each level should be formatted, and what numbering mode to use for each level.

You can change any or all of these options:

◆ *Number of Levels.* You can choose to display from one to five levels in a table of contents. If you only want to include level 1 headings (chapter titles, for example), leave the number of levels set to 1. If you want to include one or more additional levels of headings, enter the number of levels you want.

◆ *Styles.* WordPerfect has a default paragraph style for each table of contents level. To change the appearance of all table of contents entries at a given level, you can edit the appropriate style or create your own styles. For example, if you want all your level 1 entries to be bold, you can edit the `TableofCont1` style and add a `[Bold On]` code. See "Styles" for information on editing styles.

◆ *Numbering Mode.* By default, WordPerfect formats all table of contents page numbers flush right with dot leaders, but you can choose other numbering modes.

TIP

When you decide where to place your table of contents, use hard page codes to create an empty page, type an appropriate title, then add several hard returns to move the cursor somewhat down the page, before creating the table of contents definition.

Create a Table of Contents Definition

1. Insert hard page codes to create an empty page for the table of contents, type a heading for the page, and add several hard returns.

2. Choose **T**ools, Ta**b**le of Contents.

3. Choose **D**efine.

4. Choose **N**umber of Levels and enter the number of levels you want displayed in the table of contents.

5. Choose OK.

6. Move the cursor to the first page of body text.

7. Choose **L**ayout, **P**age, Page **N**umbering.

8. Choose Page **N**umber, New **N**umber, and enter 1.

9. Choose OK to close all open dialog boxes.

Troubleshooting

If you need to change the number of levels, style, or numbering method after you have inserted a table of contents definition, turn on Reveal Codes, place the cursor immediately after the [Def Mark] code, and repeat steps 2 through 5.

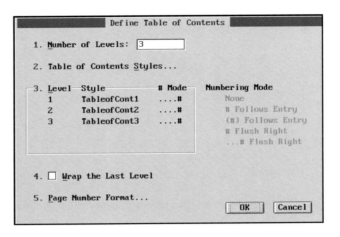

You specify the style you want for the table of contents. Just want chapter or article titles? You can specify a single level. Want to include section names or article subheadings? Add additional levels as you see fit.

Page Numbering Concerns

The length of the table of contents depends on the number of entries. If the table of contents is more than a page long, WordPerfect automatically adds pages to the document. If the table of contents is numbered in sequence with the main part of the document, each extra page changes the page numbering for the rest of the document, immediately making the page numbers in the newly generated table invalid.

To prevent this problem, start the page numbering sequence again at the beginning of the body of the document. The title page, table of contents, and other introductory material then shares one numbering sequence, and the main body of the document starts at page 1, no matter how long the table of contents grows.

Table of contents entries marked? Location and style specified? You're ready to generate the table!

After you define the location and appearance of the table of contents and mark the entries you want included, WordPerfect can generate the table of contents. When you tell WordPerfect to generate, the program scans through your document for entries marked for a table of contents. At the same time, the program automatically scans for entries marked for inclusion in an index, in lists, table of authorities, and cross-references. Each time WordPerfect encounters a reference, it copies the information between the paired mark codes and notes the page on which the reference appears. The program makes several passes through your document, looking for different types of codes.

After WordPerfect has copied all the references in your document, the program assembles those references and inserts them at the position of the appropriate definition code—such as the table of contents definition—and adds pages to the document if necessary.

For each table of contents entry, WordPerfect applies the paragraph style specified in the definition for that level. The program also inserts the page number after each entry, following the numbering mode specified in the definition.

Regenerating References

When WordPerfect generates references, the program places a pair of [Begin Gen Text] and [End Gen Text] codes around the generated table of contents text and any other generated document references. These codes tell the program where the generated text begins and ends.

If you make further changes to your document and want to update the table of contents or other references, tell the program to generate again. Once WordPerfect has created document references the first time, when you tell the program to generate, it deletes *everything* between the [Gen Text] codes. The program also builds a completely new table of contents or other reference list.

Don't edit or reformat a table of contents if you think you might need to generate again. If possible, make any necessary format changes in the table of contents paragraph styles so that when the program generates, WordPerfect automatically formats each entry the way you like.

Generate Document References

1. Choose **T**ools, Generate.

2. Choose OK.

WordPerfect generates the table of contents and other document references.

Troubleshooting

If you see errors in the generated table of contents, the same errors also appear in the headings or other entries from which the table of contents is generated. Correct the errors in the entries and then regenerate the table of contents.

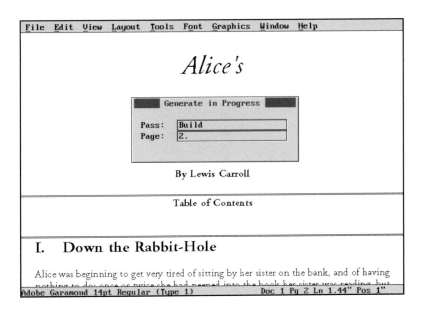

While WordPerfect generates the table of contents, the program displays this message box so you can monitor the process.

A generated table of contents.

DOCUMENT REFERENCES

WordPerfect can generate many kinds of document references: lists, an index, a table of authorities, and cross-references.

The procedures for creating lists, indexes, tables of authorities, and cross-references are similar to those for generating a table of contents. You mark the text you want included, define a location and style for the references, and tell WordPerfect to generate the references.

Lists

Your document may include several lists, such as figures, tables, illustrations, maps, and other types of information. You mark items to be included in a list much as you do table of contents entries. When you mark a list item, however, you indicate in which list the item should be included. The first time you mark an item, you type a list name, which can be any word or phrase you want. The next time you mark an item, WordPerfect supplies the name of the previous list. You can accept the name or type a new name for a second list. After you name lists, you can choose from the existing list names.

TIP

If you create captions for graphics boxes, you can include those captions in a list. When you define a list, choose **C**reate or highlight an existing list name and choose **E**dit. Then choose **I**nclude Graphics and select a box type, such as Figure Box, Table Box, or Equation Box.

Indexes

When WordPerfect generates an index of terms, it sorts the entries into alphabetical order and arranges them as headings and subheadings. To create an index, you don't need to select a block of text before marking an index item. If you do select a block, however, the program suggests the blocked text as the index entry. You can accept WordPerfect's suggested entry or edit the entry to a more concise form. Any index entry can be a heading, such as Index, or a subheading, such as Index, Define.

An index usually appears at the end of a document. Before creating an index definition, insert a hard page code to create an empty page and type an appropriate title for the index page.

If you don't want to go through a document marking entries to be included in the index, you can create a *concordance* file. A concordance file is a separate document listing all the words and phrases you want in the index, each on a separate line. If you include the name of a concordance file in an index definition, when you generate the index, WordPerfect scans your document for every occurrence of each entry in the concordance file.

Tables of Authorities

A *table of authorities* (ToA) is a list of citations in a legal brief that includes each occurrence of cases and statutes. You can create several sections in a table of authorities, such as cases, federal statutes, and state statutes.

Typically, the first time a case is cited in a brief, the full citation form is used, including case name, date, and the volume in which the case can be found. If the case is cited again, a shortened form is used. WordPerfect lists full-form and short-form citations of a given case under one entry.

When you mark a citation, you tell WordPerfect whether it's a full-form or short-form entry. When you mark a full-form citation, you specify the section name or number in which the citation needs to be included, and indicate the short-form version of the citation. When you mark a short-form citation, you can type a short-form name or choose List Short Forms (F5) to select from a list of short forms you have already created.

You must create a definition for each section of a table of authorities.

Cross-References

When you want to refer a reader to another place in a document, you use a *cross-reference*. With WordPerfect's Cross-Reference feature, you can refer to specific page numbers in a document, without knowing in advance what those page numbers are. Cross-references work somewhat differently than other document references. Instead of marking entries and creating definitions, you mark references and targets.

A *reference* is a place in your document which points a reader to a different location, such as "see page #." The page number location to which a reference points is a target. You also give each target a *target name*, which lets WordPerfect identify which reference goes with which target.

You can mark references and targets in any order, or mark both at the same time. When you mark a reference, you specify the target name for the reference. You can type a name or select from a list. Several references can refer to the same target.

When you generate cross-references, WordPerfect updates all references with the page numbers on which the targets are located.

To provide a reference for material quoted from a book or magazine, you use a footnote.

WordPerfect lets you create as many *footnotes* as you want and puts them at the bottom of the correct page. You can also create *endnotes*, which appear at the end of the document, but are otherwise identical to footnotes.

How Footnotes Work

When you tell WordPerfect to create a footnote, the program opens a window that looks like a normal document window. A footnote is essentially a minidocument, somewhat like a header or footer, but the footnote only prints on that one page. You can type any text you like into a footnote window, and apply any formatting codes. When you finish, exit to the document window, and WordPerfect inserts the footnote in the document. In Reveal Codes, you can see the footnote as a [Footnote] code. In the document, WordPerfect displays a footnote number.

When you print the document, Word-Perfect properly formats and prints each footnote at the bottom of the appropriate page, but doesn't display the footnote on-screen in Text mode and Graphics mode. You can only see the footnote in your document if you use Page mode.

Footnote Styles

WordPerfect uses footnote styles to control the overall appearance of footnotes and footnote numbers in text. By default, WordPerfect formats footnote numbers in text as superscripted numbers, but you can choose Edit Style in **D**oc from the Footnote submenu, and then add parentheses, remove the superscript codes, or make any other changes you like.

In the footnote text, WordPerfect automatically inserts a tab, then superscripts the footnote number. You can choose Edit **S**tyle in Note from the Footnote submenu to add an indent, remove the superscripting, or make other changes.

Footnote Numbering

WordPerfect automatically numbers footnotes with numerals, but you can use letters, Roman numerals, or characters instead. You can choose **N**ew Number from the Footnote submenu and then choose Numbering **M**ethod to select a different appearance.

Create a Footnote

1. Choose **L**ayout, **F**ootnote.

2. Choose **C**reate.

3. Type the text of the footnote.

4. Press F7 to return to the document window.

Troubleshooting

If you need to edit a footnote, choose Layout, Footnote, Edit, and enter the number of the footnote. You can then edit the footnote contents like a normal document, and press F7 when done. If you want to delete a footnote, you can delete the footnote number like any other character.

Shortcut Key	
Footnote	Ctrl+F7

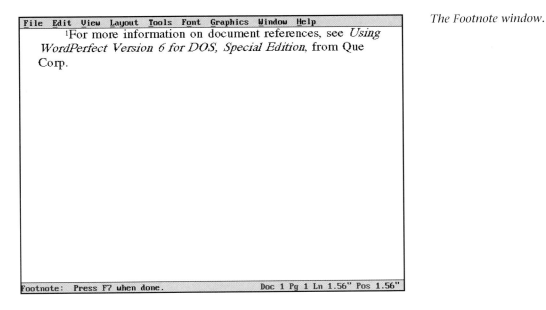

The Footnote window.

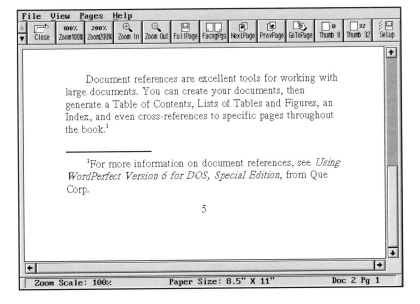

The footnote as it appears in the document preview.

Part Five

Section 13—Button Bar

The Button Bar is a row of shortcut buttons you can click on with your mouse. Instead of selecting a command from a menu or dialog box, you can click on a button for the command instead. You can also edit the Button Bar by adding buttons for the tasks you perform frequently, and create specialized Button Bars to make complex tasks easier. And you can customize the appearance of the Button Bar, choosing whether each button displays a picture, text, or both, and choosing where on-screen to display the Button Bar.

Section 14—Macros

A macro is essentially a recorded sequence of actions. Just as you can record music and play it back, you can tell WordPerfect to record your actions in a macro and then play the macro back to repeat your actions. When you perform a task frequently, you should record its steps as a macro. WordPerfect then can repeat those steps far more quickly than you can—and without making a mistake.

Section 15—Customizing

Your computer isn't exactly like anybody else's computer. Even if you have exactly the same computer model as a friend or colleague, you store your files in your directories and subdirectories; your friend has completely different files and directories. Also, even if you start with identical machines, you may add different peripherals such as a mouse or a modem. After you have used WordPerfect for some time, you may want to customize the program for your documents, your hardware, and your preferences.

The Button Bar can speed your work dramatically by providing mouse shortcuts for most WordPerfect features.

The Button Bar is just what its name implies—a bar of buttons on-screen. You can click any button to activate its feature, just as if you selected the feature from a menu or dialog box.

Note: *You must use a mouse with the Button Bar.*

Choosing a Button Bar

You can select between different Button Bars. WordPerfect provides several sample Button Bars, including one for tables and another for outlines. When you work with a specialized feature, select the Button Bar designed for that feature.

A Button Bar may contain more buttons than fit on-screen. If so, one or both of the scroll arrows at the left edge of the Button Bar is black. When you click a scroll arrow, WordPerfect displays another partial or full row of buttons.

Button Bar Options

You can edit Button Bars or create your own. For example, you can add a button for any menu item and for many items that aren't in a menu, such as Speller and Grammatik. You can change the order of buttons on the Button Bar, or delete some or all of the buttons. See "Customizing the Button Bar" for more information.

You can also assign a macro to a Button Bar button. You then can play back the macro simply by clicking its button.

TIP

You can choose to display only icons or only text on each button; doing so makes the buttons smaller, enabling WordPerfect to display more buttons on-screen. You also can choose where on-screen WordPerfect displays the Button Bar—across the top or bottom, or along the right or left side of the screen. See "Customizing the Button Bar" for help in changing the appearance or position of the Button Bar.

Select a Button Bar

1. Choose **V**iew, Button Bar **S**etup.

2. Choose **S**elect.

3. Highlight a Button Bar name and choose **S**elect.

Troubleshooting

If you click the wrong button, you can back out of a dialog box or undo an action just as if you had selected that feature from the menus.

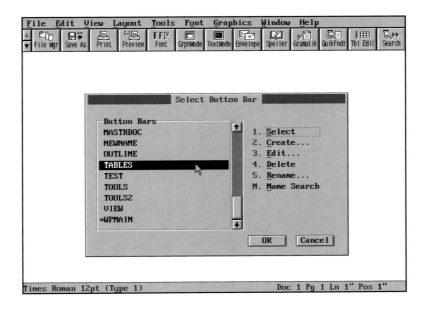

To use any of the buttons on the Button Bar, just click the button with the mouse.

The Default Button Bar

WordPerfect comes with several predefined Button Bars. The default Button Bar (WPMAIN) includes these buttons:

◆ *File Mgr* calls up the File Manager.

◆ *Save As* saves the current document.

◆ *Print* opens the Print/Fax dialog box.

◆ *Preview* accesses the Print Preview window.

◆ *Font* displays the Font dialog box.

◆ *GrphMode* changes the screen display to Graphics mode.

◆ *TextMode* changes the screen display to Text mode.

◆ *Envelope* calls up the Envelope dialog box.

◆ *Speller* starts the Speller.

◆ *QuikFndr* opens the QuickFinder dialog box.

◆ *Tbl Edit* changes to Table Edit mode.

◆ *Search* accesses the Search dialog box.

◆ *BBar Sel* displays the Button Bar Select dialog box.

◆ *BBar Opt* calls up the Button Bar Options dialog box.

BUTTON BAR

The Button Bar is one of WordPerfect's handiest tools. You can make the Button Bar even more useful by specifying its location on-screen and by creating custom Button Bars with the features you use most frequently.

When you first select the Button Bar, WordPerfect displays it across the top of the screen, below the pull-down menus, and below the Ribbon or Outline Bar if they're displayed. By default, each button contains both an *icon*—or picture—and a text description of the button. You can change the Button Bar settings to change the location or the look of the Button Bar.

You also can create your own custom Button Bars, and edit any Button Bar—whether your own or WordPerfect's—to add, delete, or rearrange buttons.

Caution: *If you edit WordPerfect's sample Button Bars and then update or reinstall the program, WordPerfect installs new copies of its own Button Bars over any changes you have made.*

Editing or Creating a Button Bar

To create a new Button Bar or edit an existing one, you use the options in the Edit Button Bar dialog box:

◆ *Add Menu Item* lets you add items from the pull-down menus. After you select this option, browse through the menus to select an item; WordPerfect adds the selected item to the end of your Button Bar.

◆ *Add Feature* lets you add features that aren't in the pull-down menus, such as the Speller, Grammatik, or QuickFinder. When you choose Add **F**eature, the program displays a list box of all features you can add (including those in the menus). When you select an item from the list, WordPerfect adds the item to your Button Bar.

◆ *Add Macro* and *Add Button Bar* let you add macros or other Button Bars. You then can start a macro or select a different Button Bar by clicking a button. With either option, you can choose from a list of available macros or Button Bars. All macro buttons display the same Macro icon, but the button text displays the macro's name. Buttons that select Button Bars act similarly.

◆ *Delete Button* lets you delete buttons you no longer need. If you choose **D**elete Button, the program prompts you to confirm the deletion.

◆ *Move Button* lets you rearrange the order of your buttons. The command acts like a combined cut and paste command, letting you change the position of a button name in the dialog box list of buttons.

TIP

Create a "main" Button Bar with the features you use most often. To switch between Button Bars quickly, add Button Bar Select to this Button Bar. On the other Button Bars, add a button to select the main Button Bar again.

Positioning the Button Bar

The Button Bar position options let you choose where on-screen the Button Bar should be displayed. The default position is across the top of the screen, but you also can choose the bottom, the left side, or the right side. When you choose the top or bottom position, the document window is a few lines shorter. When you choose left or right, the document window is narrower.

Note: Button Bar options apply to all Button Bars. If you change options and then select a different Button Bar, the second Button Bar is displayed with the new options.

TIP

WordPerfect displays a different number of buttons depending on what combination of options you choose. Text-only buttons are much wider than they are tall, so you can display more text buttons if you also choose the left or right side. Picture-only buttons are similar in proportion to your screen, so you can display about the same number, either horizontally or vertically. If you have a Super VGA monitor, you can display even more buttons on-screen.

Choosing a Button Bar Style

Button Bar style options let you change the Button Bar's appearance. The default appearance displays both picture and text on each button. You also can choose to display only pictures or only text. If you display only pictures or only text, the buttons are smaller, which allows WordPerfect to display more buttons on-screen.

more ▶

BUTTON BAR

Create a Button Bar

1. Choose **V**iew, Button Bar **S**etup.

2. Choose **S**elect to display the Select Button Bar dialog box.

3. Choose **C**reate and enter a name for the new button bar.

4. Do any of the following:

   Choose Add M**e**nu Item and select one or more items from any pull-down menu. Press F7 or click OK when you're finished adding items.

   To add a feature not in the menus, choose Add **F**eature and select a feature from the list that appears.

   To delete a button, highlight the button's name and choose **D**elete Button.

   To move a button, highlight the button's name and choose **M**ove Button; then scroll to where you want to insert the button and choose **P**aste Button.

5. Choose OK.

Troubleshooting

If you add the wrong button, finish adding buttons, including the button you originally intended, highlight the button you added by mistake, and choose **D**elete Button. You can also choose **M**ove Button to rearrange the order of buttons after you add them.

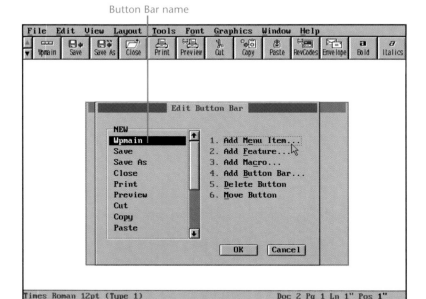

Creating a Button Bar.

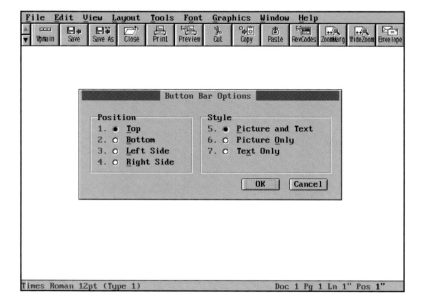

This Button Bar shows the default position and style.

Change Button Bar Options

1. Choose **V**iew, Button Bar **S**etup.

2. Choose **O**ptions.

3. To change position, choose one of the following: **T**op, **B**ottom, **L**eft Side, or **R**ight Side.

4. To change appearance, choose one of the following: **P**icture and Text, Picture **O**nly, or Te**x**t Only.

5. Choose OK.

Troubleshooting

If you don't like the appearance of your Button Bar, repeat the steps and choose different options.

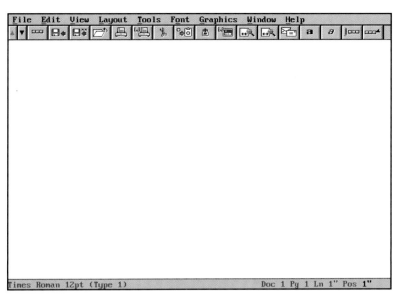

This version of the Button Bar shows how the buttons look with pictures only, in the top position.

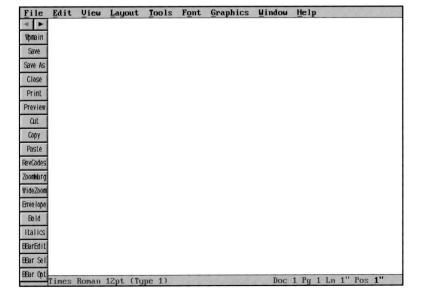

Notice how many more buttons can fit on-screen when you use the left position and text-only options.

Using macros, you can record an action or a sequence of actions and then have the program repeat those exact actions quickly and accurately.

Recording a macro is as easy as using a tape recorder. You simply tell WordPerfect to start recording your actions. As you perform the actions you want recorded, WordPerfect stores those actions in a file. When you finish the task, you tell the program to stop recording, and it saves the macro file. When you replay the macro, it repeats all the actions.

Before You Record

Here's what you should do before you record a macro:

◆ Decide what actions you want to record. You may want to select a font, change the tab set or margins, create a table, start a merge, and so on.

◆ Try the actions before recording to make sure that you know what steps you want to follow and in which order. If the macro is complicated, you may want to write down the steps.

◆ You may need to "set the stage" before recording so that the document in which you record the macro is similar to the document in which you will play back the macro. If you want your macro to block a word and convert the block to uppercase, for example, a word must be available to block.

Naming Macros

When you tell WordPerfect to record, the program asks you for a file name and automatically adds a WPM extension. When you play back the macro, you enter the macro's name or select it from a list.

You can use two types of names for macros. First is a normal file name, from one to eight characters in length. You should use names that are short and easy to remember, because the whole point of macros is to speed up your work. You can use **vty**, for example, to name a macro that types "Very truly yours," and adds your name and other closing information.

You also can create Alt+key macros. Instead of typing a normal file name, hold down the Alt key and type a letter. If you press Alt+V, for example, WordPerfect inserts the name ALTV. You can play back Alt+key macros by pressing the same keystroke combination.

Caution: *Because the pull-down menus also use Alt+key combinations, you should not use Alt+F, Alt+E, Alt+V, or any other Alt+key combinations that WordPerfect uses for its main menus.*

Record a Macro

1. Choose **T**ools, **M**acro.

2. Choose **R**ecord to open the Record Macro dialog box.

3. Enter a file name and choose OK or press Enter.

   The dialog box disappears and WordPerfect begins recording your actions.

4. Perform the actions you want recorded.

5. Choose **T**ools, **M**acro, **S**top.

Troubleshooting

◆ If you make a mistake while recording a macro, the easiest way to fix it is to stop recording and then rerecord the macro. You also can finish recording and then edit the macro if you're familiar with macro commands.

◆ When recording, WordPerfect displays Recording Macro in the status line. Turn off macro recording when you're done—or WordPerfect continues to record actions until you exit the program.

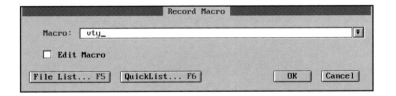

After you specify the macro name, WordPerfect records all of your actions—including any errors you make.

How Recording Works

WordPerfect 6 macros store keystroke *results*. If you select a font in a macro, for example, the macro records the font you selected, not the keystrokes or mouse movements you used to select the font. You can browse through menus or open and close dialog boxes, and WordPerfect doesn't record anything until you actually change something. If your macro involves cursor movement or selecting a block of text, though, you must use the keyboard commands. WordPerfect lets you use a mouse only in menus and dialog boxes while recording.

Shortcut Keys

Record	Ctrl+F10
Stop	Ctrl+F10

MACROS

After you record a macro, you can play back the macro as many times as you like.

When WordPerfect plays back a macro, it repeats the recorded actions in the same order you originally performed them. To play back a WordPerfect macro, all you need to do is tell the program the name of the macro you want to play.

> **TIP**
>
> Instead of typing the macro's name in the Play Macro dialog box, you can choose File List (F5) to display a listing of the files in the default macro directory, and then select a macro from the list.

Macro Methods

You can play back a macro with any of these methods:

◆ Type the name in the Play Macro dialog box. WordPerfect assumes that all macros are in the macro directory specified in the Setup Location of Files dialog box. If you have saved a macro in a different directory, you must enter the path and file name of the macro so that WordPerfect can find the file.

◆ If you gave an Alt+key name to the macro, press that key combination.

◆ If you assigned a macro to a Button Bar button, click on the button to play back the macro. See "Customizing the Button Bar" for information on adding a macro to a Button Bar.

> **TIP**
>
> WordPerfect includes a sample MACROS Button Bar. If you select this Button Bar, you can play many of WordPerfect's sample macros by clicking a button. The Bullet macro, for example, places bullets in front of a paragraph and indents the paragraph.

Play Back a Macro

1. Choose **T**ools, **M**acro.

2. Choose **P**lay.

3. Enter the name of the macro you want to play back.

4. Choose OK or press Enter.

   The program plays the macro.

After you specify the macro you want to play back, Word-Perfect immediately repeats the actions in the macro.

Troubleshooting

If WordPerfect cannot find a macro with the name you type, the program prompts Path not found and displays the macro name again. If you made a typo, you can correct the typo and choose OK. If you think you have typed the name correctly, choose File List (F5) and scroll through the list of macros to see whether your macro is listed or whether it has a slightly different name.

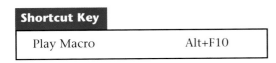

Shortcut Key	
Play Macro	Alt+F10

Why specify the path over and over? In one step, you can tell WordPerfect where to store and look for the files that the program uses most often.

The main WordPerfect program consists of two files, WP.EXE and WP.FIL. When you install the program, you also install hundreds of auxiliary files, including fonts, graphics images, printer files, macros, Button Bars, and files for the Speller, Thesaurus, and Grammatik. The Install program automatically creates several directories to hold these files. The directory's *path* specifies the location of the directory.

By storing auxiliary files in several directories, WordPerfect keeps them organized and prevents individual directories from becoming cluttered. This storage method simplifies sharing files with other network users, or with other programs from WordPerfect Corporation that use the same printer drivers, speller, thesaurus, and other files.

As you work in WordPerfect, you may create files such as macros and styles. When you create a macro, for example, the program automatically stores the macro file in the macro directory. When you play back a macro, the program automatically looks in the macro directory to find the macro file you want to play. You need to tell WordPerfect where to find these files, as well as files that you create using other programs, such as spreadsheet and graphics programs.

TIP

Never store documents in the same directory as your program files. You risk confusing the two types of files, and accidentally deleting or moving important program files. Also, every time you want to look at a list of your documents, you have to sort through many program files to find your document files.

Types of Files

You can specify a location for the following types of files:

◆ *Backup files*. By default, WordPerfect stores its timed backup files in the same directory as its main program files, usually C:\WP60. You may want to change this location to your main document directory. This action prevents you from having to change directories if you need to find a backup file to open.

◆ *Macros/keyboards/Button Bar files*. These three types of files are stored in one directory. WordPerfect automatically creates a MACROS subdirectory under the WP60 directory to store these files. Any macros, Button Bars, or custom keyboard layouts you create are automatically stored there. If you specify a shared and a personal directory for macros, the program automatically saves any new macros you create to your personal directory and lets you use macros located in the shared or personal directory. If both directories have a macro of the same name, WordPerfect uses the macro in your personal directory unless you type the full path and name of the shared macro. See "Macros" for more information on using macros.

◆ *Writing tool files*. Files for the Speller, Thesaurus, and Grammatik are stored in this directory. The default directory is C:\WPC60DOS. When you check the spelling of documents, WordPerfect creates a supplemental dictionary of words you use that aren't in its main dictionary. Choose **W**riting Tools and make sure that **S**upplementary is set to the same location as **M**ain. See "Checking Spelling" for more information.

◆ *Printer files*. This directory is where Word-Perfect stores printer drivers, the files the program uses to communicate with your printer. By default, the location is C:\WPC60DOS. You don't need to change this location unless you're on a network.

◆ *Style files*. This directory is where WordPerfect stores style libraries. You can enter a path for style files and the name of your default style library. If you have not created a personal library yet, you can enter a name such as PERSONAL.STY, and WordPerfect creates an "empty" style library to which you can copy styles as you create them. See "Creating a Style Library" for more information.

◆ *Graphics files*. When you tell WordPerfect to retrieve an image to put in a graphics box, WordPerfect looks first in this directory. WordPerfect's Install program creates a subdirectory named GRAPHICS under the WP60 directory and installs several dozen images in WordPerfect's WPG format. If you use another graphics program or have many graphics images stored in another location, you may want to change this entry to the directory that holds those other files.

◆ *Document files*. Unless you select a different directory during installation, WordPerfect automatically creates a document directory named C:\WPDOCS. When you start WordPerfect, this directory becomes the default directory. If you have documents stored in another location, you may need to change this entry to the location of those files.

◆ *Spreadsheet files*. If you frequently import spreadsheets, you can enter the location of those spreadsheet files.

◆ *QuickFinder files*. When you create QuickFinder index files, the program stores the files in this directory. In fact, you can't create an index until you specify a directory for this entry. If you leave the **U**pdate QuickList box checked, when you make any changes to locations of files, WordPerfect adds the changes to your QuickList.

◆ *WP.DRS file and *.WFW files*. These are files used by WordPerfect for displaying fonts on-screen, and by default are located in C:\WPC60DOS.

◆ *Graphics fonts data files*. For these files, you can specify directories for four types of font files that WordPerfect supports: Bitstream Speedo, CG Intellifont, TrueType, and Type 1 (PostScript). If you want WordPerfect to use any of these types of fonts, you must indicate their location.

more ▶

CUSTOMIZING

Personal and Shared Files

For most types of files, particularly macros and styles, you can enter a *personal path* and a *shared path*. If your computer is connected to a local area network, the shared path may be a shared directory on the network that all users can access, and the personal path may be a directory that only you can access. If your computer isn't on a network, you can leave a shared path empty, or supply the location of a second directory that you use to store a particular type of file. If you share your computer with another person, one of you can store files in the personal path location and the other in the shared path location.

Indicating the Path

The Location of Files dialog box lets you specify the directories that WordPerfect uses for different types of files. Changing an entry in the Location of Files dialog box doesn't move the files for that entry. If you enter the wrong location, WordPerfect can't find the files. But you can move files to a new location by using the File Manager and then change the corresponding entry in the Location of Files dialog box.

TIP If you choose a Location of Files option and enter the location of a directory which doesn't exist, the program asks you if you want to create that directory. If you choose **Yes**, the program creates the directory for you.

Specify File Locations

1. Choose **F**ile, Se**t**up.

2. Choose **L**ocation of Files.

3. Choose an option and enter a new location or change the existing location.

4. Choose OK.

Troubleshooting

If you enter the wrong directory for a particular type of file, such as macros, Word-Perfect won't be able to find that type of file when needed, and you will receive a `file not found` error message. If this happens, use the File Manager to verify the actual location of the files; then either change the Location of Files setting or move the files to the specified location.

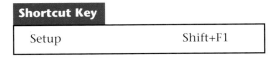

Shortcut Key

Setup	Shift+F1

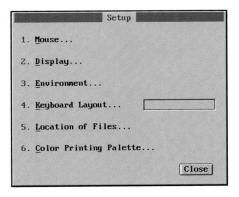

By changing the settings in this dialog box, you can customize Word-Perfect to speed and simplify your work.

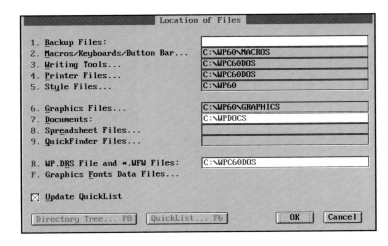

Indicate which files go where with the options in this dialog box. You don't need to change all the settings at once.

A mouse can make WordPerfect 6 very easy to use. In fact, you can't use several features, such as the Ribbon, Button Bar, or scroll bars, if you don't have a mouse.

WordPerfect needs to know what type of mouse or trackball you own to use it properly. You tell WordPerfect the type of mouse by selecting a *mouse driver*—a file containing information about the type of mouse you have. When you install WordPerfect, the program automatically installs mouse drivers but doesn't attempt to specify the type of mouse. Before you can use a mouse, you must identify the type or tell the program to select a mouse type. You only have to perform this operation once.

Most pointing devices provide a driver, often named MOUSE.COM. If you're using a mouse driver, you can use that driver instead of a WordPerfect driver, which saves some memory.

Mouse Options

When you identify your mouse, you can specify these options:

◆ *Type.* Choose from various brands and models of pointing devices. Some models, otherwise identical, use different types of connections—usually serial, PS/2, or bus. You must choose the right brand and connection type. If you already use a driver, choose Mouse Driver (MOUSE.COM).

◆ *Port.* If you have a serial mouse, you must tell WordPerfect which serial port your mouse uses. Choose COM1 or COM2.

◆ *Double-Click Interval.* Double-clicking a list item is a shortcut method of selecting an item—you rapidly click the left mouse button twice. If the second click isn't fast enough, WordPerfect doesn't treat it as a double-click. This option lets you control how much time you have to double-click. The default is one half second (50 100ths).

◆ *Acceleration Factor.* This option controls how rapidly WordPerfect moves the mouse pointer on-screen compared to the distance you actually move the mouse. If the mouse pointer darts around the screen, enter a smaller number; if the pointer moves too slowly, enter a larger number.

◆ *Left-Handed Mouse.* Most mice and trackballs have two buttons but use only the left button for most purposes, which is convenient for a right-handed person to click with the right index finger. To use the mouse with your left hand, however, you may prefer to click the right mouse button by using your left index finger. This option lets you swap which button WordPerfect uses.

Select a Mouse Driver

1. Choose **F**ile, Se**t**up.

2. Choose **M**ouse.

3. Choose **T**ype, then select a mouse or trackball from the list.

4. If you use a serial mouse, choose **P**ort and select COM1 or COM2.

5. If mouse movement appears too fast or too slow, choose **A**cceleration Factor and enter a different value.

6. If you want to swap the primary mouse button, choose **L**eft-Handed Mouse.

7. Choose OK.

Troubleshooting

If you select the wrong mouse type, Word-Perfect may not recognize your mouse. If you aren't sure what type to select, choose **A**uto Select, and WordPerfect attempts to detect your mouse. The program may not be able to detect your exact brand and model, but it can usually find an equivalent type of mouse that uses the same commands.

Shortcut Key	
Setup	Shift+F1

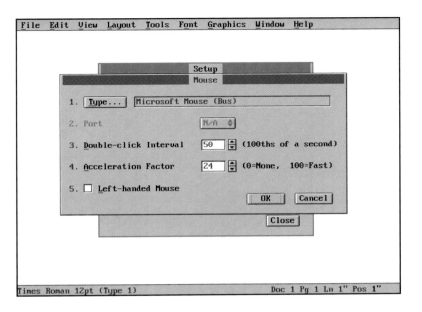

WordPerfect can use a wide variety of mice, trackballs, and other pointing devices.

CUSTOMIZING

Does your monitor's display look a bit fuzzy? Maybe your display options need to be changed.

To display information in Graphics mode, WordPerfect needs to know what kind of display adapter you have. With a Super-VGA computer monitor and display adapter, for example, Word-Perfect can display higher-quality text and graphics on-screen.

VGA versus Super-VGA

Most personal computers sold in the last five years can display VGA graphics—the current standard. A VGA monitor displays 640 pieces of information (*pixels*) across the width of the screen and 480 pixels from top to bottom, 16 colors at a time. If your computer can display Super-VGA graphics, however, you can display 800 by 600 pixels or even 1024 by 768 pixels, 256 or more colors at a time.

If your system can display more than VGA's 640 by 480 pixels, WordPerfect can use higher-quality fonts, making text easier to read. Graphic images and lines look sharper. If your system can display more than 16 colors simultaneously, color graphics also appear much more realistic on-screen.

Caution: Displaying more pixels or more colors on-screen can slow WordPerfect—dramatically. And at higher resolutions, the characters in menus and dialog boxes appear smaller on-screen.

Hardware Considerations

The kinds of graphics WordPerfect can display depends on your computer monitor (screen) and the display adapter that sends information to the monitor. A monitor that can display more than 640 by 480 pixels is often called a multifrequency, multisync, or Super-VGA monitor.

You cannot use Super-VGA graphics unless both monitor and display adapter can handle Super-VGA. In many cases, the display is also limited by how much memory (*RAM*) is on the adapter card. When you select a display type, the list of "screen types" WordPerfect displays is actually a list of common video adapters.

After indicating the type of video adapter, select the resolution and number of colors to display. For most systems, use 16 colors unless you work with many color graphic images in WordPerfect. Choose 800 by 600 pixels if your system can display that resolution; otherwise, choose 640 by 480. Choose 1024 by 768 only if you have a monitor that is 16 inches or larger.

Choose a Display Adapter

1. Choose **F**ile, Se**t**up.

2. Choose **D**isplay.

3. Choose **G**raphics Mode Screen Type/Colors.

4. Choose **S**creen Type.

5. Highlight your display adapter and choose **S**elect; or choose **A**uto Select.

6. Highlight a resolution and color option, such as SVGA 800x600 16 color, and choose **S**elect.

7. Close all open dialog boxes by choosing Close.

Troubleshooting

◆ If you don't know what type of video adapter you have, you can choose **A**uto Select, and the program tries to detect your adapter type.

◆ If you're unable to see the screen after making a selection, you can still use the program. Press Ctrl+F3, T to select Text mode, then repeat the steps to select a different screen type.

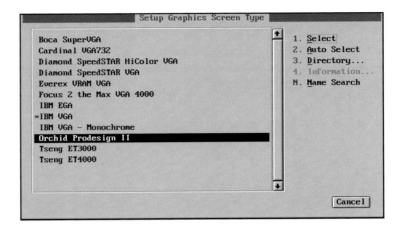

WordPerfect lists the available video setups. If you don't know what kind of adapter your computer uses, try the Auto Select option.

The default WordPerfect settings may not be the best settings for you. For many WordPerfect features, however, you can specify how you want the program to work.

You can set a wide number of WordPerfect options—for example, to control the cursor speed or specify how frequently the program makes backups. These options are the most useful:

◆ *Backup Options.* You can set the timing for timed backups. See "Working with a Timed Backup" for details. You can also make original document backups every time you save a file. WordPerfect saves the previous version with a BK! extension.

Caution: Backups take a lot of disk space!

◆ *Cursor Speed.* This option controls how rapidly the cursor scrolls across the screen when you hold down a cursor key. It also controls how rapidly WordPerfect inserts characters if you hold down a character key. You can choose settings between 10 and 50 characters per second (cps), or choose Normal— your computer's default cursor speed.

◆ *Allow Undo.* The Undo feature reverses the most recent change to a program. By default, Undo is enabled, and Word-Perfect stores the most recent document change in memory. If you deselect this option, you save memory, but you cannot Undo. You can still Undelete, however.

◆ *WordPerfect 5.1 Keyboard.* Earlier versions of WordPerfect used F3 to access Help and F1 for Cancel. The industry standards, however, are F1 for Help and Esc for cancel. With Version 6, WordPerfect has adopted these industry standards. If you prefer the previous settings, choose this option to switch defaults.

◆ *Auto Code Placement.* In earlier versions of WordPerfect, all formatting codes were inserted at the cursor position. WordPerfect 6 now places many formatting codes at the beginning of the current paragraph or page, depending on the type of code. If you turn off this option, the program reverts to placing all codes at the cursor position.

◆ *WordPerfect 5.1 Cursor Movement.* In earlier versions of WordPerfect, you couldn't see codes on-screen without turning on Reveal Codes, but the cursor acted as if the codes were visible. For example, to scroll past a boldfaced word, you had to press the cursor key an extra time to move past the [Bold On] and [Bold Off] codes. You could even delete codes by pressing Backspace or Del. In Word-Perfect 6, the codes are "invisible" to the cursor—and to delete codes, you must turn on Reveal Codes. If you turn off this option, the program reverts to 5.1 cursor movement.

Change Environment Options

1. Choose **F**ile, Se**t**up.

2. Choose **E**nvironment.

3. Specify the desired options.

4. Choose OK.

Troubleshooting

If you don't like how WordPerfect acts after choosing one of these options, repeat the steps and choose different options.

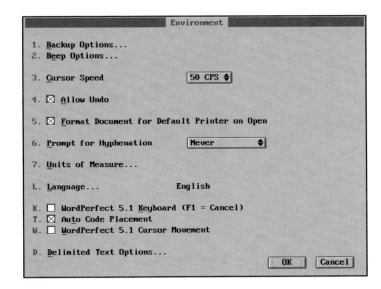

*Many environment options require you to specify additional options. To specify a timed backup interval, for example, choose **B**ackup Options, choose **T**imed Document Backup, and then type the desired number of minutes between backups.*

CUSTOMIZING

Appendix

Before you can use WordPerfect, you must install the program and its auxiliary files. These files are in compressed form on floppy disks; you can't just copy the files onto your computer's hard drive. Instead, you must run Word-Perfect's Install program.

Install creates directories to hold all the files, then expands and copies the files from the floppy disks to the hard drive. You specify the kind of video card you have, the printer model, and whether you have a fax board or sound card. Install copies drivers for those devices, and automatically configures the program.

After WordPerfect has been installed, you can run Install again at any time to add drivers for a printer, graphics card, fax/modem, or sound card. You can also use the WordPerfect Font Installer to install additional fonts.

Installation Options

You can install WordPerfect in three ways: standard installation, custom installation, or network installation.

◆ In a *standard* installation, you specify the hardware and the disk drive. Install copies all the program files to the default directory locations.

◆ In a *custom* installation, you also select directories for various program files. If the hard disk is short on space, you can tell the program not to install certain files.

◆ In a *network* installation, you install the program on a network file server and identify the network type. A network installation should only be performed by a network supervisor.

Hardware Options

For WordPerfect to use your computer properly, you must identify the type of graphics card and printer(s) you use. WordPerfect then installs *device drivers* that help the program interact with your specific hardware. If you have a fax modem or a sound card, you can also install drivers for those items.

more ▶

The install program asks you to identify this hardware:

◆ *Graphics Card.* The type of graphics card determines how the computer displays information on-screen in Graphics mode. WordPerfect always installs the driver for a VGA card, which most computers can use; however, if your card is more powerful, WordPerfect can display a higher-resolution image, which is easier to read. If you don't know what brand you own, choose **A**uto-select, and the Install program tries to determine what type of card you have.

◆ *Printer.* WordPerfect supplies drivers for nearly 1000 different printer models, including laser, inkjet, dot-matrix, and even daisy-wheel printers. Identify the exact printer model if possible so that WordPerfect can make use of all the printer's capabilities. If the printer isn't listed, your printer manual may suggest an alternate printer with similar capabilities. You can also obtain additional printer drivers from WordPerfect Corporation. If you use more than one type of printer, you can install several printer drivers.

◆ *Fax Modem.* If you own a fax modem, WordPerfect can send a fax much like it prints a document, including fonts and graphic images. The program has drivers for three types of fax modems: FaxBios compatible, Intel SatisFAXtion, and Class 1 or Class 2 Fax Modem. Consult your fax modem's manual to determine the hardware type. If you don't have a fax modem, you can skip this selection.

◆ *Sound Board.* If you own a sound board, WordPerfect can record and play sound clips in a document. Select the appropriate board, or skip this selection.

Installation Progress

Install immediately asks several questions about hardware, then begins installing files. The program always tells you which file is being installed, the directory in which the file is being installed, and what percentage of the file has been installed. In a separate window, the program shows the total progress of the installation.

You need to swap disks several times during installation. Each time, Install prompts you with the name of the next disk to insert. Press Enter to continue the installation. If you press Esc, you cancel the installation process.

Reinstalling WordPerfect

After you install WordPerfect, you can run the Install program again to install newer versions of program files, additional drivers, or other auxiliary files. Instead of installing the entire program, you just install the files for a particular option. Start Install and select from the following options. Follow the prompts that appear on-screen.

◆ *Device Files* adds additional hardware drivers.

◆ *Update* adds updated versions of program disks when WordPerfect Corporation releases them.

◆ *Install Disk(s)* installs *all* the files from an installation disk, such as all the printer files.

◆ *Graphic Fonts* runs the WordPerfect Font Installer from outside WordPerfect if you don't have enough memory to install fonts with WordPerfect running.

◆ *Additional Language* adds support files that help you use WordPerfect with foreign-language documents.

Installing Fonts

You can install additional fonts in WordPerfect by using the WordPerfect Font Installer program. When you install WordPerfect, you automatically install several fonts. If you currently own additional fonts or purchase new fonts, you can also install those fonts for use with WordPerfect. The program supports six font formats: Autofont, Bitstream Speedo, CG Intellifont, Type 1, TrueType, and HP LaserJet (bitmapped fonts).

The WordPerfect Font Installer (WPFI) is a separate program you can run from within WordPerfect. WPFI always runs in Text mode, so if you normally run WordPerfect in Graphics mode, don't be surprised when your display changes.

WPFI doesn't install fonts on your hard disk. Instead, it scans font files already on your hard disk and adds the information in those files to WordPerfect's list of available fonts, including the characters available in each font and their relative sizes.

WPFI needs to know the location of the font files and any supporting files. The program assumes that fonts in each format are in the most common location for that font type. For example, Adobe Type Manager installs Postscript Type 1 fonts in C:\PSFONTS, and Microsoft Windows 3.1 installs TrueType fonts in C:\WINDOWS\SYSTEM. WPFI also needs to know the location of WP.DRS, the WordPerfect file that identifies the names and location of font files. Accept the defaults offered if they're correct, or change them if necessary.

The program then scans the font directory for available fonts and displays a list of the fonts you can install. You can install any or all listed fonts. Choose **P** to unmark printer fonts, **G** to unmark all graphics fonts, or Home, * to unmark all fonts. Press * to mark or unmark individual fonts.

When you choose **I**nstall Marked Fonts, WordPerfect adds the fonts to your printer driver. WPFI must read the font files for information on character maps and font metrics. This information tells WordPerfect what characters are in each font and the relative width of each character. This process may take some time.

When WPFI is done installing fonts, the program returns to WordPerfect's Font Setup dialog box.

more ▶

Install WordPerfect

1. Insert the Install 1 disk in your computer's drive A (or drive B).

2. From the DOS prompt, type **a:install** (or **b:install** if you're installing from drive B) and press Enter.

3. Install asks if you see red, green, and blue colored boxes. If you do, choose **Y**es.

4. Choose **S**tandard Installation.

5. Install asks if you want to change the drive you will be installing from or the drive you will be installing to. Choose **Y**es to select a different drive letter; choose **N**o to continue the installation.

6. Install shows you how many bytes are available on the selected drive, compared to the 14,500,000 bytes (14.5 megabytes) that the program files require, and asks if you want to continue with the installation. If you don't have enough room to install all the files, choose **N**o, then delete some files to make room for the program before installing. If you do have enough room, choose **Y**es.

7. Install asks how to handle replacing existing files. If you're installing for the first time, you have no files to replace, so any option is fine. If you're reinstalling, choose **S**mart Prompting, and Install asks you whether or not to replace any files you may have customized.

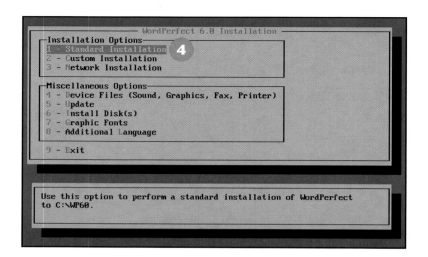

8. Install asks if you want to add the WordPerfect program to your path. Choose **Y**es unless you prefer to modify the path yourself later.

9. Install asks if you want to install a graphics driver. Unless your computer has an IBM VGA or EGA graphics card, choose **Y**es.

10. Highlight your brand of card and press Enter. Then choose **Y**es to confirm the brand you have selected. If you aren't sure of your brand, press A to auto-select, and WordPerfect will attempt to identify your graphics card for you.

11. Install asks if you want to install another graphics card. Choose **N**o.

12. Install asks if you want to install a printer driver. Choose **Y**es if you will use WordPerfect with a printer.

13. Highlight your printer model and press Enter. Then choose **Y**es to confirm the model you have selected. If your printer isn't listed, select a printer recommended by your printer manual or one of the emulations WordPerfect suggests.

14. Install asks if you want to install another printer. If you do, repeat steps 12 and 13; otherwise, choose **N**o.

more ▶

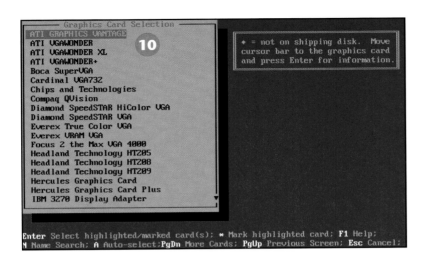

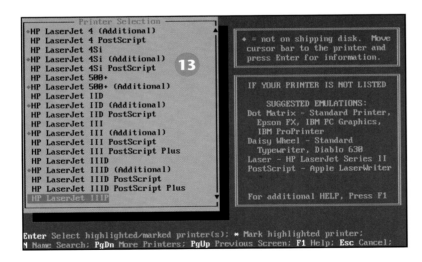

15. Install asks if you want to install a fax driver. Unless you own a fax modem, choose **N**o. If you own a fax modem, choose **Y**es, select the fax modem type, specify the directory for the fax files (the default is the WordPerfect program directory), and indicate whether or not to add the fax driver files to your AUTOEXEC.BAT file. You also have to answer some setup questions for the fax software.

16. Install asks if you want to install a sound board. Unless you own a sound board, choose **N**o. If you own a sound board, choose **Y**es, highlight the brand, press Enter, and choose **Y**es to confirm the brand you have selected.

After installing all the disks, Install loads WordPerfect to complete the installation and prompts you to enter your license number. This number is located on your license agreement.

17. Type the number and press Enter. If you cannot find the number, press Enter.

Install completes the installation, setting the default location of files, graphics card type, and installing the selected printer driver.

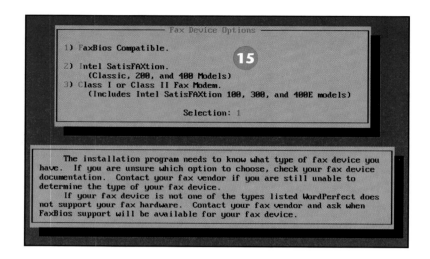

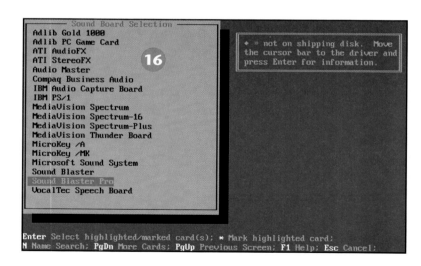

Troubleshooting

If you select the wrong graphics card, printer, or other hardware, you can install another driver after the main installation finishes. If you don't have enough room on your hard drive, abort the installation and delete some files before installing. Or if you have another drive with more room available, tell WordPerfect to use that drive.

Install Fonts with WordPerfect Font Installer (WPFI)

1. Choose Font, Font.

2. Choose Setup; or press Shift+F1.

3. Choose Install Fonts.

4. Select a font type, such as Type 1.

5. If WPFI displays the Location of Files dialog box, select an option to change a directory. The help text on-screen indicates which file types are necessary to install the fonts into WordPerfect.

6. If desired, unmark some fonts or unmark all fonts and then mark selected fonts.

7. Choose Install Marked Fonts.

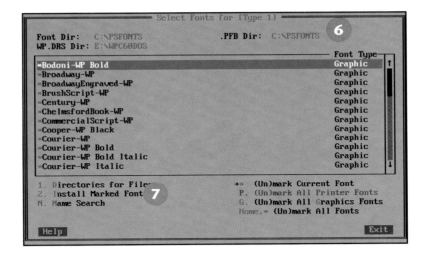

Troubleshooting

If WPFI cannot find font files, it displays a Location of Files dialog box. You must change the directory for one or more font file types until WPFI locates the essential files. If WPFI doesn't proceed to the following menu, you haven't selected the proper directory or you don't have all the files necessary to install the fonts.

Index

A

absolute tabs, 70
accent marks, 68
addresses, 239
    return, 238-239
    scanning documents, 238
aligning
    columns, 170-171
    text, 34-35
Alignment command (Edit menu), 35
Alignment command (Layout menu), 33
Alignment Decimal command (Edit menu), 35
Alignment Flush command (Edit menu), 35
Alt+key combinations, 274
antonyms, 54-55
attributes
    cells (tables), 182
    fonts, 64-67
    text, 30-31
AUTOEXEC.BAT file, 294
automatic page numbering, 82-84
auxiliary files, 278
Avery label definitions, 240

B

Back Tab (Shift+Tab) shortcut key, 33
Backspace key, 19, 27
backup files, 279
    options, 286-287
    timed, 126-127
Backward Search (Shift+F2) shortcut key, 41
Balanced Newspaper columns, 171
bar codes (postal), 239
BBar Opt button, 269

BBar Sel button, 269
bit-mapped fonts, 60
black and white images, 201
blank graphics boxes, 199
Block (Alt+F4 or F12) shortcut key, 23
Block command (Edit menu), 23
block protect codes, 97-99
blocks of text, 22
    attributes, 30-31
    breaks, 97-99
    case conversion, 46-47
    copying, 24-26
    deleting, 24-27
    moving, 24-25
    Parallel columns, 172
    selecting with keyboard/mouse, 23
    undeleting, 28-29
undoing actions, 28-29
body text, hiding in outline, 230-231
Bold (F6) shortcut key, 31, 66-67
Bold command (Font menu), 31
bold text attribute, 30-31, 64
Bookmark (Shift+F12) shortcut key, 45
Bookmark, Create command (Edit menu), 45
Bookmark dialog box, 45
bookmarks, 44-45
    borders, 92
    graphics boxes, 211-212
    pages, 94-95
    paragraphs, 93
boxes
    check, 10-11
    graphics, 198
        attaching to elements, 205-206
        borders, 211-212
        captions, 215-216
        creating, 199-200
        editing, 198

INDEX

Crystal Clear WordPerfect 6   299

Reveal Codes command (View menu), 37
Reveal Codes window, 36-37
Ribbon, 12, 100-103
    Columns button, 166
    selecting paragraph styles, 157
Ribbon command (View menu), 13, 102
right justification of text, 34-35, 72
Roman family (fonts), 59
rotating
    images, 201-202
    text in graphic boxes, 203
rows, spacing in columns, 171
rows in tables
    deleting, 178-179
    formatting, 186-187
    inserting, 178-179
Run Merge (Ctrl+F9) keyboard shortcut, 255

S

sans serif fonts, 60
Save (Ctrl+F12) shortcut key, 108-109
Save (F10) shortcut key, 108-109
Save As button, 269
Save As command (File menu), 109
Save command (File menu), 108
saving files, 106-109
scalable fonts, 60
scaling images, 201
scanning documents for addresses, 238
screen tools, 12-13
scroll bars, 12-13, 20
Search (F2) shortcut key, 41
Search button, 269
Search command (Edit menu), 40-41
Search dialog box, 38-40

searching
    for codes, 38-41
    for files, 142-143
    for text, 38-40
Select Button Bar dialog box, 272
Select Page command (Edit menu), 22
Select Paragraph command (Edit menu), 22
Select Sentence command (Edit menu), 22
serif fonts, 59
Set QuickMark (Ctrl+Q) shortcut key, 45
Setup (Shift+F1) shortcut key, 281-283
Setup Display command (File menu), 285
Setup Environment command (File menu), 287
Setup Location of Files command (File menu), 281
Setup Location of Files dialog box, 160
Setup Mouse command (File menu), 283
shadow text attribute, 30-31, 64
shadows, graphics boxes, 211-212
shared files, 280
Shared Library, Style List, 161
shared style files, 160
shortcut keys, 8
    Alt+key combinations, 274
    Back Tab (Shift+Tab), 33
    Backward Search (Shift+F2), 41
    Block (Alt+F4 or F12), 23
    Bold (F6), 31, 66-67
    Bookmark (Shift+F12), 45
    Brightness (.=more), 202
    Brightness (,=less), 202
    Center (Shift+F6), 35
    Codes (F5), 39
    Columns (Alt+F7), 177
    Columns/Tables (Alt+F7), 167
    Compose (Ctrl+A), 69

Contrast (<=less), 202
Contrast (>=more), 202
Copy (Ctrl+C), 26
Copy and Paste (Ctrl+Ins), 26
Covert Case (Shift+F3), 47
Cut (Ctrl+X), 25
Cut and Paste (Ctrl+Del), 25
Date (Shift+F5), 49
Decimal Tab (Ctrl+F6), 35
deleting rows (Ctrl+Delete), 179
Document # (Home, #1-9), 115
Edit (F7), 125
End Field (F9), 249
Enlarge (PgUp), 202
Exit WP (Home, F7), 125
File Manager (F5), 129
Find QuickMark (Ctrl+F), 45
Flush Right (Alt+F6), 35
Font (Ctrl+F8), 61
Footnote (Ctrl+F7), 265
Go To (Ctrl+Home), 21
Graphics mode (Ctrl+F3, G), 7
Hanging indent (F4, Shift+Tab), 33
IndentÆ (F4), 33
IndentÆ¨ (Shift+F4), 33
inserting rows (Ctrl+Insert), 179
Italic (Ctrl+I), 31, 66-67
List Short Forms (F5), 263
Merge Codes (Shift+F9), 249
mnemonic characters, 68
Move (Ctrl+F4), 25
Normal (Ctrl+N), 66-67
Outline (Ctrl+F5), 223, 231
Outline Edit (Ctrl+O), 233
Paste (Ctrl+V), 25-26
Play Macro (Alt+F10), 277
Print (Shift+F7), 123
QuickList (F6), 145